# Foreword and De...

This collection of material is a non-scholarly, amateur atte... communities and significant sites that exist within Jasper Cou...y, ..... ceased to exist. As I witnessed their demise I came upon the idea to record what I could w..... still possible. This effort has spanned over two decades of my life and materialized in the form of a small website that I operated for an equal period of time. Because neither myself or the website can last forever, I decided to put the materials into the more lasting form of a book.

This body of work could not have been accomplished without the generous help of many people who appreciated what I was attempting to do. They contributed information, suggestions, old photographs, old newspapers, encouragement, permission to trespass, a few hikes, and several truck rides. I also thank my family for their understanding in allowing me to indulge in this time consuming effort. A special thanks goes to my distant cousin Bill Eddins who went out of his way to help far too many times to mention.

Copyright 2018
Keith E. Wilkerson
All Rights Reserved

Printed in the United States of America

ISBN
9781983014253

# Index

1. The Original Settlers
2. The Birth of Jasper County
3. J.M. Kennedy – The Original Jasper Historian
4. Paulding – Queen City of the East
5. Davisville and Old Salem
6. Bay Springs
7. Garlandsville
8. Rose Hill
9. Montrose
10. Dushau
11. Vossburg
    - Vossburg School
    - Vossburg Methodist Church
    - Vossburg Cemetery
12. Shady Grove First Baptist Church
13. Heidelberg
    - The Oil Boom
    - Heidelberg High School
14. Mineral Springs
    - Stafford Springs
    - Lithia Springs
    - Marria Springs - Eucutta
15. Swimming Holes
    - Utopia Lake
    - Lake Bounds
    - Lake Waukaway
    - Phalti Lake
16. Pachuta
17. Claiborne
18. Stringer
19. Oak Bowery
20. Jasper County Review
21. The Civil War – McCormick
22. World War II – Key Field & Bombing Range
23. Local Industry
24. Forgotten Cemeteries
25. Obscure Jasper Locations and Post Offices

# The Original Settlers

Throughout my reading and research, I have encountered numerous facts and accounts relating to the Choctaw people who once thrived on the lands for which this book is dedicated. The information paints a sad story of a people whose most precious worldly asset was taken by force, their lives and heritage forever altered. I will not attempt to reconstruct all of the supporting facts, but I highly recommend that you take the time to read the details of the nine treaties signed between the United States and the Choctaw Nation between 1786 and 1830.

*A group of Choctaw children at a unknown church location, probably near Sandersville, MS. The teacher, Julia Dyess Arledge, stands on the back row behind the unidentified woman holding a child.*

*Pushmataha*

# The Birth of Jasper County

If you read between the lines regarding the growth of the United States, expansion boiled down to more people needed more land. As eastern settlers families grew, their children needed their own turf to farm and European immigrants also needed land. When the US government finalized the treaty of Dancing Rabbit Creek with the Choctaw Indians in 1830, a large section of northern Mississippi became available for legal settlement. Many early settlers had already staked illegal land claims prior to this treaty by way of personal agreements with the Choctaw. None of that was binding by any laws so any such settlers were forced to file for land patents in the new territory along with the newcomers.

In the case of Jasper County, land patents were applied for, in person, at official designated government offices. The district office for the Jasper area was near Hattiesburg know as the Augusta Land Office.. Land was sold for a nominal price and some was awarded for previous military service. Most settlers of Jasper could not afford more than a 40 or 80 acre partial.

As an example of the process I have records of the purchase of Jasper land by my Great-Great Grandfather. He brought his wife and children to Jasper soon after the treaty was finalized and chose a small piece of land near the development that became known as Davisville. There they built a cabin and lived on that site the balance of their lives.

The lives of these early settlers had to be harsh. If you pause to imagine the circumstances, there were no shelter until you built one, no stores to purchase provisions, no gardens yet established to grow food, no medical help, no anything if you didn't bring it with you. The term hard scramble farming is very real. Just imagine arriving in a heavily wooded area and turning it into a self subsidence someplace with no more than a ax and a lot of self determination.

The following are copies of my Great-Great Grandfather's original file for a land patent in Jasper County at the Augusta office. This process was typical for all settlers in the newly opened land.

> I William Eddins Claiming the right to enter under the Provisions of an act of Congress entitled an act to graduate and reduce the Price of Public Lands to actual Settlers and Cultivators approved august the 4th 1854 The SW¼ of SE¼ Sec 26 T2 R13E Subject to entry at augusta Mississippi do Solemly Swair that I enter the Same for the use of an adjoining farm or Plantation owned and occupied by Myself and that together with Said entry I have not acquired from the united States under the Provisions of Said act More than three hundred and Twenty acres according to the established Surveys,
>
> William Eddins
>
> I Oliver C Dease Receiver at the Land office at augusta Mississippi do Certify that the above affidavit was taken and Subscribed before me this the 28th September 1854
> 2d October
>
> O C Dease Rec

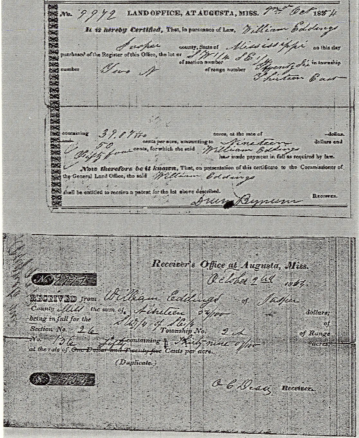

No. 9949 LAND OFFICE, AT AUGUSTA, MISS. 7th Oct 1854

It is hereby Certified, That, in pursuance of Law, William Eddings of Jasper county, State of Mississippi on this day purchased of the Register of this Office, the lot or SW 1/4 S E 1/4 of section number Two N of range number Township Ni in township Thirteen East

containing 39.0740 acres, at the rate of
50 cents per acre, amounting to Nineteen dollars and Fifty four cents, for which the said William Eddings has made payment in full as required by law.

Now therefore be it known, That, on presentation of this certificate to the Commissioner of the General Land Office, the said William Eddings shall be entitled to receive a patent for the lot above described.

Drury Bynum Receiver.

Receiver's Office at Augusta, Miss.
October 7th 1854

RECEIVED from William Eddings of Jasper County Miss the sum of Nineteen 54/100 dollars; being in full for the SW 1/4 of S E 1/4 of Section No. 2 Township No. 2 N of Range No. 13 E containing Thirty-nine 07/100 acres, at the rate of One Dollar and Twenty-five Cents per acre.
(Duplicate.)

C. C. Deas Receiver.

## FORM OF PROOF

REQUIRED UNDER THE
SPECIAL ACT OF 3d MARCH, 1857, STATUTES FOR 1856 AND 1857, PAGE 248, CHAPTER 112, IN THE CASE OF ENTRIES FOR THE USE OF "ADJOINING FARMS," WHERE THEY HAD BEEN MADE AT A LESS RATE THAN THE TRUE GRADUATED PRICE, IN THE CHOCTAW CESSION OF 1830.

---

I, William Edding, do solemnly swear that I entered the SW¼ S E¼ of section 26 in township 2 N of range 13 E the 2nd day of Octr 1854, at the Land Office at Augusta Mississippi, under the graduation act of the 4th of August, 1854, per Certificate No. 9972 for the use of an "adjoining farm" owned and occupied by me, which farm is situated on the E½ SE of section 26 in township 2 N of range 13 and that I now own and occupy and have continued to own and occupy the same.

William Edding

Sworn and subscribed before me the 21 day of July, 1857.
Jonathan B. Gough Esq
Justice Peace Jasper County

### CORROBORATIVE PROOF.

I, John Fisher, do solemnly swear that I am acquainted with William Edding, who subscribed the above affidavit, and the land entered as above described, and from my own knowledge know the contents of said affidavit to be true in every particular.

John Fisher

Sworn and subscribed before me the 21 day of July, 1857.
Jonathan B. Gough Esq
Justice Peace Jasper County

(NOTE.—The official character of the attesting officer must be certified under seal if other than a Register or Receiver.)

# J. M. Kennedy – The Original Jasper Historian

The following clips are copies of newspaper articles written by Mr. J.M. Kennedy. This weekly series, published in the Jasper County News, began January 3, 1957. The title of this admirable body of work, History of Jasper County, speaks for itself. I have not been successful in learning any life details of Mr. Kennedy, but it is very clear that he was learned and passionate educator. Contained in the later articles, beginning with the June 26th, 1957 publication, he mentions holding the position of Jasper County Superintendent of Education from 1932 through 1940. Deeper in the articles, we learn that he was educated in the earliest schools of Jasper County and later attended Milsaps College. We certainly owe him our gratitude for bringing together a rich and accurate collection of local history. Great thanks go to a cousin (B.E.) for his efforts in obtaining copies of the articles and permission from the Jasper County News to use them.

The final Kennedy installment appeared in the September 5, 1957 issue of the JCN and the series unceremoniously ended. I offer my apologies up front for the small text and the quality of the scans. The only copies available were made on a Xerox machine from a previous Xerox copy of the original newspaper clips. The scans were manipulated to obtain the most readable images but you can only do so much.

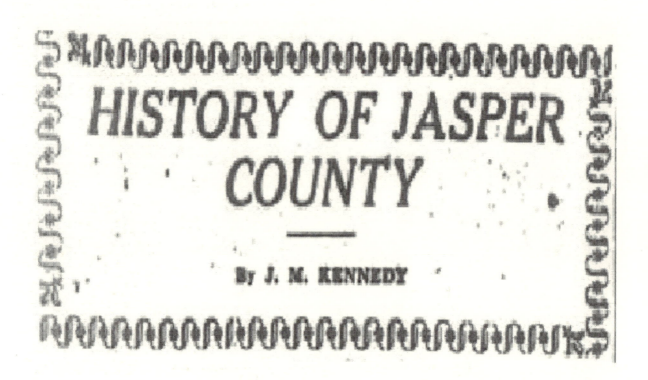

## January 3, 1957

# HISTORY OF JASPER COUNTY

### By J.M. Kennedy

### FORWARD

History is one of the most important subjects in our course of study in our schools and Jasper County has one of the greatest histories in the state. A few days ago some of the daily papers had the picture and history of a beautiful home in Jasper County but did not name the man that built the home and first lived there (one of the great producers of the country). He built cities and named them but his name was not mentioned concerning his home.

One of the greatest Indians of the country, buried in the Congressional Cemetery at Washington, D.C. followed there by a line of people one mile long. It is said that this Indian kept our ancestors from being massacred. He gave the land for our capitol, lived in Jasper county. Our teachers are taught to teach most subjects of the schools by the inductive method. Applying it to history we would start with the child's community and then branch out to other communities which would cause the child to think.

Bacon says that history makes men wise, poets, witty; mathematics, subtle; natural philosphy, deep; moral, grave; logic and rhetoric, able to contend.

Senator James Gordon in his farewell to Washington said: "A man always loves his home better than any other place. I love the particulars spot where I live better than any other spot, and you do the same. We have there ties of friendship and love and everything that we do not have anywhere else".

I have quoted in some instances from other writers, such as Mrs. Smith's History of the Choctaw race; of B.H. Thigpen and the late J.B. Lightsey, late Skates Moore. Department of Archives and History of Mississippi, City Library of Jackson, State Library, Jackson, Bureau of Census, Federal Government reports and most of my own knowledge and experience in the county. Other writers who I have quoted, will be credited in my writings.

So let us study Jasper history for a short while.

J.M. KENNEDY

### PREFACE

Some say, "Why do you dig in those old books and papers, it is nothing but junk." But I have to read of the old, I like to meet old friends. I am like David Moore when he wrote:

### The Old

It preciousness can not be measured
By value of silver and gold;
However pleasant new fields may be,
Fond memory still clings to the old.

New gardens of beauty and of pleasure,
And mansions of luxuries untold,
Never can fill the heart's empty measure,
Estranged from the love scenes of old.

Roses of luster and fragrance
That vie with the sun's brilliance and gold,
Are never so charming among strangers,
As pink in our rude garden of old.

The learned, refined and cultured,
Whom tongues of renown have extrolled,
Are sweet as companions, but never
Dear as our unlettered friends of old.

New friends our lives ever cheer and gladden,
Our hearts to revive them unfold;
And yet they have cause memory to sadden,
Recalling our loved ones of old.

The smiles of strangers may enchant us,
Cheer us far more than gleams of gold;
For they are the glad, glad reflections
Of our true and loved friends of old.

The music of strangers has raptures
For our hearts that can never be told;
It vibrates the cords of remembrance,
And charms us with songs of old.

The kindly deeds of civil strangers
We estimate far more than gold;
Yet there is lacking in their kindness
That true and sweet sympathy of old.

Ah! through every land we may journey,
And where ever the sea has rolled,
But we can never meet the pleasure
Known in our humble homes of old.

The laughter loud or joyous strangers,
Altho like bells of pleasure tolled,
Discordant rack the friendless spirit,
And start the tears for scenes of old.

And thus it by memory's magic,
No matter where we may have strolled,
The fondness, dearest scenes of gladness
Still linger in our homes of old."

When in a county meeting, I was always ready to take up for my home town; when in a state meeting I was ready to defend Jasper County; when a national meeting I always fought for my state.

One of our presidents closed his speech with the words: "Remember our forefathers; Think on our posterity."

I have paid a tribute to the ones of old; and now let me quote you a poem for the young:

"Strive not to win vast wealth,
It must depart;
The love of gold should not hold
In chains thy heart;
Gold can not beat life's crucial test;
Wealth can not bring thee peace and rest.

Strive not for fleeting fame—
Men will forget;
Thy very name the dust shall claim
Thy star shall set;
Yea all that thou can ever see
Will surely shortly cease to be.

Subdue thyself, within
Be thou a king;
This path alone unto a throne
Thy soul will bring
Know thyself; thyself control;
For thus thy feet shall gain the goal."

The great philosopher has said: "What will thou have? Pay the price and take it."

And here is a verse for both;

"So live, that when they summon to join
The innumerable caravan, which moves
To that mysterious realm, where each shall take.
His chamber in the silent halls of death,
Thou go not, like the quary slave at night,
Scourged to his dungeon, but sustained and soothed
By an unfaltering trust, approach thy grave,
Like one who wraps the drapery of his couch
About him, and lies down to pleasant dreams."

And now from the Bible for both. Rom. 12:2 "Be not conformed to this world but be ye transformed by the renewing of your minds". READ good books and journals. It is said that the Americans do not read as our great crime record. Some say teachers do not read much, terrible. I hope some may find pleasure in reading what I have gathered in past life from places, people and books.

Author

### JASPER HISTORY IMPORTANT

Garlandsville is perhaps the oldest town in the South as it was the Capitol of the Choctaw nation until 1824 when Greenwood Le Flore was elected chief, when it was moved to French Camp. The Choctaw Indians were perhaps the most civilized Indians in America because they were not savage and produced all kinds of farm crops. The black fertile land in their domain was without forest and they worked this land first with wood equipment. I have seen the old Indian harrow which was made with a forked piece of wood hewn down flat with wooden pegs through it. The old mole board was wood used to turn the soil. Later they put a piece of sharp rock in front of it; the white man put a metal piece in front of it. At one time the French settlements were cut off from the mother country on account of war; they would have starved to death if it had not been for the Choctaws. Garlandsville was one of the first post offices in east Mississippi, it was one of the gathering places for the Indians to leave for Indian Territory; the whites came in before the Indian left. It was laid off in blocks and streets, people of the gulf cities came to Garlandsville to spend the summers.

It is the only county in the state that has two old highways crossing in it. The oldest highway in the state, "old Jackson Military Highway" and the "Three-Chopped-Way" crosses three miles north of Bay Springs on the old Holder place. The Old Jackson road, the records say, from New Orleans to Nashville but at first from New Orleans to Garlandsville (after the whites came). The Three-Chopped Way from Savannah, Ga., to Natchez, was one of the first mail routes and was the first road through Alabama. Creek Indians would not allow a tree cut in their territory till old Sam Dale confered with them as they were afraid of him (called him Big Sam). He laid out this road. Most of the settlers from the east came over this road.

The greatest Indian that ever lived, Pushmataha was chief of the Choctaw nation and lived in Garlandsville. He is the only Indian that was ever buried in the Congressional cemetery at Washington, D.C. Andrew Jackson made a great speech and a parade a mile long followed him to his grave. He is the only chief that defied Brig. General Tecumseh who persuaded most of the Indian tribes to fight the Americans during the War of 1812, telling them that their hunting ground will soon be gone if they did not take this opportunity. He gave the land for our state capitol at Jackson, Miss.

January 10, 1957

# HISTORY OF JASPER COUNTY

### By J. M. KENNEDY

The greatest mission to the Indians was established at Missionary, Jasper County, on the Three-Chopped-Way. Dates differ as to the establishment of this mission but we know that it was there when the county was formed. This is said to be the most beautiful piece of land in east Mississippi. It was thought at first that the county site would be here as it was on the Three-Chopped Way and the Indians had a road to their capitol at Garlandsville and in many other directions as they had their ball games, cries, dances, on this level land. The settlers in the southern part of the county objected to the Missionary for the county site, saying it was too far to the north for the county site and so a compromise was made and it was located at Paulding.

The above mission was Catholic and when the Indians left for the Indian Territory they built a large church at Paulding which was struck by lightning in 1942 and burned. The Irish Catholics began to settle around this church at Paulding and so many came that a section around Paulding became known as Irish Town. So many came and settled there that they affected county affairs. They now have a large tract of land between Missionary and Paulding on which is located one of the three Cistercian Monasteries in the United States, the other two being at Milwaukee and Dallas.

Soon after Paulding was made the county site a contract was let for a large courthouse; soon two newspapers were located there; prominent citizens came to Paulding to live; one of the first telegraph lines was built from Paulding to New Orleans. A road was built from Paulding to connect with the Old Jackson Highway, whereby citizens made frequent trips to New Orleans. This brought the first bridge in east Mississippi, over Tallahala Creek which is still known by the name of the man that built it, Ramboo. Citizens from the surrounding counties brought their legal notices to be published in the papers; candidates made their announcements in them. Products of the rich black land, worked by slaves, were brought to Paulding for market.

The Eastern Clarion became the largest paper in the state, having ten columns, netted ten thousand a year. It is now the Clarion-Ledger. The True Democrat was edited by Oliver Dease, whose family held more offices than any in the county; Brame and McFarland held office longer.

John J. Mellen was one of the first citizens of Paulding. He later became governor. Capt. W. M. Hardy, said to be one of the greatest promoters in the state. Gov. Lowrey married at Montrose. Pushmataha, perhaps the greatest Indian in the U. S. lived at Garlandsville. Sam Dale often visited the county. Judge Deavours at one time was head of the University Law School, had lived at Paulding.

A rural public school was established in the county soon after its establishment. This is said to be the first of that kind in the state. It was fostered by Noah Barber, Rose Hill.

Jasper County has more mineral springs than another county in the state. Stafford, near Vossburg, was known to have medicinal qualities by the Indians. Its water has been shipped to all parts of the world, even the King of England having used it. It is still visited by many patients.

The mineral springs at Montrose are heavy in sulphur and alum. It is claimed that sulphur will keep the hair from turning gray. The alum is said to be a good kidney medicine. It is reported to have cured kidney cases where the doctor has failed.

Nature's Remedy is produced by dripping the earth found west of Bay Springs and is being shipped to all of the U. S. as a general medicine. The town spring at Bay Springs is a good medicine for indigestion.

South of Lake Como a large spring gushes from the bank of Tallahoma Creek, having the appearance of containing several minerals. A mineral spring is on the old Duncan McLaurin place, near Antioch.

Indian names: Souinlovie, Tallahala, Muke Flupper, Tallahoma, Tallahatta, Bougahoma, Pachuta, Shubuta.

### An Indian Ball Game.

The writer as a small boy attended a number of Indian ball games at the old Missionary, where it had been the custom to play their games and have other contests on that level land. One, I especially remember, was between the Six Towns and the Mucalushes. They began to arrive two days before hand, when they would have a cry that night. This paid respects to their dead. On the second night they would have a dance. Preparing for the game, they would go into the woods and select a tall pine, about one foot in diameter, and cut off a piece about fifteen feet in length and split it open and erect this and another similar one, about one hundred feet apart, with the split side facing each other. Sides were taken and in the rear of each, all the belongings of each was placed as they were to forfeit all they possessed on the game.

On the morning of the game each would meet on the grounds and make exhibits of strength, etc. Each player was nude except hippings with animal hides, with the tail sticking up behind. A large crowd of whites gathered on the side they were rooting for. The players were arranged like basket ball players, so many in the middle and so many at each goal. The players must handle the ball with ball sticks made from a piece of hickory about three feet long with one end trimed flat and turned to the handle and tied with a piece of hide which made a little cup for the ball to rest in held there by the second stick which was made the same way. They could throw the ball much farther than by the hand as they had a greater swing. Four players from each side were in the middle and goals making in all twenty four players. I was told that this number could vary. There seemed to be no rules as the affair was a knock down and drag-out affair. Sometimes they would hit each other with those sticks, bringing the blood, but the players seemed not to notice that act as he seemed to be after the ball. I was told that one who fought was not considered a good player as he should be after the ball. An old chief would throw the ball up in the center and all players would be holding up their sticks for it. They could catch the ball with the stick and I have seen them throw it from behind one goal and hit the face of the other which was a game. If the ball fell on the ground and one reached for it another Indian would run his stick between the player that had the ball, forcing him to drop it, then all the players were in a circle after the ball with their tails sticking up behind which would last for several minutes which I thought was a beautiful sight. Sometimes when a player had the ball and his opponents were after him, all would gather their opponent which would leave the two playing ball. I noticed that they always grabbed their opponent from behind so he could not strike with his sticks. The side that lost would begin to leave walking, but the white man with whom they were living did the best he could to provide for them.

### PUSHMATAHA*

That the great Chief Apushmataha rendered a service to the white people of this continent, beyond any human expression, will be clearly set forth in the following pages. This book would not be complete without the records of his life, which are set down in the history of the United States of America. To show our deepest gratitude, I shall not omit a brief story of his life. Without doubt, Pushmataha saved the white settlers of Mississippi, Georgia and Alabama from total extermination.

During the War of 1812, when England was at war with the colonies in the West, she put forth every effort to engage the Indians in this fight agianst the Americans. The English turned their special attention to the Indians of the South, known as the five civilized tribes: the Choctaws, Chickasaws, Cherokees, Creeks and Seminoles. These tribes were the most dreaded because they were the shrewdest and bravest of all Indians of North America.

Tecumseh, the great Shawnee Chief, a Brigadier General in the English Army—one of the bravest and most renowned of all Indian warriors who made their way over trackless forest, through dense canebrakes, swimming creeks and rivers as they journeyed. They passed through the country of the Chickasaws, and arrived in the country of the Choctaws. They pitched their camp in the district over which Apakifulleuhi was Chief, at a place known as Plymouth, five miles north of Columbus, on the Tombigbee River. There were thousands that gathered for this Council meeting, amid great excitment and wildest imagination.

When Tecumseh approached with his 30 warriors the circle around the great heap of blazing logs, left open for twenty or thirty feet, closed in about them and they were surrounded by thousands of strangers. He made use of forceful figures and no one could use them to better advantage than the Indian, nor could a race of people understand them better than Indian, for they are noted for their beautiful word pictures, their figures and metaphors.

Indians were told that they had met together to thrash out a very serious matter, the question of which was NOT whether we have been cruelly treated and wronged, but "what punishment we shall exact to avenge ourselves of that wrong. The whites have already determined THEIR proceedings, unless we unite to give a check to their consuming desire to annihilate us. They will soon subdue us and we shall be driven off our native soil." To use Tecumseh's exact words:

" Look abroad over this once beautiful country, and what do you see now? Naught but the ravages of the paleface destroyers meet your eyes. So it will be with YOU, Choctaws and Chickasaws! Soon your mighty forest trees (under the shade of whose spreading branches you have played in infancy, sported in boyhood and now dest your weary limbs after the fatigue of the chase) will be cut down to fence in the land which the white intruders dare to call their own. Soon their broad roads will pass over the grass of your forefather's graves, and the peace of their rest will be blotted out forever. The annihilation of our race is at hand unless we unite in one common cause against the common foe; your people too will soon be as failing leaves and scattered clouds before the blighting breath, and as leaves are driven before the wintry storm. Shall we give up our homes, our country bequeathed to us by the Great Spirit, the graves of our dead and everything that is dear and sacred to us without a struggle? I know you will cry with me, 'Never! Never!' "Then let us in one united blow, destroy them all. I am at the head of many warriors, backed by the strong arm of English soldiers. Now listen to the voice of duty, of honor, of nature and your endangered country. Let us form one body, one heart, and defend to the last warrior our country, our homes, our liberty, and the graves of our forefathers."

*From "Greenwood Leflore and the Choctaw Indians of the Mississippi Valley," by Allene DeShazo Smith.

January 17, 1957

# HISTORY OF JASPER COUNTY

By J. M. KENNEDY

### PUSHMATAHA*

Though the North American Indian shows no visible signs of feeling, whatsoever, the dazzling light of the fire reflected a far more significant look in the fierce and piercing eyes of that vast multitude which gave Tecumseh assurance that he had driven his message home with greater promise of success than he had ever dreamed. Some of the Choctaws as well as the Chickasaws, came to the center of the circle from which Tecumseh had retired. Most of them agreeing but some of them doubting him.

Tecumseh was exalted because his talk seemed attended with overwhelming success. But he did not know that there was a listener around this campfire, who had been as silent as the stillness of the night, who had listened with rapt attention. A splendid specimen of nature's unlettered manhood; wonderful to look at. As he stood up, drawing himself to his full height, all eyes were turned to this undisputed leader of the Choctaws, for he was none other than the renowned Pushmataha, eloquent in speech, unsurpassed in bravery, unequaled in dignity and a true and lasting friend to the American people. This was the man whom Tecumseh had to reckon with! The expression of the dauntless Choctaw commanded respect.

. . . . We can better understand this truly great man by using his own words:

"My friends and fellow countrymen, you now have no just cause to declare war against the American people, or reek your vengeance upon them as enemies since they have ever manifested feelings of friendship toward you. It was not my desire in coming here to enter into a disputation with anyone. But I appear before you, my warriors and my people, not to throw in my plea against the accusations of Tecumseh, but to prevent your forming rash and dangerous resolutions upon things of higher importance through the instigation of others. Nor do I stand up before you tonight to contradict the many facts alleged against the American people. We should consult more in regard to our future welfare than our present. Remember: the American people are now friendly toward you. You have no cause to declare war against them. It is, besides, inconsistent with your national glory and with your honor as a people to violate your solemn treaty; and a disgrace to the memory of your forefathers to wage war against the American people merely to gratify the malice of the English.

"The war which you are now contemplating against the Americans is a flagrant breach of justice, yes, a fearful blemish on your honor, and also that of your forefathers. If you, examine it carefully and judiciously it forebodes nothing but destruction to our entire race. It is a war against a people whose territories are now far greater than our own, and who are far better provided with all the necessary implements of war, with men, guns, horses, wealth far beyond that of all our race combined; and where is the necessity or wisdom to make war upon such a people? Where is our hope, if thus weak and unprepared, we should declare war against them? Let us not be deluded with the foolish hope that this war, if begun, will soon be over, even if we destroy all the whites in our territories and lay waste their homes and fields. Far from it! It will be the beginning of the end that terminates in the total destruction of our race. Be not, therefore, guilty of rashness, I pray you; which I never as yet have known you to be. Therefore, I pray you not to break the Treaty, nor violate your pledge of honor, but to submit your grievances, whatever they may be, to the Congress of the United States, according to the articles of the Treaty existing between us and the American people. If not, I here invoke the Great Spirit, who takes cognizance of oaths, to bear me witness, that I shall endeavor to avenge myself upon the authors of this war by whatever methods you shall set me an example.

"Remember: We are a people who have never grown insolent with success or become abject in adversity; but let those who invite us to hazardous attempts by uttering our praise never elevate our spirits above our judgment, nor an endeavor to exasperate us by a flow of invectives to be provoked the sooner by compliance. From tempters equally balanced, let it be known that we are warm in battle and cool in hours of debate. Listen to the voice of prudence, oh, my countrymen, ere you rashly act. But, do as you may, know the truth, I shall join our friends, the Americans. In this war."

A hush over the vast throng, then a murmuring, then a scattering of the whole assembly and a stealing away to their homes, followed these words of Pushmataha:

"Know the truth, I shall join our friends, the Americans, in this war."

This noble declaration of this great Choctaw Chief, was the means of saving the thinly scattered inhabitants of this broad land from total extermination; and for this noble act, he should be renowned for more than his celebrated orations, his illustrious statesmanship, his fame as a fighter; for had Tecumseh succeeded in his terrible scheme there would have been hardly a single white person left in all this broad land, to have given an account of the horrible slaughter.

Pushmataha's military ability was recognized when he, as Brigadier-General, with seven hundred warriors, aided General Jackson in the Creek War, given unstinted aid and allegiance. Then also in the Battle of Orleans 500 warriors were courageous and worthy lads in the sure aim of their deadly rifles.

"Apushmataha's last request of President Jackson was, "Let the big guns be fired over me." The Government took charge of the funeral for we did not know how to proceed. He was buried in *Arlington National Cemetery with the honors of war. There were two bands of music, several military companies and the Marines from the Navy Yard. It was a long procession and with the body of our departed Chief, we passed through the long lines of several thousand people. We laid him in the grave. The minister prayed for us. When it was over, he was covered with cold clay and we left him, in the midst of many hundred people.

"I am thankful that there was so much honor paid our departed Chief. Many Congressmen and President Jackson treated us with great kindness. I can truly say that we have received every mark of friendship and brotherly love from the white people since we have been among them."

*Congressional Cemetery, there was no Arlington then.

* * * * *

"The Choctaws, milder in their savagery than other tribes, had some customs that were more barbarous than any of them. One of these was the compressing of the heads of infants. The child was placed in a recumbent position with a weight upon its forehead, which was kept there until the shape of the growing skull was affected. On this account, the Choctaws were often called 'Flat Heads.'"**

*From "Greenwood Leflore and the Choctaw Indians of the Mississippi Valley," by Allene DeShazo Smith.
**"Mississippi History," by H. L. Riley, Ph.d.

---

When the white man came to Jasper County he found the Choctaw Indians living here. How long these Indians had been here no one knows. There are a number of mounds over the state, some few in Jasper County. One of the Rufus McLaurin place, between Lake Como and Bay Springs. Another near Mt Moriah Church near the Newton County line, one on the old Murray place, east of Rose Hill. Early settlers thought these mounds were made by the Indians, some thought as a burying ground. A number of people think differ- "The early explorers that came to America found the Indians and the mounds together and the conclusion was that the mounds were Indian mounds. This is a lie that has been handed down in our histories. Men who have studied the habits and character of the Indian deny this. The Indian man was a hunter and a warrior and his wife did the rest."

Thus we have people who think that a race of people lived in Jasper County before the Indians.

The first white people were the French from New Orleans and Mobile who came to where Garlandsville is, to trade with the Indians, as the chief of the Choctaws, Red Shoes, lived at Garlandsville. The road from New Orleans to Garlandsville later became known as the Old Jackson Military Road. The next white came with Sam Dale, who had secured the right from the Creek Indians to open a road through their territory (most of the state of Alabama). This road ran through the center of the county (Jasper) on to Natchez. This road was used by settlers from South Carolina and Georgia, to make their way to the Natchez district. James Street has written about this trek in his book, "Oh, Promise Land." He claims that a part of these settlers came back to Jasper after it was formed. By the Dancing Rabbit Treaty with the Indians, Jasper was included in this grant, sixteen counties in all being in this grant. Jasper County was formed out of that part of the Choctaw cession which is north of Jones County (which was already formed). The northeast part of the county was mostly black prairie land which was very productive. The southeast was mostly lime clay, the west part was piney woods. The streams in the county ran mostly south and were Tallahoma, Nuke Fupper, Tallahala, McVey, Goodwater, Twistwood, Pachuta, Tallahatta, Bogahoma, Souinlovie and Penantly. The forest in the eastern part of the county was mostly hardwood and short leaf pine. In the swamps, mostly hardwood; in the west, long leaf pine.

The north line of Jones County ran a little noreast and a base line was needed to measure the land of all of these counties. This line was established about where Stringer is situated and east to Heidelberg. All the land of these counties is measured from this line north and east from meridian 90 (runs about Jackson) except the small part south of the base line which is measured from 31st degree or near Poplarville. The part above the base line is a perfect square. 1, 2, 3, 4, Townships and 10, 11, 12, and 13 Ranges East. As soon as the county was open for settlement large numbers of people from Jones County, Alabama, Georgia, South Carolina, and North Carolina rushed to take up the rich land. The people from Alabama, Georgia, South Carolina and North Carolina came over the road that was laid out by Sam Dale, known as the Three Chopped-Way.

January 24, 1957

# HISTORY OF JASPER COUNTY

By J. M. KENNEDY

About ten years before the county was established some white people came from the East and established a mission at Missionary. This was a Catholic mission and is said to be the cause of the large influx of Catholic Irish in that section. It was later called Irishtown.

Around this mission is said to be the most beautiful tract of land in the county and as it was a great gathering place for the Indians it was thought that the county court house should be located there, but the people in the southern part of the county objected and so it was located five miles south of there.

Little is known of Pushmataha in early life. We know that he loved to travel and visited other tribes of Indians. The early settlers of Wayne county tell of his frequent visits to them (Wayne was settled much earlier than Jasper), and how much they enjoyed his visits but they must not have any colored folks about. After he was made chief of the Choctaws and lived at Garlandsville the capitol of of the Choctaw nation, we find him at the Choctaw Council in 1812 when the great chief from the north, Tecumseh was visiting all the Indian tribes telling them that now (War of 1812) is their time to attack the whites and redeem their hunting grounds. The English had made him (Tecumseh) a general. The old books at Jackson say that the Choctaw council was held near Chunky River, West of where Meridian now is situated. Pushmataha's speech to this council in answer to Tecumseh's is recorded at Jackson and is a masterpiece of oratory. The council decided in his favor that they would remain friends to the whites. Pushmataha was soon at the head of Choctaw warriors, headed for Alabama to help Gen. Jackson fight the terrible Creeks who soon massacreed the people at Fort Mims. Jackson, with the help of the Indians, defeated the Creeks and drove them into Florida. Jackson then defeated a great English force that landed at Mobile and New Orleans; Pushmataha and his warriors were with him in all these battles. Jackson made a trip with him over the old Jackson Military road, stopping at Garlandsville with him. In 1820 Jackson and Hinds met Pushmataha at Doak's Stand and Pushmataha gave the land on which our capitol stands. Pushmataha visited Jackson at Washington, D. C., where he died and was buried in the Congressional Cemetery. He was buried with military honors. Jackson making a speech at his grave in which he said that Pushmataha was the greatest Indian that ever lived.

From an old volume of Lowrey and McCaudle history found in the State Library: "The commissioners to organize Jasper County in 1833 were Samuel Grayson, Asa Hartfield, Robert James, William Ellis, H. W. Ward, Henry Hale, George Evans, C. Dyer, N. Martin, and J. Bidwell.

"Among the early settlers were: Thomas C. Heidelberg, John McCormick, Joshua Terrall, James S. Terrall, Fountain Land, Thomas Denn, L. L. Porter, William C. Bounds, Reddick Rogers, Drew Sumrall, John Caraway, Edwin S. Caraway, William Jones, Archibald McColum, Robert Cooper, Henry Miley, Howell Hargrove, Uriah Millsaps, Ransom J. Jones, Thomas S. Newman, Thomas Newell, Ansa Hartfield, Ruben Hartfield, William Hartfield, Oliver C. Dease, who was at an early day prominent in state politics. He served in both houses of the state legislature and is the father-in-law of Capt. James J. Shannon at one time editor of the Eastern Clarion at Paulding. He was grandfather of John H. Miller, a forcible writer and experienced journalist, is now and has been for years editor of the Tupelo Journal in Lee County; Seth Fatheree, John D. Fatheree, James Dupriest, Peter Loper, John Loper, Aaron Bolton, Farr Procter, John D. Ratcliff, James Thigpen, John Parker, Henry W. Ward, William Ellis, Simon B. Ellis, James E. Wata, Henry W. Ward, Hamilton Brown, L. B. Brown, Elias Brown, Alfred Brown, Alford McCarty, Luke Barnett, William Bridges, Noah Barbour, William Hosey, William Bridges, John McDonald, Robert Crawford, Wiley Meeks, Larkin Collins, James A. Chapman, John Watts, John Lightsey, Samuel Grayson, Adam Ulme, J. C. Moffit, John R. Brinson, David Lightsey, John Millow, Benjamin Moss, Zachariah Thompson, Abel Merrill, Walden Lewis, John J. Williams, William Rogers, N. McKinstry, Levi Hollyfield, James M. Seala, R. R. Abney, Bartlett V. Gammage, the father-in-law of Gov. Robert Lowrey, Malachi Sharbrough, Thomas Nelson, Willis Holder, Richmond Craven, Jack Craven, Zedekiah X. Raynor, Francis Martin, John Williams, Thomas Hodges, John A. Hodges, Isham Hodge, Robert James, Phillip James, Vigil Randle, Ezekiel Wimberly, Ichabod Kelly, Dan B. Johnston, Hugh Brebman, and John Anderson."

More copy from Lowrey & McCardle: "Paulding, the county site

Paulding, one of the captors of Major Andre, Adjutant General of the British Army, and was for many years a thrifty and prosperous town. Forty five years ago it was called the "Queen City of the East". Fifty four years ago the Eastern Clarion was established in Paulding by John J. McRea, referred to in the preceding pages. The paper while owned by John J. McRea, was conducted by Need and Duncan. Simeon R. Adams succeeded the founder of the Clarion, under whose management it became a power in the state. He was elected state senator from the senatorial district in which he resided. After the death of Mr. Adams and during the late war, the paper was removed to Meridian and after cessation of hostilities was removed to the capitol where its editorial columns were controlled for a number of years by Hon. E. Barksdale. A few years ago, the Clarion, then under the management of Col. J. L. Power and the State Ledger, published and edited by R. H. Henry, united under the name of Clarion-Ledger and is now edited and published by R. H. Henry and J. L. Power.

"Among the early lawyers of Jasper County was John Watts, who was circuit judge for nearly twenty years, was the father of Dr. Josiah Watts of Newton. Captain Joseph Watts of Scooba, and Thomas Watts of Hickory and the uncle of Major A. H. and Captain S. B. Watts of Meridian. James McDougal, a native of Scotland, who worked at his trade, that of a tailor when he first came to the county, studied law and became a most excellent advocate. He was elected to the state senate from the district from which he resided. Joseph Hayfren, a native of Ireland, an accurate and strong lawyer. While Judge T. Sterling was on the bench he occasionally indulged in a glass of toddy, and upon an occasion while a little under the influence of liquor he was annoyed with the pertinancity of the Irish lawyer in the conducet of a case, who persisted in desiring to read an authority. The Judge said: "Mr. Hayfren, the point has been decided by the court." Mr. Hayfren replied: "I understand, your honor, but I wanted to show you how profoundly ignorant was Sir William Blackstone."

"Henry Calhoun, father of Henry Calhoun of Scott County, and father-in-law of Gen. J. A. Smith, was a lawyer of good attainments. Henry S. Mounger, a native of Georgia, a lawyer by profession and a thorough Christian gentleman, settled in Paulding and married the daughter of an old and prominent citizen, Judge Uriah Millsaps. He was elected circuit judge and was on the bench four years. He was the father of Rev. Edwin H. Mounger and father-in-law of Rev. Ransom J. Jones, both distinguished divines and members of the Methodist Conference of this state." His son, W. H. Mounger served several terms as sheriff of Jasper County.

"The towns now in the county are Paulding, Garlandville, Lake Como, Heidelberg, Vossburg.

"The principal streams are: Tallahala, Tallahoma, Swannee, Ettahoma, Tallahatta, Shubuta, and Town Creek.

"The New Orleans and North Eastern Railroad runs through the southeastern corner of the county.

"The prairie, bottom and hammock lands are excellent, and the uplands average with the adjacent counties.

"The population is intelligent and reasonably prosperous.

"Jasper County has 67,101 acres of cleared land; average value as rendered to the assessor $4.17 per acre."

---

### "Choctaw Mission Station in Jasper County"

By A. J. BROWN

"The Six Towns Mississippi Station was established about the year 1825, by a gentleman by the name of Bardwell. It is thought that he was a native of one of the New England states, probably Massachusetts. He came by way of from Mobile, Alabama, which was about one hundred and twenty miles from the Station. The Indians among whom this station was located were known as the Six Town Tribe. They occupied most of the county of Jasper. The station was situated in Section 15, Township 3, Range 12.

"The missionaries began their work by laying out part of the road leading from Mobile to Jackson. They erected a comfortable loghouse two stories high, which was used for a dwelling. It had a stick and dirt stack chimney, and large cellars under two of its rooms. They also built a school house and a church, the latter of which was supplied with a bell. Two or three other houses were erected for different purposes.

"The missionaries had vegetable gardens, and a separate graveyard from that originally planned by the Indians. They kept horses, cattle and hogs, and had an abundance of milk, butter and cheese. The location of this place was one of the finest sections of land in Jasper County. It was a beautiful tableland with no hills or large streams to mar its beauty. It was destitute of water except a spring of large volume which came out of a solid rock, and had furnished sufficient water for a city of two thousand inhabitants. This spring is situated about four hundred yards from where the missionaries built their houses. It is strange that they should not have settled nearer to what was necessarily their only water supply; there was no chance to obtain water from wells, as no one would have been very difficult to make at that place. A gentleman now living on the site of this station has the water brought to his residence by a hydraulic ram.

"The growth of timber was principally oak and hickory; some magnificent specimens of oak trees grew in front of the houses. Only a few of the original trees now remain. The missionaries planted china trees, also, which grew to be a large size. All traces of those trees have disappeared."

(To Be Continued)

# January 31, 1957

## HISTORY OF JASPER COUNTY

### By J. M. KENNEDY

"The missionaries supplied the natives with church and school privileges. Their work of eight years, though done in a spirit of self-sacrifice, seems not to have amounted to a great deal, as their influence and teachings were little observed after their departure. The missionaries left Jasper County in the latter part of 1833, or early part of 1834.

"Mr. E. E. Chapman, late of Newton County, occupied the premises and lived in the houses in the years 1934-1935. His son states that the tillable land on the place must have been between fifty and seventy-five acres. This land was very fertile, being a deep, sandy loam, with a clay foundation, very level and easy of cultivation. One year Mr. Chapman made thirty-three bales of cotton on thirty-three acres of it. This tract of land was so level that a straight race course was made on it in after years, and here many of the best horses of the country had their speed tested.

"This valuable tract of land was bought from an Indian, it is said, for a horse and cart. The purchaser was Col. John H. Horne of Wayne County, who became one of the wealthiest men and largest slave-holders in the state.

"Col. John Johnson, who was an Indian Agent, also bought a claim on the land from an Indian and the title became so clouded that no real purchase was made for nearly thirty years after the departure of the Indians.

"After the War Between the States, Judge John W. Pewel succeeded in quieting the adverse claimants. It was then bought by Mr. A. Russell of Newton County, who now (1902) occupies it. The present owner of the place writes of it as follows:

"Houses of modern architecture have taken the places once occupied by the rude huts of these Indians. Golden harvests are annually gathered from the fields nearby and views of majestic scenery when obtained from the surrounding hills, lend a charm and a degree of loveliness to the wide extent of the neighboring landscape.'"

### EARLY TAX PAYERS

**1836**
Phillip H. James, William James, Robert James, Samuel Grayson, William Hosey, William Ellis, Several Cooleys, Jake Blackwell, N. R. John Hillman, P. Ed. Tobias.

**1838**
Adam Ulmer, Jim Windham, John McCormick, James McCormick, Tom Newel, Calendar McCarty, Nathan Tyner, Samuel Tyner, John Tyner, Thomas Tyner, Levi Tyner, Jim Terrall, Edward Terrall, Joshua Terrall, Willis Lewis, Tom Heidelberg, Jim Evans, John Evans, Asa Hartsfield, Isum Clayton, Felix Blackwell.

**1840**
Alf Brown, L. B. Brown, Hamp Brown, Edward Ball, Aaron Boulton, William Clayton, John Chatham, Hugh Chatham, Spence Chatham, L. B. Ellis, James Foley, Aaron Green, Barlett Gammage, Abner Hosey, William Hosey, Hezekiah Hosey, Isaac Hosey, R. J. James, L. J. James, Hutto Morgan, Lewis Morgan, Ben Morgan, Dave Morgan, John McDonald, Abe Merrill, Henry Mounger, Leroy Morrison, Enoch McCarty, James Thigpen, Henry Mounger, Jack James, Phebe Terrall, John Terrall, Edward Terrall, E. Y. Terrill, Thomas Terrall, Ben White, William Stringer, Thomas Stringer, Ujriah Millsaps, Tom Bingham, S. A. Reid, John Read, Amos J. Reid, Abraham Reid, G. W. Ryan.

It is said that very few paid taxes in the early days. His household goods were very few. A rifle, ax, cart, oxen, sometimes one, sometimes 7, quilts, pot and fryer, a lean to. His ox could earn his own living by grazing. The man hunted and fished for his meat, beet up some corn for bread. If he did not like his location or neighbors, he could move in a short while. The citizen who had prairie or hammock land was generally satisfied to stay there and began to build a home and secure more household furniture.

Comment on early settlers: Of the old families that settled in the county, the Lewis family is the largest. A few years back some one examined the registration books of Rose Hill and said he found 176 Lewis' there beside the kin of other names. The farm land around Rose Hill is above the average and they claim to have had the first rural free school in the state and the first junior college in the county. Some became prominent in public affairs. They claim Jack Lewis as the first white child born in the county; he was later postmaster at Twistwood; and his son, Mill, was a member of the state legislature. Wyck Lewis was a member of the legislature for two terms. Rev. Joe Nicholson, a prominent Methodist minister, married Jack Lewis' daughter and she is still living in Laurel.

The James family is perhaps the next largest family in the county and they are scattered to all parts of the county. Quite a few are in the public limelight. One was county commissioner, another first officer (as has been mentioned). W. W. James was a prominent lawyer in Newton, Miss. Amon James is superintendent of schools at Drew, Miss., and an officer in the Mississippi Education Association. Tom James is principal of the high school at Natchez, Miss. Ollie James has and is principal of the school at Duckhill, and has been for 23 years. Farmer James was Bilbo's assistant in Washington, D. C., his brother-in-law, C. H. Wall, was a member of the board of supervisors, Dr Franklin James is a member of Millsaps College faculty.

The Lightsey family is the third largest family of the county. One was the first officer of the county (been mentioned before). John and Clarence have been members of the board of supervisors. Ada Lightsey Douglas has written a book, "The Veteran's Story," a Civil War story, mostly about Gen. Lee.

The R. J. Jones family was not only prominent in the county but in the state. He was a Methodist minister and is said to have been in every part of the state. He had three sons, Kenneth, Ransom II, Will, and a son-in-law, Dart Huddleston. All three sons were Methodist ministers who stood high in the Conference of the state. They claimed Kenneth as the first white child born in the county. He preached mostly in north Mississippi and was the father-in-law of Judge Lamb of Eupora, who, in turn, is the father-in-law of Pete Portner, cashier of the Bank of Eupora. Ransom II. was the father of Walt Jones, bookkeeper for Marks Rothenberg, also Charlie, secretary of the East Mississippi Asylum, and Mrs. Reid, whose husband was the cashier of the First National Bank at Meridian. Will Jones has been clerk of the Mississippi Methodist Conference for a number of years. He has a son, Dr. George Jones, who is editor of the Methodist Journal at Nashville, Tenn., another son, Dr. Jones at Forest, Miss., also Henry Jones of the Health Department, at Jackson, Miss. The Rev. Bart Huddleston had a son, Kenneth, who was assessor and a member of the legislature.

R. J. had a brother, Jeremiah, who was a school teacher and farmer, and had 27 children. Also a brother, Henry, who was a minister and was known as "Hellfire" Jones, because he preached so much about hellfire and damnation. He had a son, Lazarus, who was first assessor and minister. He had three sons, Fred, of New Orleans; Walter, Jackson, Roy, of Hattiesburg. Henry also had a son-in-law, P. H. House, who was a member of the Conference for a long time. Another brother of R. J. Jones was Judge Wiley Jones, who had a large farm south of Paulding, which was sold to F. J. Cook in 1887 and he moved to Texas. Another brother was L. J. Jones, who was a member of the legislature (speaker) for a long time.

George Jones is a Doctor of Divinity. Three generations of his family have graduated at Millsaps College. The only family that has this honor.

R. J. Jones had a sister, Mrs. Martha Jones Kennedy, who lived in the county and was the grandmother of the writer, and Postmaster Hugh Kennedy of Louin, and great grandmother of Dr. J. T. McIlee of Louin, and Mrs. W. P. Tally (deceased). The Rev. H. C. Castle is a grandson-in-law. He has been a member of the Mississippi Conference for a number of years.

The McCormick family has been prominent in the county and state. The first act of John McCormick was to establish Hopewell church and John II was an officer of the county. Forest McCormick was the first citizen of the county to secure a Ph.D. degree, and is now teaching at M.S.C.W. at Columbus, Miss. Arch McCormick is head of one of the schools in Jackson. Miss Stella McCormick is supervisor of elementary schools in this county; first cousin, Mr. Overby, is now superintendent of schools of the county.

The R. R. Abney family was perhaps the most prominent in business. R. R. was president of the board of supervisors and postmaster at Montrose. J. P. was postmaster and had a large business at Montrose. Foster was very prominent as a merchant. Bill and his sons, Sam and John, were popular merchants at Heidelberg and Pachuta. R. R. II owns quite a bit of property at Bay Springs. R. R., III, has a large department store in Bay Springs. Bill, proprietor of the Abney Motor Co., at Bay Springs. R. L. has been mayor of Bay Springs for 30 years. R. L., II, is a member of the board of aldermen. J. T., was a member of the Mississippi Conference for a number of years. They have more space in the Goodspeed publications than any other family. Else Abney is a member of the school faculty of the City of Laurel. Annie Mae Abney Horn is assistant postmaster in Bay Springs.

NOAH BARBOUR, president of first school known in Jasper. Said to be the first rural free school in state.

# February 7, 1957

## HISTORY OF JASPER COUNTY

**By J. M. KENNEDY**

The Thigpens established the town of Lake Como and soon took active part in church, schools and public life of the county. S. F. was a teacher and was elected county superintendent of education in 1891, and then served four years in the legislature. He was later editor of the Bay Springs News and is now in the mercantile business. His son, Argie, is state welfare agent. Another son, S. F. Jr., is on his second term as mayor of Bay Springs.

Mike was editor of the Jasper County Review, then lawyer, state senator. He was later judge in Vicksburg. Wiley was a merchant, county treasurer and state senator.

The town of Heidelberg was named for the Heidelbergs. Tom and Irve ran a large mercantile business there. Tom's son, Roy, is the owner and operator of the Heidelberg Hotel at Jackson. Irve's son, Jim, is connected with the Deposit Guaranty Bank & Trust Co. at Jackson. Dan moved to Shubuta and became judge. He had a son, Harvey, who was superintendent of schools at Clarksdale, Miss., for fifty years. Another son, Roland, was judge in Hattiesburg. W. W. was in the legislature for a long time. His son, Hinkle, is a prominent lawyer at Pascagoula.

The Stringer family is said to be very large in Jasper, Jones and Smith counties. M. B. was a member of the board of supervisors for several terms. S. L. was superintendent of schools, Louin, Richton and Crosby. Then president of the Mississippi Education Association, member of the Department of Education and is now retired. Charlie was superintendent of schools in Smith County for a long time. L. J. was superintendent of schools in Jones County. Roscoe is president of a college at Booneville, Miss. John has been a doctor at Stringer for a long time. Will is district attorney in Missouri. Minnie Stringer Ford has been a member of the Mississippi Southern College faculty for a number of years.

Through the kindness of Miss Myra Pruitte, a daughter of our only Forty Niner, we were given a record book which she found in her home that turned out to be of the first rural free public school in the state. It did not give the location only that it was a school in T 3 R 12. Some think it was just south of the old Twistwood church which was at the intersection of Highway 18 and the old Three-Chopped-Way or where the Rose Hill cemetery is located. This ran from 1836 in the fifties. It was a leather bound book written with a goose quill. It was signed Noah Barbour, president. He and his son, Henry, built the Twistwood Baptist church which some say was the first in the county. Henry was a Baptist preacher and was the organizer of many churches in Jasper, Clark, Smith and Newton counties. He went to the Civil War and carried his four sons and his son-in-law. He lost one son, another was severely wounded at the battle of Atlanta, and a telegram was sent to his daughter at Enterprise, Miss., that her husband was killed. His daughter prayed over the matter that night and rose the next morning to go

to Atlanta. The people tried to stop her but she told them that it had been revealed to her that he was alive. She had a small baby but carried a twelve year old daughter to help. It was a terrible journey as it was in 1864 when the country was full of free Negroes and Yankees, and most of the property had been destroyed. When she reached Atlanta she found it in ashes and was told that the Confederate wounded were 100 miles from there. She kept on, found her husband, nursed him a month and brought him home and he lived till 1905. In 1937 Chas. Tally's picture was given in The Jasper News as the 7th generation of N. Barbour that has lived in the county.

B. F. Moss was at one time sheriff and the town of Mossville was named for him. He has a son in Jones County, B. L., who is a big land owner; Jubal is a member of the county school board.

Gabe Ellis was at one time county treasurer; Jim Ellis was a member of the board of supervisors and sheriff. A large connection of this family has always lived in the southern part of the county.

Judge Sam Terrall was considered one of the most brilliant Chief Justices of the Supreme Court that the State of Mississippi has ever had. Georgie Terrall was deputy chancery clerk for a number of years. Terrall Graham, a relative of the Terralls is county assessor.

The Brown family has always been very large in the county. G. N. was county attorney and a member of the board of supervisors for 20 years.

Gen. James A. Smith came to Paulding and taught school after the Civil War and married the daughter of Judge Henry A. Calhoun who lived southeast of Paulding, where the Bergins now live. He was later state superintendent of education. The Smiths have been many and prominent during the life of the county. Rev. Jackson Smith settled in the northwestern part of Beat One and most of his children and grandchildren have settled around him and so we have Smithtown. Bob was a member of the board of supervisors for a number of years and is now a member of the welfare board. J. C. was a member of the board of supervisors and a member of the legislature for two terms. Jewell Smith is now a member of the state senate. R. L. was a member of the county school board for 30 years. Rev. Jim Smith is a noted evangelist. Col. John Smith was a state senator, a member of the Constitutional Convention in 1890. Mill was a popular preacher of the county.

The Clasthams have stood high in the county for years. Lum has been a member of the legislature; Ben, post master at Montrose, and Earl the same at Rose Hill. John, a member of the board of supervisors for two terms. John has a son who is a member of the Mississippi Methodist Conference.

The Merrills were high class citizens. Green was a judge, Miss Sue was a teacher, John stood high in business in Meridian. Humphries is a member of the State Department of Agriculture. Will Alexander was a...

state of Bay Springs. Marzell was a member of the state legislature. John D. and John F. were postmasters at Baxter. Miss Lena is a teacher in the Gulfport schools. Eunice Alexander Eley belongs to the State Library Commission. Chessie, with her husband, John W. Eaton, has charge of the Blind Institute at Jackson. LaGetta is a Presbyterian minister at Greenwood, S. C.

Richard Simmons was the first county superintendent of education of the county and later was sheriff. Dr. W. C. Simmons is said to have had the largest practice of medicine that the county has ever had. Dr. Ona was a large practice at Newton. Dr. Cloura was state veterinarian. Dr. Shubert has a good practice at Newton. Irl is judge at Gulfport. L. W. is superintendent of schools at Meadville. Miss Geneva, teaches in the college at Meridian. Verba has been chancery clerk for 20 years. Velma has been postmaster at Louin. Viva's husband is a member of the board of supervisors.

Jim Bassett was sheriff for two terms and has been a member of the board of supervisors for 20 years. Rev. Dowe was a Baptist minister of the county for his adult life. Levi did the same work also, and was postmaster at Louin. Alex was also a member of the board of supervisors. Charlie is a saw mill operator. Rev. Dowe was also a member of the county school board.

W. J. McFarland was sheriff longer than any man in the county; was also circuit clerk and a member of the legislature. His son, Alex, was county attorney. His grandson, Joe Alex, is now on his second term as district attorney. Mrs. Blanche McFarland represents the State Department of Health at Bay Springs.

C. E. Boulton was circuit clerk for two terms, also postmaster at Lake Como. His wife and son, also, Welby is in business in Bay Springs.

William Hosey came to Jasper County before the Indians and his descendants have lived in the southwestern part of the county since. Bill H was mayor of Laurel. Earl is an employee of the government at Meridian. John, Hillman, N. B. and J. H. were doctors. William was first assessor. Sam is still a large land owner in this section.

William Pugh was one of the first members of the board of supervisors. R. C. was president

Central Mississippi and Northwest Mississippi Junior Colleges. Charlie was superintendent of schools in Mississippi for more than 30 years. Lacy was in the Bureau of Education at Washington, D. C., for a long time, also with the Insular Possession Schools. W. E. and Garfield were deputy sheriffs for a long time. Rivers belongs to the Mississippi Methodist Conference.

The Buckleys have owned a large tract of land in the northeastern part of the county where they had a post office called Buckley's store. The Buckleys are prominent in business in Enterprise, Laurel, Meridian and Newton. Hardee has been a member of the board of supervisors for a number of years.

Steve Sims has been a member of the board of supervisors for nearly 20 years. J. L. has been justice of peace for a long time. The Sims family is old and very large.

The Ulmer family has three members in the Mississippi Methodist Conference. It has been a family of fine citizens for many years. One is county attorney.

It is said that the Reed family spelled their name only one way when they came to the county but now spell it three ways—Reed, Read and Reid—and that they came from the same family. Walter Reid was a member of the board of supervisors for eight years, also a member of the school board. B. C. Reed is a member of the school board now. They are very fine citizens. Fred is county surveyor.

Clarence Thomas has been member of the board of supervisors for eight years. He comes from a fine family that has always lived in the southeastern part of the county. J. C. Thomas was a member of the legislature.

George Ryan was one of the first citizens and was probate judge. His son, Milton, was at one time representative to the state legislature. Marion was a prominent teacher. Sid was a large property owner in Bay Springs. Grandsons, W. P. and L. R. Massey were preachers; L. P. Davis a superintendent of schools at Pachuta.

Bill Massey was a large land owner and had a son, Tom, who was county superintendent of education, and also a son, Lee, who held this office for three terms. His grand-daughter, Prof. Lel Massey, is professor in Ohio Wesleyan University.

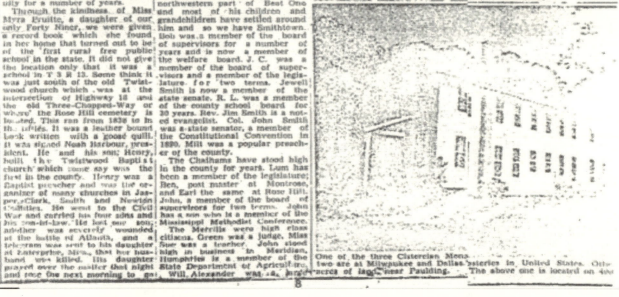

One of the three Cistercian Monasteries in United States. Other two are at Milwaukee and Dallas. The above one is located on 400 acres of land near Paulding.

**February 14, 1957**

# HISTORY OF JASPER COUNTY

### By J. M. KENNEDY

ERATA: G. N. Brown was county attorney, representative and senator. Deavours Brown has been supervisors 20 years.

R. C. Alexander was sheriff of the county.

The Huseys came to the county before Indians left.

There were five dentists in the T. L. Massey family. Dr T. L. and his four sons; Dr Jewett (deceased), John Oates, Orris and Mark.

There were several doctors in the Lyon family. Dr Wilson Lyon is now president of Pamona College in California. He is a Rhodes scholar.

N. D. Graham was a large property owner near Rose Hill. N. D. Jr. still lives in the beautiful old home. A son-in-law, Brogan Holifield, is a member of the Mississippi Methodist Conference; another son-in-law, John Chatham, was a member of the board of supervisors for several terms.

Bill Brame was a Confederate veteran and was later elected sheriff of the county and was killed defending the county treasury. His son, Tom, was chancery clerk for 44 years. The Brames are still prominent in the county. Bertie is postmaster at Paulding.

Capt. Sartor fought in the Indian wars. Jeff was a member of the board of supervisors for a number of years. A son-in-law, Herbert Crisler, is editor of The Jasper County News. A grandson, Havis, is a member of the legislature; another, G. T. Roberts, was in the legislature.

The Grissoms are popular citizens of the southwest beat, and have given us our popular circuit clerk. Mrs Grissom Conner is postmaster at Stringer.

The Lands have been in the county since its organization. Dr Land has practiced at Louin for many years. John was postmaster at Byena.

John Ball was constable and deputy sheriff most of his life. His father was killed in the Battle of Atlanta. William was a Baptist preacher. O. C. is a mail carrier.

One of the first officers of the county was a Parker. They are still with us. Allison is editor of the Prentiss Headlight. Dr E. U. is at Laurel.

### The First Settlement

Excerpts from the Choctaw Mission in Jasper County, by A. J. Brown. Brown is the author of Newton County History.

The Six Town Mississippi Station was established about the year 1825. Some records give it earlier than that. The man's name was Bardwell and thought to be from New England. The Indians around this section were known as Six Town tribe of the Choctaws. They occupied most of what is now Jasper County. The station was afterwards surveyed in Sec. 15, T. 3 R 12 East.

The location of this place was one of the finest sections of land in the county. It was a beautiful table land with no hills or streams to mar its beauty. The site was at the edge of this tableland and just down the hill was a spring which gushed from a solid rock and gave enough water to supply a city of 2000 people. Later, water mills were placed on this stream. Later settlers forced this same water into a tank by a hydraulic ram.

Two-storied settlements were built with logs. Living quarters, church and school. The graveyard was located about 3 or 4 hundred yards a little east of north. They located on the old Three-Chopped-Way which ran to Natchez where they had to make their reports to the bishop (this being a Catholic mission). They soon began to lay out a road to Jackson, the new capitol.

The writer has attended gatherings here of the Indians, their ball games, cries, dances, etc. Great crowds of Indians and Whites attended. When the county was first organized this was thought to be the place for the county site but people in the Southeast thought it was too far north and sco acompromise was made to place it five miles south where there was plenty of good clay to build a courthouse. A few Irish Catholics had settled near this place and so when the courthouse was located at Paulding a catholic church was located there and thus we had what was called Irishtown. At one time an Irishman, Mike Hanly was President of the board of supervisors for many years. Many attempts were made to defeat him but no success as there were so many Irish and the taxpayer said he looked after their interest.

### And the Stars Fell

Science tells us that Haley's comet comes near the earth about every seventy years and showers us with a quanity of small meteors. They say that there meteors coming through the air so fast that they become heated and look like fire at night. The Writer has seen them so large that they would light the whole heavens at night. He saw the one that fell near Pelahatchie about 45 years ago. It fell about nine o'clock in the morning creating a loud noise and smoke. It was seen and heard over most of the state.

Uncle Heck was my negro helper in using the hoe in the crops. The farmers did more hoeing then than now. In plowing the small crops they used to say, "run on one side and knock it down and come on the other side and cover it up." So the plowman had to pull off from the small crops and depend on the hoe hand to do the work. The writer fixed a double stock so that you could plow both sides of the crop at the same time lapping the dirt around the small plants and hoeing was not so important. So Uncle Heck and I as we pulled the hoe from sun till sun would indulge in a number of conversations. He said that the showers were light the first few nights and then they began to come thick and fast. The old man in the community that was a Bible student told the people that it was the sign the world was coming to an end. Both white and black quit work and all were very much disturbed, children crying and old folks praying, some fainting. A preacher lived about five miles away and all decided to go to see him. When his crowd arrived, many people were there. The preacher told them that the time had come and for all to meet it bravely, telling them that if they had done anything wrong to confess it and pray, if they had done a wrong to anyone to go and confess it and ask for forgiveness. A great many astounding facts came to light even with man and wife. Alabama has a book, "Stars Fell On Alabama."

As soon as the report went out that the Choctaw nation had agreed to move to the Indian Territory (This agreement was made at the Dancing Rabbit-Creek in Noxube County in 1830) people began to come from North Carolina, South Carolina, Georgia, Alabama, Tennesee and from some of the old counties such as Wayne and Jones. It was said that so many people came from Jones that there were not enough left to have a county government and hence the "Free State of Jones."

The black lands in the county was much in demand as there was no fertilizer at that time. It was said that you could plow it up in June and plant it in corn and you could have a good crop. The people that came from North Carolina, South Carolina and Alabama, came mostly over the Three-Chopped-Way. Those from Tennessee and North Alabama came over the Old Jackson Highway. Many settle even before the county was formor organized and before there were land lines. The settlers would decide on his location, build a shack and mark off his land one half mile each way. He would have to be careful about Indian claims as the Indian claim stood ahead of all others. It took the Indians some time to prepare for their journey; prepare food, make wagons, boats, etc. They were to gather at Missionary and proceed to Garlandsville for their journey. A book has been written "The Trail of Tears." All who wished could remain but would be under the laws of the state. There was talk of rebellion as they did not trust Greenwood Leflore so much as he was a half Frenchman. He remained in the state and built a great mansion near Greenwood. Jasper was one of the first counties surveyed as it was decided to establish a new base line about where Stringer and Heidelberg is now situated and survey north.

As soon as the county site was selected a log courthouse was built as the contract for the old courthouse was not let till 1838 by J. E. Watts of Garlandsville. The brick were made at Paulding by slaves. Before the courhouse was built John J. McRea came to town and established a news paper and named it the Eastern Clarion. The Newton Record of 1901 says that the Clarion was the only paper in East Mississippi.

The W. H. Hardy home at Paulding, which was later occupied by M. Hanly, president board of supervisors for many years after the Civil War. Then Judge Stone Deavours, prominent lawyer and director of University Law School resided there. The residence is now owned by the Read family.

**February 21, 1957**

# HISTORY OF JASPER COUNTY

By J. M. KENNEDY

The Newton Record says: "There were very few newspapers in the State before the year 1860, probably not more than forty. Now there are probably 182. There was no newspaper in Newton County until after the war. An attempt had been made to establish one at Decatur in 1861, but there was probably not a 'copy issued. The paper that had the circulation in this county (Newton) for about twenty years before the war, was the Eastern Clarion published at Paulding, in Jasper County, about twenty miles from the railroad. This paper was owned and edited by Simeon R. Adams, who was a man of marked ability as a journalist. The Clarion was the largest paper in the state, had the largest circulation, an advertising medium in the towns and county, to say nothing of its foreign business, which was large."

Pages from An Old Scrapbook: Great Men, Early Newspapers They Edited for Mississippi, by Anabel Power:

"The following story is from the files of the writer's father, the late Col. J. L. Power, who was owner and publisher of The Clarion at a later date, with Major Barksdale continuing as editor.

"Away back in the 'forties, there were two noted newspapers published in this State. One was the Paulding Clarion, published at the county seat of Jasper by Simeon Adams, and the other other, the old Mississippian, at Jackson, by Charles M. Price and George R. Fall, with Price as the editor and Fall as the general manager.

"The Clarion was perhaps the largest single sheet ever published in this State. It was of huge dimensions — a single sheet would cover a large bed. It was not only a newsy paper and well edited, but its columns were filled with advertisements.

"These were the days before railroads when the farmers of East Mississippi carted their cotton to Mobile and returned with the supplies necessary for 12 months. The merchants in Mobile, a wide-awake set, used the columns of this widely circulated sheet for advertising their goods and business, and its columns teemed with their advertisements.

"Two Noted Newspapers

"The Paulding Clarion was to the people of east Mississippi, what the old Mississippian was to the entire State. Though they did not exactly swear by it, they all took it. It was a sad day to East Mississippi, and especially to Paulding, and the old county of Jasper, when Simeon Adams was called to his father. He was a Mason and when his brethren met to pay the last sad tribute to their deceased brother and consign his mortal remains to that narrow resting place, it was lamented that there was no music to escort the honored dead to the little cemetery situated among the long-leafed pines of old Jasper.

"An Improvised Band

"A gentleman by the name of Tannebaum, who taught music in the little village, was importuned to arrange music for the occasion. He improvised a band consisting of a violin, flute, guitar and an accordion, and heading the procession, the quartette played a melancholy dirge as they marched at the head of the procession to the grave and there, amid the tears of family, friends and brethren, was consigned to the grave the remains of one of the most remarkable men who had ever wielded the pen in an editorial sanctum in Mississippi."

The Record says that the Clarion was the largest paper in the state, and had the largest circulation and that it made $10,000.00 net. McRea did not stay with it long as he moved on to build Enterprise. His old home still is occupied at this time. He became governor of Mississippi in 1852. The writer has perused the pages of the old Clarion in the Department of Archives in Jackson. It looks like a bed sheet, having ten columns and being long. It had "ads" from New Orleans to New York. Legal notices and announcements of candidates from all parts of the state. Simeon R. Adams took charge of the paper when McRea went to Enterprise, and ran the paper for about twenty years when he died. The Jackson paper says that a great funeral took place at Paulding then. James J. Shannon was editor after Adams. In 1852, it had an "ad" for a cotton picker.

In 1842, O. C. Dease established the True Democrat at Paulding. It was a seven-column paper. Dease was the first senator from Jasper County. He was a member of the Secession (State) Convention and later county superintendent of education.

At first the people were at a great disadvantage about a market but in the fall of the year great crowds would make a trip to Mobile to buy for the year. The slogan then was to make your living at home. Two water mills were soon constructed on Town Creek, also two on Goodwater The big business of these mills was grounding corn for bread. Round and McDougal put the two in on Town Creek and Morris and Green the two on Goodwater, near Missionary.

In 1836, Sterling Lodge No. 54 was installed at Paulding. Some of the early members were: B. Hunt, James E. Watts, S. B. Leftwitch, W. M. Ellis, James McDougal, J. D. Dabney, J. H. Saxon, S. Fatheree, James A. Chapman, K. J. Jones, the famous preacher.

Harrison Lodge No. 87 was granted at Garlandsville in 1842. Early members were: J. E. Watts, Isaac Hodge, John A. Hodge, Thomas Watts, Samuel B. Watts, Seaborn J. Brown, William Garry, Hamilton Brown.

Oak Bowery Lodge No. 186 was granted in 1855, early members were: L. J. Jones, W. M. Jones, F. R. Loper, John H. Cook, Henry P. Cook, Henry T. Jones, secretary; James M. Rambo, Jared M. Windham, Williams Gresham, S. A. Allen, Allen Bridges, Utley Bufking, Gabrel Collins, Riley Cooper, Isaac Downs, T. W. Grayson, Z. K Dempsey, John Garner, George W. Garvin, Ancrew Garvin, Israel C. Harris, Seaborn W. Jones, Leroy S. Morrison, G. D. McCormick, L. L. Porter, William Pearce, Cary Patterson, John R. Stockman, A. C. Towler, S. P. Windham, R. R. Abney, D. W. Windham, T. W. Linder, O. K. Dyas, L. W. Carroll, Riley Cooper, F. B. Loper, A. C. Fowler, E. F. Moss, Isaac Horsey.

With its newspapers and reputation Paulding was a great place for political gatherings. A story is handed down that at one time when Gen. Foote was speaking against secession, he pictured a terrible condition if the country should be divided. Bryant Morris (owner of the Missionary) cried with a loud voice, "Hasten the time when that may be." Foote, coming back with renewed vigor, called on the "mighty men of Jasper" not to let this happen. Thence the saying, "Ye mighty men of Jasper."

Garlandsville was the first post office and leading town as it was the Indian capitol. When the French first settled in New Orleans (1718)), they soon made their way to Garlandsville to see the chief of the Choctaws, Red Shoes, for the purpose of trading with the Indians. This trail passed where the town of Columbia is situated on to Williamsburg and Taylorsville, and when Gen. Jackson was taking charge of the Gulf Coast he used this road on his way to Nashville. The government at one time kept it up. The other old highway was the Three-Chopped-Way which the first whites (missionaries) traveled to Natchez, which was the seat of the Catholic diocese in Mississippi, was the first road through the Creek nation which covered most of the state of Alabama. The first settlers who came to Wayne County, brought their household goods on horseback and some rolled it in barrels. Same Dale secured this road from the Indians and helped to clear it out.

Statement About the Three-Chopped-Way

In the early days after the county was formed, my father came from South Carolina and settled near Rocky Mount (six miles southwest of Paulding). He soon decided that he wanted to move on the Three-Chopped-Way where he could see more people. I remember the old hand-carved mile boards marked from Raleigh to Enterprise. We could see all kinds of traveling, wagons, horseback, walking, whites and Indians. I still live on this highway, near Antioch Church.

Signed, J. O. BISHOP.

The writer remembers that someone asked why this road was not marked by Paulding. The old man answered that this road was here long before Paulding came into existence. Some of the maps give it marked by Paulding and on to Quitman but there was no Paulding or Quitman when this road was laid out and you could not cross the river at Quitman. The Chickasaway river forks at Enterprise which makes fording possible. It is said that a private mail route was established along this route from Natchez to Savannah, Ga. Later, the government took it over and changed to Monticello and Augusta because of ferries and the land office at Augusta. This road crosses the old Jackson Highway in the western part of the county about three miles north of Bay Springs on the Risher Holder place. Jasper County has the two oldest roads in the state crossing in the county. S. F. Thigpen (now ninety-three years of age), says when a boy he loved to talk to Billy John (the oldest Indian in the county, said to be one hundred and fifteen), who lived about five miles north of Bay Springs. He could tell about seeing Gen. Jackson pass with his soldiers.

As the settlers came to this county they only had these two roads and no bridges; they either had to ford the stream or swim it, but soon roads were laid out, mostly to the county site. Garlandsville had a road to Missionary (by the Indians); it was soon opened to Paulding. A road was soon opened south to Oak Bowery settlement and to Lake Como. The first bridge built in the county was on the road to Lake Como, named in honor of the man who built it, Rambo. This road proceeded beyond Lake Como into the old Jackson Highway in Smith County and was the road traveled to New Orleans from Paulding. Churches soon were springing up. Among the first were: The Catholic Church at Paulding; Hopewell, a Methodist Church, established by John F. McCormick, still stands; Twistwood, a Baptist Church, on the hill east of the creek, bearing the same name. There is nothing there now but a cemetery. On the Three-Chopped-Way — Shady Grove in the southeast part of the county. Of course, the churches at Garlandsville, Montrose, and Lake Como were some of the first churches. Henry Barbour seems to be one of the earliest Baptist leaders and the Jones brothers seemed to be the earliest Methodist leaders. It is said that the first rural free school was established in this county, supported by the 15th Section funds. Miss Myra Pruitt, a daughter of our only "Forty-Niner", presented to the county a record book which was leather bound and written with a goose quill, which seemed to be the records of this school from 1838 to the fifties. It was signed by Noah Barbour who was the father of Henry Barbour.

# February 28, 1957

## HISTORY OF JASPER COUNTY

### By J. M. KENNEDY

**Postoffices and Postmasters of Jasper County**

The first postoffice in the county was Garlandsville as it had been the Indian town for many years. Tallahoma was the next one and it is said to be south of Lake Como as William Hosey settled in that part of the county before the Indians left here. Paulding was third.

Garlandsville—H. W. Ward, 7-5-1834; James Watts, 6-13-1835; M. F. Beard, 1-31-1840; I. V. Hodges, 2-11-1841; B. F. Reynolds, 1-3-1843; James M. Williams, 1-18-1845; W. N. Payne, 2-24-1853; F. B. Loper, 1-2-1857; Wiley Flanagan, 7-9-1866; Stephen H. Barnes, 9-10-1868; Western Spann, 12-10-1877; Josie Williams, 7-2-1883; B. D. Williams, 3-21-1928; Henry Weir, 1-13-1930; Robert Weir, 12-22-1943; Levi E. Weir Jr., 10-1-1946. Discontinued, 12-31-1953.

Tallahoma — William Bridges, 11-22-1834; Allen Jones, 7-10-1856; J. B. Hart, 2-3-1857; R. O. Cain, 12-1857. Discontinued 8-26-1859.

Paulding—William Ellis, 5-25-1835; W. M. Mead, 6-2-1837; Berry Hunt, 10-5-1837; Simeon R. Adams, 4-20-1841; J. D. Knox, 12-10-1845; R. W. Thompson, 12-28-1848; W. P. Cherry, 3-8-1850; L. A. Kidd, 9-20-1851; W. B. Ferrall, 9-13-1852; Simeon Easterland, 4-20-1853; J. B. Gough, 11-29-1855; John G. Markham, 4-43-1859; Sam Castell, 12-26-1865; James Sampson, 6-20-1868; Zachariah Windham, 7-13-1868; John E. Green, 7-1-1867; John B. Weathersby, 10-25-1869; E. H. McKinstrey, 2-7-1871; Margaret C. Chapman, 11-23-1881; Ella Round, 4-16-1912; Ella Foley, 4-2-1917; Leila Street, 1-15-1927; Virginia A. Hawkins, 10-31-1928; Leila McDevitt, 1-26-1929; Mrs. Berdie Brame, 9-28-1933.

Claiborne—E. L. Caraway, 1-8-1840; O. C. Rhodes, 5-15-1844; Labon Caraway, 6-3-1845; C. J. Caraway, 1-21-1847; Josiah Jones, 6-10-1847; J. H. Terral, 9-17-1855; Geo. D. McCormick, 4-7-1857; William Rose, 7-15-1858; Ellis Caraway, 10-5-1858; T. C. Moffit, 12-28-1858; W. W. Tate, 8-18-1650; John Lindsey, 2-5-1874; D. H. Price, 11-29-1887; Al M. Dorter, 11-15-1882; Mary C. Donald, 7-22-1884; D. H. Price, 6-18-1885; S. Q. Donald, 7-31-1887; Henry James, 5-17-1898.

Montrose—Ezekiel Harris, 4-27-1846; William Caldwell, 4-2-1855; Ezekiel Harris, 7-29-1855; R. W. King, 9-1-1855; Birhard W. Burge, 11-1-1855; James Campbell, 12-22-1858; Henry Addy, 6-8-1871; Robert R. Abney, 1-27-1873; John M. Cole, 2-29-1872; James P. Abney, 3-30-1874; Mary L. Burnett, 5-14-1872; Ezra W. Abney, 2-1-1898; Robert F. Abney, 11-22-1900; John Burnett, 5-16-1901. (Three fine citizens came from Smith County to live in Jasper: John, Don and Bob Burnett. The Burnett's have the oldest dry goods store in Bay Springs). Jesse M. Elry, 4-27-1904; Ben Chatham, 3-21-1922; James W. Abney, 1-31-1953; Bernice L. James, 10-7-1955.

Hough's Store, 9-22-1847; Buckley, 12-22-1855. Discontinued, 1-21-1867.

Davisville—J. R. Tenal, 1-4-1852; D. A. Morris, 5-1-1857; Henry Lyman, 12-7-1871; O. C. Thompson, 4-6-1874; Sue Terrall, 6-7-1876; Hattie Hudson, 1-21-1878; Terrall Smith, 2-27-1878. Discontinued.

Twistwood—N. F. Ferguson, 8-23-1855; A. J. Lewis, 7-18-1854; William L. Kennedy, 5-27-1857; John M. Byrd, 9-18-1874; D. J. McKinnon, 1-15-1878; W. C. Day, 3-18-1854; James A. Granberry, 11-2-1884; G. F. Peek, 7-5-1885.

Rose Hill-9-22-1868; Pat James, 6-27-1896; Sallie H. Avera, 1-2-1900; Milton A. Ryan, 6-20-1900; Wofford M. Merrill, 11-3-1913; Rodney E. Chatham, 1-30-1933.

Etohoma—W. J. Sugg, 7-29-1856; Frazier Bridges, 9-16-1858; John W. Jones, 7-1-1873; W. M. Flanagan, 1-25-1877; Thomas Bowden, 1-6-1878.

Turnerville—S. S. Turner, 8-12-1857; John R. Jones, 6-1-1877; F. J. Turner, 8-15-1881; Wm B. Pool, 8-3-1887; Alfred T. Burton, 1891; Robert L. Smith, 10-7-1897; Ollie Burton, 1-13-1898; B. F. Richardson, 10-30-1903; W. F. Windham, 1-28-1904; James L. Waldrup, 1-6-1905; James M. Waites, 2-15-1906. Discontinued, 3-31-1909.

Prairie Line—C. A. Hatch, 7-14-1857; Nathaniel Barnett, 10-3-1858.

Roaring Creek—Lovie Shelby, 9-16-57. Discontinued, 3-23-1859.

Colemana—B. F. Ellis, 9-18-1857; W. S. Thompson, 11-6-1857; to Lake Como—4-26-1859; Urial H. Oliphant, 7-1-1873; B. F. Duke, 6-13-1876; Chas. Thigpen, 6-8-1894; C. E. Boulton, 3-27-1912; Maggie L. Boulton, 1-2-1923; Welby Boulton, 4-30-1942. Discontinued, 7-31-1951.

Holt—Mose — Lovitt, 8-30-1060. Discontinued, 5-17-1867.

Shady Grove—S. E. Selby, 11-24-1860; Henry M. Shoemaker, 8-16-1871; John A. Boyd, 11-8-1892; Mary J. Boyd, 8-11-1893. Discontinued, 7-6-1901.

Crosswell—Tharrel R. McCormick, 12-10-1873; Seaborn W. Jones, 3-8-1875; M. W. Lovitt, 1-15-1878; Urial H. Oliphant, 4-19-1878. Discontinued, 3-18-1880.

Jewell's Hill—John B. Gray, 5-21-1878.

Otho—Thomas E. H. Robinson, 01-1878. Discontinued, 12-18-1882.

Mabel—J. J. Perdue, 3-18-1880; A. H. Windham, 12-20-1881. Discontinued, 1882.

Brevel—J. F. McCormick, 5-12-1881.

Vosburgh—C. C. Thompson, 4-17-1882; Sallie B. Buckin, 6-11-1856; Mary Frances Voss, 8-20-1889; Delilah J. Voss, 2-13-1891, to Vosburg — 12-18-1893; Jessie Mamblin, 12-18-1893; Ida Voss, 11-13-1897; Ida Bounds, 6-15-1903; Kate B. Martin, 2-19-1915; Katie M. Thornton, 10-2-1918; James S. Andrews, 5-26-1922; Rose P. Singleton, 2-6-1924; Aden N. Utsey, 2-17-1925; Bill J. Martin, 12-16-1930; Mrs Eloise T. Martin, 1-30-1932; Bill J. Martin, 2-6-1933; Mrs Lottie D. Martin, 9-2-1941; Mrs Gertrude H. McGee, 4-11-1942, Name to Vossburg, 11-1-1950.

Stringer—Bettie Stringer, 5-3-1895; Sloan Stringer, 5-3-1900; R. A. Welborn, 3-24-1903; Viola Moss, Viola Stringer, 7-9-1909; Nola M. Price, 4-15-1910; Monnie Grissom, 8-19-1910; Ida Terry, 6-14-1913; Everett Welborn, 2-17-1915; Ervin Anderson, 4-5-1921; George H. Hosey, 2-15-1926; Ruth Johnston, 4-20-1926; Joe G. Ishee, 5-26-1935; Pearl W. Ishee, 6-30-1952; Rufus A. Ware, 10-15-1954.

Bolton—Sim G. Graham, 9-21-1882; W. L. Allen, 4-23-1886. Discontinued 4-9-1890.

Hamlet—Jeremiah Holder, 12-21-1882; James Richard, 10-13-1887; B. T. King, 11-19-1888; G. W. Ainsworth, 6-1-1889; W. B. Ainsworth, 11-11-1895; Maggie Windham, 1-30-1901; J. E. Waters, 8-30-1907; W. H. Ishee, 1-7-1908.

Heidelberg—D. M. Gatlin, 2-13-1883; J. A. Taylor, 1-19-1885; Mary C. Bounds, 15-13-1887; Susan R. Cook, 8-22-1889; Kate Terral, 8-23-1893; Marcia Cook, 5-13-1897; Mary Wilkins, 3-23-1900; G. M. Morrison, 9-28-1906; Pink H. Morrison, 1-6-1915; J. Truett Carr, 6-1-1942; Elizabeth M. Carr, 8-20-1943; Rusie King, 4-19-1945; J. Truett Carr, 4-30-1946; Rusie M. King, 3-16-1949.

Missionary—S. D. Russell, 12-22-1884. Discontinued, 10-14-1905.

Acme—T. A. Mervin, 8-17-1886; John D. Tyner, 3-16-1888; Sarah Tyner, 1-16-1890; W. M. Tyner, 7-31-1899; James T. Brinson, 4-9-1901; B. F. Morgan, 7-2-1901; Agnes Kuydendall, 4-21-1909.

Alto—G. W. Clayton, 2-25-1888; F. L. Cook, 4-21-1898; Martha Lighsey, 10-6-1908; Sarah Bethea, 1-30-1915.

Massengale—Curtis B. Massengale, 6-30-1888; Discontinued, 1-22-1903.

Leona—C. W. Pryor, 2-25-1890; Ida J. Pryor, 5-24-1894; John R. Nealy, 10-1-1895; W. M. Heard, 3-31-1903.

Viola—Spence Wade Jr., 8-21-1894. Discontinued, 9-7-1895.

Weems—John J. Weems, 10-3-1895; Walter Eckels, 9-26-1894; Allie J. Weems, 1-14-1894; James C. Gardner, 4-8-1907.

Penanity—W. E. Foley, 8-12-1891. Discontinued, 10-9-1906.

Ferman—Albert G. B. Graham, 9-5-1891. Discontinued, 7-25-1895.

Bay Springs—Joe B. Blankinship, 4-12-1892; L. L. Denson, 5-6-1900; John T. Cook, 2-27-1901; Minnie E Keown, 7-1-1902; Addie Tyner, 1-5-1915; Sarah A. Tyner, 12-26-1918; Fannie C. Shoemaker, 7-3-1930; Charles O. Yelverton, 7-8-1935; Lily B. McDonald, 1-23-1936.

Vernon—Wm Hosey, 5-23-1893. Baxter—John D. Alexander, 5-22-1894; John F. Alexander, 11-5-1902.

Hyena—John L. Land, 5-25-1897. Discontinued.

Hosey—Robert H. Hosey, 4-22-1895; Bryant Harrington, 9-13-1896. Discontinued, 4-4-1897.

Addins—Corine McLaurin, 4-26-1895. Discontinued, 7-31-1906.

Ras—W. L. Green, 10-4-1895; Florence Green, 10-7-1897.

Hero—John W. Bonner, 5-5-1899; Ezra Abney, 5-9-1905.

Alford—John J. Weems, 5-22-1899; John E. Harris, 11-31-1899.

Vrue—Joseph T. Waldrup, 6-19-1899; Major W. Lovitt, 9-25-1900; W. E. Mathis, 12-2-1903. Discontinued, 1-31-1916.

Otoe—Susan Johnson; James J. Johnston, 12-1-1901; Ella McLoughlin, 5-12-1900; Charlie Wilson, 12-2-1905.

Stafford Springs—John M. Perry, 4-19-1919; R. L. McLendon, 12-20-1929; C. A. Chancellor, 5-31-1930; Evan M. Gavin, 12-5-1932; Mary B. Gavin, 2-26-1935; Evan M. Gavin, 4-16-1937; May B. Gavin, 11-25-1939; Nona C. Risher, 11-1-1943; C. B. Rawlings, 8-29-1944; J. L. Banks, 5-15-1947. Discontinued, 7-1955.

Vale—Lawrence Harper, 4-10-1901; Amanda McCarty, 7-14-1904. Discontinued, 1906.

Louin—Zack Ishee, 3-22-1900; Mary A. Long, 8-19-1902; Allie Tullos, 12-17-1903; D. F. Kitt, 5-26-1926; J. V. Simmons, 2-15-1933; Levi G. Bassett, 2-10-1934; Hugh A. Kennedy, 7-7-1943.

Success—W. C. Harris, 4-23-1901; W. T. Sumrall, 10-3-1903; John E. Harris, 1-11-1904.

Gridley—Lula Read, 7-2-1901; Katie Read, 12-15-1902; W. M. Read, 1-6-1908. Discontinued, 10-31-1922.

Text—Wm Upton, 10-1-1901; George F. Upton, 8-6-1902. Discontinued, 8-15-1907.

Verba—J. J. Smith, 10-31-1901; Fannie B. Smith, 12-21-1901; Jas. J. Smith, 3-21-1903; F. M. Brady, 7-21-1905; Queen V. Brady, 8-5-1907; Lillie Brady, 2-1-1946, discontinued, 2-15-1951.

Cooley—W. R. Brasher, 2-16-1903; Elia McDaniels, 1-30-1905; Sallie Brasher, 5-31-1905. Discontinued, 12-15-1905.

Wadesboro—Annie R. Wade, 8-16-1903; S. R. Moffitt, 3-9-1904. Discontinued, 1-4-1906.

Moss—Virgie V. Moss, 2-10-1904; J. M. Robbins, 7-25-1905; T. L. Bulloch, 1-6-1915; B. R. Bulloch, 12-20-1927; Susie V. Mauldin, 8-23-1929; Claudie E Chadwell, 7-1-1949.

New—Earley N. Lee, 7-16-1904 Discontinued, 4-30-1906.

Waldrup—B. F. Waldrup, 7-6-1907; Margaret Windham, 2-28-1916; Amelia A. Pittman, 2-1-1940. Discontinued, 4-31-1952.

Fouke—Mamie F. Bannon, 8-29-1918; Sam R. Parker, 2-6-1920; Elbert R. Pugh, 8-9-1921; W. M. Read, 12-19-1923; W. M. Morgan, 10-31-1924; J. G. Pugh, 8-16-1926; Minnie B. Windham, 1-10-1927. Discontinued, 4-15-1931.

Dushau—R. O. Wilkins, 9-5-1924; John W. Hill, 6-21-1927; J. B. Causey, 10-1-1927. Discontinued, 6-30-1931.

Kelona—Lillian Millsaps, 9-7-1923. Discontinued, 9-15-1933.

**March 7, 1957**

# HISTORY OF JASPER COUNTY

By J. M. KENNEDY

With the establishing of post offices, opening of roads, the building of bridges, churches, homes, signs of progress were everywhere. The Catholics erected a large church at Paulding in 1840 which led to the influx of Irish Catholics around Paulding. These Irish settled near each other on small tracts of land as they were not use to much land in Ireland. They were different from other settlers in that they were never able to speak English in a clear tone. From the above facts this section of the county was soon termed as Irish Town. They loved their liquor and were always ready to fight but had a code of ethics which made it to some extent harmless. They believe in fighting with what the Maker had given you, your fist and that a person who used a pistol, stick, or knife was a coward. Also if a man hit another when down or after he had said "quits" then he was a coward. It is said that a man went to Paulding with a hickory stick and told his friend that one Irishman would get a licking that day; the two men met but the man with his stick got the licking by one without a stick.

O. C. Dease, editor of the True Democrat and J. U. Shannon, editor of the Eastern Clarion were Catholics. From this section came the story of the "Lost Irish Girl." J. J. Shannon and his family made a trip to New Orleans which people often did. The Sisters told him that the girl's mother died at birth and that her father left the baby with his father and mother and left for America. He later learned that his father and mother were dead and that the girl had been given to some neighbors. She was then ten years old. He sent money and asked that the girl be sent to him at Washington, D. C., The girl, Mary, was given the money and sent to Liverpool, where vessels embarked for America. Mary kept looking and asking for a vessel to Washington, but none was found as Washington was no seaport. Someone told her that there was a vessel to New Orleans and that was near Washington. She boarded this vessel. This was a trading ship to southeast U. S. and Cuba and then to gulf ports. In about three months (sailing ship) she landed in New Orleans. The Sisters took charge of her and wrote to Washington but could never get an answer. Shannon talked to the girl and told her that there were a lot of Irish at Paulding and a lot of new ones always coming, that she would be welcomed to live with the family until she found her father and if she did not find him he would be coming back to New Orleans and would bring her back. The girl came to Paulding and heard nothing of her father but became interested in a young Irishman who had just come from Ireland and had known her people. The girl married this young Irishman but never did hear from her father. Some of the names of this Irishtown are as follows: Daly, Hanly, O'Flinn, Carr, Harrington, Skehan, Malone, Dease, Shannon, Street, (ancestors of James Street, the writer) Brogan, Bergin, McDevitt, Kerly, Dolan, Drew, Lawless, and Finnegan.

The farmers were importing slaves (mostly from New Orleans) and cultivating the rich land of Jasper county. These slaves were carried to the black and lime clay land and soon farmers had large farms, a large home and traveled in buggies and surries driven by a slave, and thus we have the rich and the poor. The writer has seen many of these ante-bellum homes destroyed by fire, wind, and sold for junk. Old bachelors and maids mostly lived in them and when the old whites died the slaves took over and now we have more negro children than whites. The writer in the nineties traveled the road from Paulding to Heidelberg which was lined with beautiful homes of the whites. Now no white family lives on this road. Perhaps the oldest home was five miles southwest of Paulding on a high hill and was the home of Judge Henry Calhoun. The home had seven fire places and the rooms upstairs and down were very large. The father and mother died, one son was killed and the only daughter married Gen. J. A Smith who was teaching school at Paulding and later became State Superintendent of ducation. The old home was left with the china and silverware on the table with the door open but no one bothered it as the old home was said t be "Haunted" two persons being killed there. An old Irish ditcher married and bought the place and reared a large family there. This family, the Bergins, are citizens of a very high type.

Another old home of about the same age is the Johnston home about four miles west of Stringer or where Otoe post office was located on Roaring Creek. The home has been changed some but most of it is like it was built more than a hundred years ago. Willie J. Wilson lives in the home now and has a very fine farm. He and his family were on T.V. at Jackson last year, showing what a fine family he had and how well he was managing the place.

Another old home that is still in existence is the old Bonner home at Garlandsville. It is said that the old home was saved from burning during a Yankee raid by a negro woman who met the raiding soldiers and told them that her mistress was upstairs with a little baby and if they would not burn it they could occupy the first floor and that she would cook for them. The soldiers had some comrades that were wounded and were in need of some place to give them aid so they accepted the negro woman's offer. The federal soldiers were fired on at Garlandsville by some local citizens. The Eastern Clarion at Paulding gave their names as Cole, Chapman, Levi, and Marshall. Years later when the Blue and the Gray had a Reunion together at Washington, D. C., a man arose and announced that he was shot by someone at Garlandsville. Miss. Cole arose and told him that he was the man that shot him. It is said that the two men spent much time together and the story was written up in the press of the nation. Cole was a captain in the Confederate army but was home on parole. The old home seems to be in a sound condition and is occupied by a Mr. Harris but still belongs to the Bonner estate as one member of the family is still living.

The old McRea home at Paulding is occupied by Hawkins but has been repaired. The Street, Ferrall, Dr. Cotton, and Capt. Bill Hardy homes are still being occupied. The Hardy home was occupied by Mike Hanly for a number of years, Judge Deavours, and now by Reads.

The Buckley home at Fellowship, the N. D. Graham home at Rose Hill, the Pruitt and McCormick homes at Moss Hill, the Thigpen home at Lake Como, the Sprinkle, Hightower and Jones homes at Heidelberg are all very old.

The Mexican War came on in 1846 but we find only two names that enlisted in that from Jasper county, Sam Caston of Rose Hill and Sim Easterlang of Paulding. The territory that was acquired as a result of the Mexican War caused great agitation of slavery and resulted in bringing on the war between the states in 1860.

Before the Civil War, Mississippi, Alabama, Louisana and Texas were infested with a large gang of robbers headed by Jim Copeland (said to be about 50 in number). Jim was caught and hanged at Augusta. Some of the others were caught and some were never apprehended. They were said to have had a camp on Etehoma east of where Bill Gresham lives now. One was brought back years later from the penitentiary to find some money that he said was burried, south of Missionary below the mill dam beside a beech tree. When he was carried to the place they found two mill ponds near each other on the same stream, the Morris and Green mills and beech trees below each dam. Some claimed they found it and some said not. Since then this has been known as the "Money Hollow."

As the county prospered and time moved on, railroad talk became rampant in the county. A road was being built by Stephen A. Douglas from St. Louis to Mobile. Railroad building then was very slow as they had no way of moving dirt only by the shovel and cart, finances were an enormous job. By 1850 trains were running on part of the road and in a short while trains were running to Mobile and Paulding had a stage coach to DeSoto and the people had a market at Enterprise and Shubuta. Some dared to make the trip to Mobile and lots of stories were told about these trips. The road was new and the train did not run more than fifteen miles per hour but the boys became excited about the speed and as the conductor would come through they would grab him and say "just a little slower if you please." Then they became alarmed about the toilet and he carried one to it and he told the conductor, "I know what you want, you get me over that place and you will run over a bush." As one landed in Mobile he said that if he had his mule he would not get back on that train. Then came talk that a railroad was coming through by Garlandsville and that trains were already running from Vicksburg to Jackson. The road was already surveyed by Garlandsville to Enterprise but the merchants at Enterprise thought that the road would cut off their trade on the west and therefore began to fight, and so the road went where it now is, crossing the Chunky River three times and making a tunnel through the mountains before it gets to Meridian. No Meridian was there then. The road from Garlandsville to Enterprise would have been without much grading and no rivers.

John N. Waddell who lived at Gainsville, Alabama, went down the Tombigbee river to Mobile and met a number of farmers from Jasper who were there to trade. He made a deal with a man for a tract of land west of Montrose and moved there. He soon opened a school at Montrose in connection with the Presbyterian Church. A few years later a man came riding by on horseback which proved to be Simeon R. Adams, editor of the Eastern Clarion at Paulding, but who had been to a session of the senate at Jackson, Adams, then being a member from Jasper county, Mr. Adams informed him that he had been appointed on a committee to establish a University for the state. Some time was spent locating the institution, they came very near locating it at Montrose. Then after it was located at Oxford, some time was spent getting a building, but the institution was opened in 1848. In the meantime, Waddell had a large two story building constructed for the church and school at Montrose. This building was not torn down till about 1900. But Waddell was soon asked to become a member of the faculty of the University which he accepted. In his autobiography he tells about making the trip from Montrose to Oxford on horseback. After serving as professor for a while he was made Chancellor. Other schools were organized in the county, Paulding, Garlandsville, Lake Como, Pleasant Hill, but all were private except the one at Twistwood.

**March 14, 1957**

# HISTORY OF JASPER COUNTY

By J. M. KENNEDY

In the fifties was a time of great agitation throughout the nation concerning slavery. The slave owners were about one fourth of the population but were wealthy, and of course, prominent. The non-slave owner was not so concerned about this matter as he and his family did their own work and existed on what they made on their farm. Most of the slave owners were good to their slaves because they wanted them to be in healthy condition for work or trade, but there were some reports of slave owners being cruel to their slaves when they were unruly.

When the non-slave owners or members of his family would come about the big house of the slave owner the slaves would whisper, "Look at the poor white trash." It is claimed that the common people hated them so and joined in mobs to kill them. In 1860, when Democratic National Convention met at Charleston, S. C., they could not agree on a candidate (Douglas having received the highest vote), the party split and thus the Democrats were defeated. The way a presidential election is conducted it is possible for a man to get the majority of electoral votes and not get the majority of the people's vote. When the major party is split then another smaller party may get the largest vote in the majority of states and thus he has the majority of the electoral votes which Lincoln had. If the Democratic party had remained intact perhaps Douglas would have been elected. A great howl was raised over the nation with the slave states were advocating secession. South Carolina took the lead and then Mississippi. A date was set for state and county convention.

The writer, when a small boy, would sit around Paulding and hear the old men tell about this convention. The slave owners were all present but none of the non-slave owners were there. Many said it did not concern them. The convention opened at ten o'clock and many speeches were made. Several speakers spoke of the North imposing on the South and if the South did not oppose them, Southerners would be cowards. He said the damn Yankees would not fight anyway. Some noticed that these statements stirred up the fighting blood of the Irish, and when they were going out of the building they were ready to fight. The slave owners sent out their surreys and gathered up all the Irish they could find. Speeches were made on both sides in the afternoon, but one speaker had been appointed to recite the many crimes that the North had done to the South and that the South would have no rights if it did not secede. By this time the Irish were applauding loudly; the vote was taken and passed. A non-slave owner arose and told the crowd that this "would mean war and he guessed he would leave his wife and children and go, but if he did and home back and you dont go (pointing to the man that made the big speech); you and I will have war then." The non-slave owner came back and the slave owner had not been on account of having more than twenty slaves. A chase took place.

C. C. Deas was elected delegate to the state convention. And thus the people of Jasper took a step which was to mean thousands to be killed and their land to be laid waste. States kept seceding and President Buchanan took no action. Numbers of people North and South believed that a state had right to withdraw from the Union if it wished. The North said "Let the South go, we can get along without them." When Lincoln became president, he took no action. Very few people on both sides thought there would be a war. Lincoln waited for the South to make the first move and it soon happened when the Federal general refused to leave his post at Charleston, S. C., he was fired on. Then Lincoln issued a call for 75,000 troops to defend the flag. Still people in the North thought there would be no war. True to their spirit the Irish were talking enlistment. On May the 21st the Jasper Grays gathered at DeSoto to take the train for the field of battle. A great crowd gathered and dinner was served.

The captains were J. J. Shannon, J. J. Walton and D. L. Duke. The lieutenants were: T. J. Hankston, W. M. Pardue, T. W. Grayson, C. A. Jennings, J. J. Walton, C. H. Wilson, E. Y. Terral, D. L. Duke, P. M. Loper, O. C. Jones. The Catholic priest Boheim was chaplain. Most of this number were Irish (Catholics) but a number of Protestant young men joined. R. J. Lightsey went and served four years with Lee and returned home, married, and moved to Daleville where he lived and died. He had a daughter, Ada Christeen, who wrote a book called The Veteran's Story, in which she gives an account of her father's four years with Lee. General Robert E. Lee fought most of the war and he is regarded as the world's greatest general.

The writer remembers some of these men who came back and lived in the county for many years. William Arledge returned and was a prominent farmer of near Phalti. He was the father of Mrs. S. Y. Thigpen. P. Bergin came back and reared a large family who are now good citizens. J. W. Brown lived near Bay Springs and now we have many prominent citizens named Brown. R. A. Byrd came back and was a traveler on foot over the county, repairing clocks and machines, etc. He was a favorite of the people and they were all glad to see him and to have him take a meal with them or spend the night. He gave them the news.

The Bradys came back and a large number are still living in the county. Clint was circuit clerk for 12 years.

Tim and John Daly came back and spent the balance of their lives near Paulding.

Marion Downs came back and spent his remaining days around Antioch.

G. E. Ellis came back and resided near Paulding. He was at one time county treasurer.

B. F. Everett returned and lived near Mulberry Church.

The Fatherrees came back and moved to Clarke County where they were prominent in politics.

The Jameses came back and now live in all parts of the county, than any other family.

The Morrises came back and settled around Missionary for about twenty years when they moved to Forrest County and named their community Morristown. They have been prominent in politics.

The McCormicks returned and resided at Penantly and Heidelberg.

J. T. McCrany returned and resided at Heidelberg.

The McDonalds returned and resided at Hopewell and Claiborne.

The Parkers came back and are still prominent in the county. A Parker edits the Prentiss Headlight.

Rambo came back and his kin are still well known in the county.

R. M. Read returned and the Reads are quite prominent in the county.

Skehan came back and spent his days in Irishtown.

Smiths returned and are many in the county now. We read their names in politics.

The Morrises came back, except one, W. B., who was killed. They are still prominent in the county.

Traylors came back and lived north of Missionary.

J. B. Thompson came back and lived in Mobile.

Welborns came back and are many in the county, mostly at Stringer.

Yarber came back and his descendants live mostly in Newton County.

At first the war looked very favorable to the South. Gen. Lee defeated eight generals in battle. The North conceived the idea that it should capture Richmond, the capitol of the Confederacy, but failing in that they decided to take charge of the Mississippi River, severing the Confederacy. This was easily done except Vicksburg. Faragut first tried it from the river but failed. Then Sherman tried from land but that failed. Then Grant himself made eight attempts but failed, but what made Grant a great general was that he would not give up. So after trying to cut the river from Vicksburg, he floated his vessels by Vicksburg and landed his troops at Bruinsburg, then he went to Port Gibson where he had a small battle and proceeded north, clearing the country of all opposition, even taking in Jackson. He then proceeded to Vicksburg, and tried to storm the breastworks but failed in that, nearly all of his assaulting men having been killed in the charge. He then surrounded the city and began a bombardment which lasted forty days before the city surrendered.

In trying to weaken the defense of Vicksburg was when Jasper County was invaded by Federal soldiers. Gen. Grierson destroyed two train loads of supplies at Newton, burned all trestles to the Chunky River, tore up the track and bent the rails around trees. He knew that the Confederate cavalry was after him from behind and therefore went south through Garlandsville and Montrose but camped at the Bender farm, west of Montrose. He said Bender's hogs and cows made fine eating. Bender had a sack of gold (so it is said), and was holding it when he saw the Yankees coming in at the front gate. He threw the bag out of the window to a Negro who carried it away and gave it back to Bender when the Federals were gone.

The capture of Vicksburg was said to be the turning point in the war. With conscription, the blockade, and heavy losses, the South was now suffering. Among the many things that the South did not have and could not get was table salt. Some was found in southern Louisiana, but the Yankees soon took charge of that. The next step with the North was to cut the Confederacy in two at Chattanooga and Atlanta.

Lincoln made the statement that he had at last found him a general and therefore made Grant commander-in-chief of the Union Army.

Sherman was put in charge at Chattanooga but fought several battles before he could move in the direction of Atlanta. This accomplished, he moved on to the sea, destroying everything in sight. Grant, after collecting a large army and drilling them for an attack on Lee; this in the latter part of 1864. Grant lost 54,000 men but kept following Lee, when Lee surrendered at Appomatox April 9th, 1865. Other generals surrendered and thus the great war was over. President Jeff Davis was arrested and placed in jail. The slaves were freed and Lincoln advised that the seceding states could come back into the Union. Thad Stephens notified Lincoln that this could not be. Lincoln was assassinated and Stephens took over. The southern states were divided into military districts and military law was declared. Slaves were enlisted and soldiers were placed at every state capitol and every county site. Most of the whites were disfranchised and political offices were held by Negroes or some northern man. The white men who came from the North to hold office were called carpetbaggers and the men from the South who held office were called scallawags. Of course this brought on trouble.

# March 21, 1957

*JASPER COUNTY NEWS, BAY SPRINGS, MISSISSIPPI — THURSDAY, MARCH 21, 1957*

## HISTORY OF JASPER COUNTY

### By J. M. KENNEDY

Dr Loughridge of Garlandville was jailed for eighteen months at Vicksburg. Riots were frequent. This went on till 1876. Negro organizations were directed by northern white men. The records at Jackson say that more than a hundred were meeting at Paulding carrying their box, their director was McKnight who was carried from his home by four Negroes; McKnight being in rocking chair. It says that Richard Simmons, sheriff, and his efficient deputy, Q. C. Heidelberg, became alarmed about such a meeting and secured an order from Jackson, saying that they could meet but not with their gun." (Excerpts from Miss. Hist., Volume 4, page 15.)

Capt. W. H. Hardy, who was active in social and political life of the state, gives the following information as to the Loyal League at Paulding, Miss.: "The Loyal League was a secret oath-bound organization, and lodges were organized in all parts of the country, and every male Negro between the ages of eighteen and seventy and all white men who would take the oath, were eligible to join. Only a few whites were members but nearly all Negro men were members. The candidate for membership was blindfolded and led to the altar and made to kneel and a short prayer was said, telling about Moses leading the Children of Israel out of bondage. He was then asked a set of questions. What is your name. Jim Cruise. Are you a white or colored man? A colored man. Were you born free or a slave? A slave. Are you now a slave or free? I am free, thank God. Who freed you? Abraham Lincoln, bless God. Who helped to free you? The army of the Republican Party. Who fought to keep you in slavery? The white people of the South, and the Democrat Party. Whom then are your best friends? The Republican Party and the northern soldiers. Whom do you want to hold all the offices? The Republicans, the friend of the poor colored people. Suppose the Democrats were in office? We would be put back into slavery. The oath: "I, Jim Cruise, do solemnly swear on the Holy Bible in the presence of God and these witnesses, that I will ever remain true and loyal to the Republican Party and the league and teach my children to do so, that I will never testify against the league or its members. For the violation of this oath of any part of it, I agree for the first offense to receive fifty lashes on my bare back, and for the second offense, one hundred lashes, and for the third offense I agree to be shot to death, so help me God."

The whites organized the Ku Klux Klan and it is said saved the South. Thad Stephens might have thought that he was helping the Negro but he got thousands of them killed.

The whites mostly remained at home during this period and tried to make a living. It was a hard go or it as taxes were high to pay for this misguided government. Carpetbaggers were here to make money and the colored thought they were entitled to it also.

The Klan kept growing and getting bolder and when time came for the election in 1876, word was sent out to every place in the state for all to get to work to win the election for white rule, a crowd was to come over the night before the election and overrun Kemper and Lauderdale Counties. At one precinct in Jasper County, quite a crowd of colored had gathered to vote, the whites started a row and began to shoot but Negroes were talking and no whites. At another box nearly four hundred Negroes had voted and so something had to be done. The election was held in a small room. A fight started and when all was quiet there was no election box and it was never found. The state election was carried by the whites. President Hayes soon withdrew the troops from the South but still there were white Republicans who tried to keep up the organizations which caused riots in some places. But by 1899 it was announced that the last Republican had been killed.

Soon after the close of the war peddlers soon began to go through the country; some tin peddlers and some pack peddlers. Grown boys and girls who had been at home all these years had never seen such beautiful things. To be sure the peddlers were soon rich. Later, stores began to appear which soon became the social, religious, financial and entertainment centers. Prof. Thomas of the University of Kentucky has written a book on this subject, "Plils, Ploughs and Petticoats". He says that the merchant soon had his baseball team; his church was built two-story for the lodge on the second floor. He sold everything and took care of all business of the community.

About 1880, there began talk about a railroad in Jasper County. Capt. Bill Hardy had moved from Paulding to Meridian and had charge of the construction of the road. He came to Paulding and told the people that he would run the road by Paulding if they wished it. An election was held and the road was "turned down". The objections were that it would kill people and get cinders on their table linen.

This road, from New Orleans to Meridian, was named the New Orleans and Northeastern Railroad. It is now a part of the Southern Railway System. We then had two railroad towns, Heidelberg and Vossburg.

Capt. Hardy twenty years later was building the road from Jackson to Gulfport, known as the Gulf and Ship Island Railroad. He also, with the help of a New Yorker, constructed the harbor at Gulfport. The city has a statue of him in front of the post-office. He is termed one of the greatest producers of the state.

After trains were running of the Northeastern Railroad, there soon was a story going the rounds. A man went to Meridian in July and came back and told that they had ice in Meridian. He was soon before his church brethren and accused of telling a lie for which he would be excluded from the church. But some being of a lenient disposition, suggested that the church send the deacons and the preacher to Meridian to investigate the matter. This was done, and the preacher and deacons came back and reported that they were not only in possession of ice in Meridian, but were making it. The preacher and deacons were dismissed from the church.

### An Old Ticket

The following is an old ticket that was found in the old court house before it burned in 1932:

Circuit Judge, James J. Shannon.
District Attorney, E. Rush Buckner.
Representative, W. H. Edmonson, D. D. McLaurin.
Probate Judge, S. W. Jones, G. W. Ryan.
Sheriff, L. B. Lassiter, Seth Travis, J. B. Gough, D. A. Morris, W. B. Ferrill.
Circuit Clerk, James U. McCormick, Thomas W. Grayson, M. W. Ellis.
Assessor, M. M. McNeal, Jno. B. Smith, Duncan McInnis, A. J. Hyde, C. Patterson, J. A. Dillard, W. F. Cain.
Treasurer, G. L. Lightsey, G. S. Collins, J. M. Kennedy.
Surveyor, T. S. Newnon, J. C. Parry, S. S. Turner.
Coroner, Josiah Jones.
Ranger, A. L. Reid.
Board of Police, Center Beat—B. F. Killen, W. M. Pugh, Aaron Green, Jesse Y. Carter; Beat 5—S. A. Allen, T. B. Heslep, L. L. Parker.

### Comment—

J. J. Shannon was editor of the Eastern Clarion and was captain of the first company that went to the Civil War from Jasper County. D. D. McLaurin was representative at one time and lived between Antioch and Tallahoma Creek.

The records show that Jones and Ryan were both probate judge.

Ryan was the father of Milton Ryan who lived near Rose Hill who was the father of Sid Ryan who lived at Bay Springs.

Jones lived south of Paulding and sold his place to F. I. Cook in the eighties and moved to Texas.

Seth Travis lived near Claiborne, married a Barber from Rose Hill, is buried at Ebenezer church, was father of Enoch and Abney Travis of Laurel. J. B. Gough lived near Paulding. D. A. Morris lived in the Salem community near Vossburg, father of W. B. Morris. W. B. Ferrill, a prominent family, lived in Paulding.

James U. McCormick, one of the pioneer families of Jasper County. Thomas W. Grayson, one of the old families of the county. M. W. Ellis, father of Gabe Ellis, at one time treasurer of the county, descendants Kelleys at Heidelberg. A. J. Hyde, old family of the county; Charlie Hyde of Vossburg, very prominent. Lirame Hyde lives at Stringer.

G. L. Lightsey, old, large and prominent family of the county. G. S. Collins, old family of Oak Bowery. J. M. Kennedy, son of Dr Kennedy, who established the post office Twistwood, which is now Rose Hill, lived at the Finnegan place, moved to Dallas, Texas, in the eighties. A. I. Reid, uncle of J. W. Reid, whose sister married Henry Read.

W. M. Pugh, father of Jim and Tom Pugh, who lived in the center of the county, grandfather of R. C. Pugh, former president of Northwest Junior College.

Aaron Green lived near Missionary, owner of a water mill, father of Dave and George Green, descendants live at Heidelberg.

There was no date on the ticket but probate judge and board of police was changed to chancery judge and board of police to board of supervisors in 1870, therefore it is about one hundred years old.

In 1890 a constitutional convention was held at Jackson and a new constitution was made which became famous over the nation because of its educational requirement for voting which was made to exclude the Negro. No more trouble existed with the Negro until the famous decision of the U. S. Supreme Court of May 7th, 1954.

About 1900 there was a report that a timber man was coming to Montrose to buy timber and that he would give one dollar per acre for the timber and let the owner keep the land. Several reports around that he was coming and he did not come. A strange boy was there attending school. He had ordered a pair of mustaches for a concert and he saw the funny side of the timber deal. He had a friend to accompany him around one night and introduce him as the timber man. They say he did a big business."

Later, the timber man did come and began to buy the timber for one dollar per acre. Eastman and Gardner was the first company to cut timber down from the North to erect a mill. They went to Ellisville to erect the mill there, but Ellisville informed them that they did not desire a saw mill their town. They came to a stop, north of Ellisville and o_ in their mill; soon three other companies came down and Eastman and Gardner gave them land to put the mills there, and soon this place, Laurel, was the largest lumber manufacturing town in the world. The company that cut most of Jasper's timber was soon rated at 60 million dollars. This business gave the people of Jasper the first money since the Civil War.

ERRATA: In last issue, it was said that W. B. Morris did not return from the Civil War, either having died or was slain. It was another Morris and not W. B. W. B. Morris returned home after the war and was prominent in county affairs.

**March 28, 1957**

# HISTORY OF JASPER COUNTY

By J. M. KENNEDY

---

**COMPANY F, 16th MISSISSIPPI**

The following roster of Company F, 16th Mississippi Regiment, was prepared after the close of the war, by the old Orderly Sergeant, John F. McCormick, from memory, assisted by his comrades.

Captains—J. G. Shannon, J. J. Walton, D. L. Duke.

Lieutenants—T. J. Bankston, W. M. Pardue, T. W. Grayson, C. A. Jennings, J. J. Walton, C. H. Wilson, E. Y. Terral, D. L. Duke, P. M. Loper, O. C. Jones.

Non-Commissioned Officers and Privates—Acker, W. F., Adams, C. R., Anderson, G. M., Anderson, R., Arledge, L. D. S., Arledge, W. M., Alexander, J., Armstrong —, Bishop, John, Bankston, D. O., Baker, John, Barksdale, L., Bergen, P., Beville, R. M., Brown, B. W., Burns, O., Bridges, J. C. C., Bridges, W., Breitharpt, J., Bruce, W. W., Byrd, R. A., Brannon, S. R., Bodie, G. W., Baulton, C. M., Bingham, C. M., Brady —, Brady —, Clark, John, Clark, J. B., Caldwell, Wm., Carter, John, Cannor, W., Crawford, John, Craven, John R., Craven, Jas. R., Cain, H. F., Cain, Thos., Cain, W. F., Chandler, T. L., Carr, J. B., Daniels, J. G., Davis, John, Daly, John, Daly, Tim, Dolan, L., Donald, W. A., Downs, J. M., Downs, D. M., Downs, D. M., Downs, Marion, Duke, B. F., Davis, W. M., Erwin, G. W., Ellis, O. K., Everett, B. Y., Everett, Sam, Fatheree, J. W., Fatheree, F. P., Fatherree, T. J., Fewox, J. M., Gandy —, Gibson, J. A., Green, L. H., Grayson, C., Gough, A. P., Gray —, Harris, J. C., Hankins, P. O., Harper, J. H., Harper, W. F., Heidelberg, G. C., Howard, Jones, Hopkins, John, Hopkins, R. H., Hudson, Eli, Hughey, J. F., Hair, G. W., James, R. H., James, R. W., James, C. P., James, Wm., Jones, D. M., Jones, Polk, Keeton, G. W., Kelly, P., Keith, J. W., Keown, R. L., Killen, G. W., Kidd, Wm., Okom, A., Langham, A., Lawless, J. W., Lawles, T. J., Lee, J. N., Lee, W. W., Lightsey, J. W., Lightsey, B. J., Linder, J. L., Loper, U. S., Markham, J. O., Mears, John, Miller, J. H., Minton, Jas., Morgan, W. M., Morris, S. J., Morris, W. B., Morris, R. C., Morris, James, Mounger, U. M., Mullins, P., Malvey, P., Mulan, P., Myer, A. B., McCormick, J. F., McCormick, U., McCormick, F. M., McCormick, J. E., McCraney, J. T., McCraney, M., McCurdy, C., McDevitt, J. A., McDonald, B. E., McDonald, H. A., McDonald, D. S., McDonald, W. P., McKinstry, J. T., McMickle, R. V., McPhail, Isaac, McNeil, M. E. T., Moody, J. D., Neely, James, O'Brien, Mike, O'Flinn, Tim, Oldham, I., W., Oliphant, J. E., Overstreet, T. J., Owens, Henry, Orr, O. J., Parker, J. F., Perry, Jacob F., Porter, M., Pierce, G. W., Rambo, J. F., Reeves, Isaac N., Register, G. B., Robinson, A. P., Robinson, Alex, Rogers, Seth, Reynolds, J. P., Read, S. M., Seavy —, Selby, G., W., Shannon, C. L., Shephard, Wm., Skehan, Wm., Smith, A. B., Smith, Hector, Smith, J. B., Smith, J. E., Smith, P. C., Smith, T. L., Smith, W. B., Smith, Sam, Snell, J. M., Starling, T. L., Starling, P. M., Steele, J. J. V., Stillman, C. H., Taylor, J. A., Talbot, N., Taylor, H. L., Traylor, J. J., Traylor, J. M., Turner, M. G., Turner, Wm., Turner, Allen, Thompson, J. B., Thompson, W. C., Ulmer, J. W., Watkins, R. M., Welborn, J. E., Whitley, H. J., Whitten, Jesse, Willingham, C. J., Whittington, J. C., Yarber, James, Young, John.

## RECOLLECTIONS OF THE CIVIL WAR

By J. B. Lightsey

(From the January 2, 1908 issue of The Jasper County Review)

We old Rebs had some laughable incidents occasionally in our little frolics, as well as things not so funny.

During the siege of Vicksburg in 1863, where for 47 days and nights we fought and bled for Southern principles, and were fed mule beef and dirty pea bread, we found it not so funny until General Pemberton turned 38,000 of us over to the tender mercies of General Grant. We got one square meal, and a parole to come home.

We reached home in July, foot sore and ragged. Some of our boys killed themselves eating roasting ears before reaching home, but those of us who reached home safely made fearful depredations on the larder: a dish of bacon and greens would grow beautifully less, and disappear as if by magic.

In about a month we were sent to parole camps, located at Enterprise, where we bivouacked until winter was over, and then were ordered to join General Joseph E. Johnson's army in Georgia. There was a squad of my command who did not go on with the main army, Captain W. D. Ferrell commanded this squad.

We boarded the train at Shubuta, where we remained over night, and there was a ball there that night, at which Lieutenant Holliday was gallanting a girl. Water was scarce, and in looking around for some one to bring in a bucket of water, Holliday espied my old friend, Sam Parker.

The lights were dim, and Sam being unshaven, he mistook Sam for a negro, and said, "Here, boy, take this bucket and bring some water and I will give you two bits."

"H—l," exclaimed Sam, "I just now offered five dollars for a drink"! The Lieutenant wilted.

The next day we reached Mobile, where we had to lay over until night. The other boys took a stroll around town, and I passed the time writing at the depot.

The only company I had was three drunken Choctaw Indians soundly sleeping in the sunshine, with mouths wide open. At this juncture a finely dressed lady came tripping up to me and said: "Are all of the engines gone out?" "No, madam," I replied, "there lies three of them asleep." She turned and looked at the Indians and laughed heartily and left without another word. I then discovered the mistake I had made in calling an Indian an "Injun." Then it was my turn to laugh.

(From January 9, 1908 issue)

We left Mobile and crossed the Bay and took the cars for Pollard, Florida. Our squad took seats in a car that a Colonel Brown with an Alabama Regiment had taken possession of.

Colonel Brown came in just as we had taken our seats and as he entered he discovered the Rev. Dan McKinnis, a Presbyterian Minister from Jasper County, Mississippi, and called out: "Hey there, you man with the stove pipe hat on, get out of this car, I want it for my men and want none but my men in it." The minister meekly obeyed.

The next man that Brown noticed as not belonging to his command was my friend and comrade, Sam Parker, of Company K, 37th Mississippi Regiment.

"What command do you belong to?" said Brown. "Is that any of your business" retorted Sam, who by the way had managed to get hold of some bug juice, of which Sam was at that time particularly fond, and had a special talent for finding, and of course had imbibed too freely. Brown was considerably angered at Sam's reply to him, and said, "You must get out of here."

Sam said, "I am not going to do any such a thing." Brown then called for two of his men with bayonets, and they laid hold on Sam, but could not move him from his seat. Brown ordered them to stick their bayonets in him, but the men pretended to try to stick their bayonets and told Brown that they were so crowded that they did not have room to obey orders.

At this juncture Captain Ferrell went to Brown and told him that Parker was one of his men and had been drinking rather freely. As soon as Brown learned that Sam was an old time friend of Captain Ferrell and that he was an ex-sheriff of Jasper County, this stopped the row.

We retained our seats with Brown and his men until we reached Pollard where we took possession of some vacant cabins, and spent some time with the salamanders and gophers.

While here Sam got even with the Brown gang, for the treatment accorded him by them on the train.

There was a widow lady living not far from our camps owning some fat hogs, one of which ventured dangerously near our camps and was taken in out of the wet by the Brown gang. The widow found the hog thief, and the widow agreed to take $10 and let them keep the hog. So it was salted down in a tub and put under their bunk for safekeeping anticipating fine breakfast of pork in the morning. They retired early and slumbered and slept, but Sam whose keen eyes had discovered where the pork was hidden decided he wanted a little fresh pork too, and did not particularly care to wait until breakfast, so he swiped the pork from under the bunk, not leaving a single piece for Brown and Company.

Then as Company K was in no hurry to go to sleep we decided to put the pot on and have a sup before we went to bed, and by next morning there was nothing left but the bones for poor Pohny Jones.

Next morning there was not a greasy spot to be found of the widow's hog.

(From January 16, 1908 Issue)

We took the train the next day for the front, passing a train of soldiers in a parallel track, we could easily grab a hat from their heads, stuck out the car window.

A Lieutenant Hopkins from Enterprise of the 37th Mississippi Regiment looked back from the platform on which he was standing and said: "Boys, now is the time to get a good hat."

The word was scarcely out of his mouth when a man on the other train snatched him baldheaded taking his fine beaver and a lock of his hair as a parting gift. Then there was a full grown Rebel yell along both lines.

Hopkins did not enjoy it as well as the other boys, and dodged back in to the car hatless until we landed at Resaca, Georgia, where the next day we got caught in a trap, set and sprung, by a little too much whiskey aboard.

The Yankees were shoving General Joe pretty closely, trying to out flank him with their superior numbers, and he like old Santa Anna, would fight and run away, to live and fight another day.

Our Commander who was under the influence of whiskey, decided that he with the 37th Mississippi Regiment could whip a Brigade of Yankees, marched us to a gap the Yankees were making for, and took a position that no sane man would have chosen. It was a little valley, bounded on both sides by a range of steep hills. After viewing the situation, I remarked: "Boys, right here some of us are going up."

We did not have time to advance our picket skirmisher before the blue coats made their appearance on the hills, surrounding us. Guns commenced popping all sides, and the cry of "Oh L—" went up as some poor fellow was hit with a bullet.

It was then that men called on the name of the Lord. Our officer soon saw that we would all be killed, or captured, he gave orders to retreat which most of us who were able obeyed with alacrity.

One gritty fellow of Company H named Pete —, would not hope according to orders, but stood by a tree loading and shooting a rifle which he had brought from home, and which he could come as near driving the cross at 10 yards, as any man in the regiment. He caused at least two of the enemy to bite the dust before he was captured.

As we retreated, the bullets reminded me of a swarm of bees, as they came whizzing uncomfortably near our ears. Some of our men preferred dropping behind logs and stumps to climbing hills in a shower of lead.

That was one time that I made good use of my legs, which were long, limber, and light. I knew that I was quite fleet in a foot race, but on this occasion, I think out of 100 men 99 were left behind me in a race of 200 yards up a hill.

When the brow of the hill was turned, there was but one man ahead of me, and it seemed that both of us believed alike—that distance lent enchantment to the view.

# HISTORY OF JASPER COUNTY

### By J. M. KENNEDY

**RECOLLECTIONS OF THE CIVIL WAR**
By J. R. Lightsey
(January 23, 1908 Issue)

We lost about 80 men in 10 minutes time from our Regiment, which was 800 at that time. Two men from Company H were killed: Duffy and Isaac Land, an uncle of Dr. Land of Louin. Among those detailed to bury him was the writer.

We had to fall back fom Resaca as the enemy with his superior forces was out flanking us. Johnson's tactics was in accordance with old Santa Anna of Mexican fame: "He that fights and runs away may live to fight another day."

After our reverses here, we crossed the Chataba River, as our scouts informed us that the enemy was crossing on pontoons c outflank us.

We retreated to Cassville, where we threw up some hastily constructed breast works, expecting to give battle to Sherman's forces who were close in our rear, our calvary having held them in check by a desultory running fight day and night with their advance guard.

Late in the evening the enemy came near enough to begin shelling our position, to which our batteries replied, and soon silenced their guns, which we learned afterwards, was owing to this attack being only a feint to cover a flanking movement.

There was but little harm done in this artillery duel. Firing ceased at night, but we lay on our guns at night expecting a big battle the next day. About midnight our scouts brought in report that Sherman was flanking again, and did not intend to give battle to Johnson, unless they could catch him napping. We were ordered to silently withdraw, and move to check the outflankers, which was done early next morning, to the discomfiture of Sherman, and the loss of many of his men.

(January 30, 1908 Issue)

Our retreat then continued until we reached Kennesaw Mountains, where another stand was made, and some severe skirmishing done, during which General Leonidas Polk was killed, while reconnoitering the enemy.

Polk was a Methodist Bishop who laid aside his clerical robe, and donned the soldier's uniform, and took up the sword, and according to Scripture, perished by the sword. He was a good general and a fine looking man.

Sherman again displayed his flanking tactics, but did not dare to come to a general engagement, notwithstanding his army was stronger numerically 3 to 1 than was Johnson's.

Every time Johnson struck him in his flank movements, he left a good many of his men to be buried.

Johnson continued his policy of falling back to prevent this flank movement of Sherman's, and this fretted Jeff Davis who removed Johnson and put General Hood in command about the time we reached Atlanta, Georgia.

On the 28th day of July, 1864, we turned back to meet General Sherman at Peach Tree Creek, where he had constructed some temporary breastworks. There was a sanguinary battle fought there, with a heavy loss on each side and Hood drove the enemy away from their position. We lost many brave, good, and noble men in this conflict, amongst whom was Wyatt Jones, our color bearer, from Co. K, 37th Miss. Regiment. He was in advance of our Company and was shot as he mounted the enemy's works. There was not a better soldier, nor a braver man in the Company, than Wyatt Jones, and his death was much regretted by the entire command.

Another brave soldier that was lost there was Jeff Fatheree of Company K.

I was on this battlefield about two weeks after this battle, and of all the sickening sights that I ever beheld it was there. In burying the hundreds of slain soldiers they were piled into heaps of 15 or 20 like heaps of logs, and not enough dirt placed upon the heaps to cover them.

When I saw them, there were many arms, legs and even skulls perfectly bare, and I saw one poor fellow that they did not pretend to bury at all, as he lay with his face to the enemy, just as he fell, resembling a shriveled mummy.

There were no scavengers of nature there, and it seemed that all nature abhorred such a sickening scene.

This is where but little fun came.

## April 4, 1957 – Part 2

### THURSDAY, APRIL 4, 1957

From the February 8, 1908, issue of The Jasper County Review.

After repulsing Sherman at Peach Tree Creek, Hood remained at Atlanta about a month, during which time Sherman was massing, and recruiting his forces, but would not attack Hood.

Having recourse to his flank movement, again he caused Hood to evacuate Atlanta, destroying much military goods which it was impossible to remove. The explosion of shells for some time was much like a battle, the incessant detonations were heard for miles, and was by many mistaken for another big battle.

I was taken quite sick just as we were marching out of Atlanta, and dropped out of ranks, lying down a short distance from the road.

I remained there until the entire army had passed, not being able to travel until the next day. My case developed into bilious remittant fever after having a chill and a roasting fever every other day for several days.

Knowing that camping nearby the roadside was dangerous, I, too, took to the woods none too soon, as the blue coat gang soon passed by following in the rear of Hood, which cut me off from my command. When able to travel, my command had got so far ahead of me that there was no chance to overtake them until 15 days after, they having stopped and given Sherman's outflank another check before I reached them; but I had many ups and downs before that took place.

More downs than ups you will agree readily when they have been related, which is the subject of the following lines.

About the fourth night after my departure from Atlanta, this being my best night as the fever had about subsided, and being in the woods resting on a bed of mother earth, with the canopy of the Heavens as my covering, with no medicine, nurse, or nourishment with the cold, pitiless rain descending in torrents, saturating me entirely from head to foot.

The next morning after disrobing, not even retaining the traditional fig leaf, and wringing out all the water that could be got out, and hanging them out to dry, I betook myself to my bed of wet leaves, which I had swine-like raked into a pile.

Soon a relentless ague had me in its clutches, but this did not last long before the fever banished the shaking ague, causing me to spend another day and night on this cheerless spot.

Up to this time I had retained my gun and accouterments, but now feeling too weak to carry them, and thinking they might not be needed, they were discarded, with but little regret.

About this time, a stray bullet from the enemy, which was near, came uncomfortably near me, causing a little uneasiness on my part, fearing a bullet from the random firing. Therefore, the distance was widened, which caused me to make slow progress toward my command.

There was another rain that evening, and about that time a farm house was espied near by, and thinking to find shelter, resolved to call, but here I found mans inhumanity to man exemplified. The farmer even denied me shelter in a woodshed, saying if the Yanks, who were near, should find a Reb hiding they would tear up his place in retaliation for hiding a Reb.

I did not have much dust on my feet, but gave them a shake and departed in an unthankful mood, but as is often the case, providence directs our footsteps, and what we think bad for us turns out to be a blessing in disguise. Poking slowly along brooding over my ill luck, and expecting to be compelled to spend another night in the comfortless condition of the previous nights, I came in view of another house. Being quite thirsty I decided to make another effort to find a shelter, and this time as I called at the gate, instead of seeing a churlish man, a handsome matron came and invited me in with a smile on her beautiful face.

After giving me water and hearing my tale of suffering, she insisted that I remain over night, and her hospitality was accepted and highly appreciated.

She and her married daughter after making a fire, which I sat by and thoroughly drying myself, prepared a nice supper of fried chicken, ham, eggs, and biscuits, with sure enough coffee.

From the February 13, 1908, Issue of The Jasper County Review.

I was breaking a fast of several days, and this was my off day from the fever, and you may well imagine there was ample justice done to the viands. Then preparing a good bed in a private apartment for me, they bade me good night, and as I tumbled in the bed, the first on which I had reposed in near six months, I thanked the Lord for his last and best gifts to man—a good woman, and wondered who invented the first good bed, thinking he or she ought to be immortalized.

What a contrast to my bed of wet leaves the night before! And to further show the goodness of Providence in being denied shelter by that selfish brother of this widow, as she informed me to be the case that night. The enemy came to his house that night and relieved him of much of his goods.

Had I remained with him, it is probable I would have been captured and sent to another prison on Rock Island. The widow blistered her brother soundly, saying that he was too mean for any use, and said she would not have treated a dog as he treated me. Next morning they provided me a good breakfast, and invited me to partake of it, but alas! that sneaking chill laid hold of me again and my appetite was gone. The ladies spread some quilts on the floor before the fire, with pillows for my head, and gave me some stimulants and let me shake a while. In the meantime, hearing a noise up the road, she saw a regiment of Yankees coming towards her home. She asked me if I wished to hide from them and I told her that I certainly did, as I was in no condition to go to Rock Island. She then hustled me off to the room that I had occupied the night before, and turned the key on me, just in time. The regiment halted in front of her gate and stacked arms and began to cook their rations. There was a glass window in my room and I could, from my bed, see them but they could not see me, as I was all covered up to the eyes. Two of the officers came in and spoke to the widow, and she gave them chairs and asked them to be seated. They complied, resting their chairs against the wall of the room occupied by me. I could hear them talking, and though they said some things I didn't like, thought best not to contradict them.

They gave the Rebs Hail Columbia! I had to grin and endure it. I remained quietly in bed watching them cook breakfast, notwithstanding my being so sick and my serious condition.

---

*Mr Lightsey was in error in stating that Bishop Polk was a Methodist Bishop. He was a Bishop of the Episcopal Church.

April 11, 1957

# HISTORY OF JASPER COUNTY

By J. M. KENNEDY

## RECOLLECTIONS OF THE CIVIL WAR

By J. B. Lightsey
(January 23, 1908 issue)

From the February 20, 1908, Issue of The Jasper County Review.

They remained here until about 3 o'clock P.M., when the bugle gave the signal to fall into ranks, and much to my relief they marched away.

As soon as they were out of sight my door was unlocked and the lady inquired how I was getting along.

Remaining there that night and resting well, I was aroused at the usual breakfast time to partake of a good breakfast, and bidding them farewell, the good lady asked for my haversack which was filled with nice biscuits, ham and fried chicken. She then asked if I had any money, and I replied, "Not a red cent." She then begged me to accept five dollars, saying that it might come in well before overtaking my commander.

I often think of that good widow's kindness to me, a stranger, and am satisfied that she has long since been rewarded for this unmistakable evidence of a Christlike spirit.

After leaving this good Samaritan's home, I had to make quite a detour through the woods to avoid the bluecoats, who were still near by.

Late in the even coming to a large two-story house near the road, and finding it vacant, I resolved to go in and spend the night there, as I was about exhausted after my day's walk through the woods.

Finding a bold spring of good water near, refreshing myself from its bubbling stone fount, I betook myself to the inside, threw down my knapsack, spread my blanket, and was soon in dreamland. Being the sole occupant of the house with the exception of a few huge rats, my slumbers were not much disturbed, although there was a large cemetery near the house, and I still had enough of my early superstition left to cause me to be lonely; and a slight display of anything out of the ordinary might have revived the old time belief in hobgoblins.

Next morning quite early my shake came on followed by the fever. Here I remained prone on my back all day and next night, not seeing either a friend or foe. Next morning, being clear of fever, and recruited for enough to travel, I bade a lasting farewell to the old house, and the rats.

Finding that I was on the track of my command travel was somewhat accelerated by following the trail of the command, and about sundown being in ten miles of them worn out and exhausted, dropping down by the roadside watching our cavalry go by, many of them home boys, and brothers in the church. I was then forcibly reminded of the parable of the good Samaritan, as none of them offered me any assistance until George Calhoun passed by, and seeing my sad plight he inquired what I was doing there.

After telling my story he jumped off his horse and said: "Mount my horse and I will take you to the command." We reached there about midnight and he then had to ride ten miles farther to overtake his command. Up to this time I did not much appreciate George, as he was thought to be rather wild, but this act of the good Samaritan caused me to shed many tears at his untimely death from the hands of a brutal Negro, Lewis Morgan, who was hung in Paulding for this dastardly assassination.

From the February 27, 1908, Issue of The Jasper County Review.

My comrades were glad to see me come into camp, and they physicked me up on willow bark tea in lieu of quinine, which did not improve my condition, and they soon hustled me off to the hospital at Cuthburt, Georgia. As is often the case, this was providential in saving my life, as the hardships of our boys in Hood's foolish march to Tennessee, where at the battles of Franklin and Nashville our losses were severe and demoralizing.

Many of the boys were barefooted and bloody tracks were seen in snow everywhere they went. The cars on which I went to the hospital were box cars with flat tops, and were so crowded that many of us had to ride on top of the cars, and if it had not been that a slow rain was falling, we would have been badly burned, as the sparks from the engine flew in our faces like snow in a snow storm.

We found Cuthburt a nice little town, and in the hospital, which was crowded, were many good doctors and nurses. I was placed under a doctor from this state, and he seemed to be partial to the boys from home and the result was good for me. My trouble had developed into bilious remittent fever of a typhoid type, and I was very sick for about 30 days after which I was convalescent.

A few days later, my doctor permitted me to go before the examining board to ask for a furlough. Desiring to make my case out as bad as possible, and knowing by a former experience how sickening the taste of tobacco was to me, I got a chew from a man on the outside and went in chewing it, getting before the board a sure enough sick man with a woe-begone expression.

"Where did you come from" said the examiner. "From Jasper County, Mississippi", was my reply.

Turning to the clerk, he said, "Give him a furlough for 60 days."

Getting out of their sight and taking emetic, and dispersing with my chew of tobacco, which had been swallowed, I felt much better, and have had no use for tobacco since. Reaching home in 'tater-digging time with my appetite well improved, you may be sure I was no laggard when it came to eating.

We had plenty of hog and hominy as cotton planting had been stopped. My furlough was extended forty days, and by that time my command was again under Joe Johnson and back in Georgia. Returning to my command, accompanied by my brother David, we spent a few days at the home of David Dixon who was a noted Georgia planter, and an uncle to my wife.

We soon reached our command at Greenwood, North Carolina, after the surrender, and were disbanded there, footing it a good part of the way home as the railroads were all badly torn up.

This ends this part of my story.

## COMPANY K, 37th MISSISSIPPI REGIMENT, CIVIL WAR, APRIL, 1862.

From The Jasper County News October 10, 1906.

A. F. Dantzler, capt., Dr. Allen Bridges, 1st Lt., W. B. Ferrell, 2nd Lt., William McCurty, 3rd Lt., A. L. Husbands, 1st Sgt., Elijah Mounger, 2nd Sgt., Ed C. Welborn, 3rd Sgt. Lawrence Gaddy, 4th Sgt., Phillip G. Cook, 5th Sgt., F. L. Hufkin, 1st Cpl., Richard T. H. Lightsey, 2nd Cpl., Peter Trest, 3rd Cpl., Elijah E. Cooper, 4th Cpl.

Privates: Henry Abney, S. W. Anderson, E. H. Anderson, John Blackledge, Tom Bingham, R. D. Bounds, Joe Byrd, Wm. Byrd, L. F. Bingham, John C. Bounds, Haynes Crabtee, Wm. Barnet, J. R. Cousins, J. H. Copeland, F. L. Cook, J. T. Cochran, G. P. Calhoun, J. A. Grayson, C. W. Holly, D. W. Hall, D. D. Hall, C. J. Herrington, E. J. Herrington, R. R. Herrington, D. W. C. Hayier, John Holdn, C. H. Hyde, Albert Hudson, J. G. Hyde, S. W. Jones, Wm. Johnson, J. M. James, Joe Lyons, Joel Loper, D. A. Lightzzy, Herriwell Parker, Wm T. Parker, M. D. Parker, H. S. Patrick, J. F. Packer, A. J. Patrick, Amos Reid, Abram Reid, J. H. Robinson, M. E. Rogers, O. E. Huston, Thos. J. Ruffin, J. F. Rice, A. G. Smith, Hiram A. Suggs, W. J. Stanley, J. W. Smith, J. A. Saderfield, John Warren, J. W. Wingate, G. A. Yarbrough, W. R. Yelverton, J. P. Yelverton, Arthur Young, D. Nelson, J. E. Cooley, W. A. Caraway, J. L. Cooper, J. F. Depriest, Bob Davis, J. T. Davis, G. W. Davis, Charley Dease, Wm. Davenport, W. P. Duke, V. G. Evans, W. H. Evans, J. C. Ellis, Sam D. Ellis, John C. Furguson, Wm. Fairchild, Tom Fewox, T. J. Fartree, John Fall, T. C. Gibson, John Linder, J. B. Lightsey, J. D. Lee, Sam Mitrrel, A. P. Moore, W. W. Myrick, J. B. Merrell, T. P. Mercer, J. P. Myrick, W. C. Myers, J. C. McDonald, J. R. Nealy, B. J. Myers, C. C. McDonald, James H. Neily, W. H. Overstreet, Samuel Parker, T. J. Noble, J. A. Sanders, D. F. Smith, E. H. Smith, H. C. Smith, Willis M. Smith, Archie Smith, Samuel Terrell, W. B. Trest, Alex Taylor, F. S. Thornton, A. C. Thomas, W. M. Temple, David Thatch, J. K. Thigpen, James Tippit, C. M. West, W. L. Walters, James A. Walters, T. L. Walters, J. E. Walters, James P. Abney, Alexander Reid, Dick Sauls, Jones Sauls, French Rizo. Signed by J. B. Lightsey.

### Comments

Capt. Dantzler was killed at the battle of Corinth, was the father of Dr. Dantzler at Heidelberg.

W. B. Ferrell returned and resided at Paulding.

William McCurty returned and was president of the Board of Supervisors. His post office was at Claiborne.

Phil Cook returned and lived near Heidelberg.

Tom Bingham returned to his old home near Paulding, later moved to Vossburg, later to Newton.

C. H. Hyde returned and moved from Paulding to Vossburg and later to Poplarville.

S. W. Jones returned and was probate judge, later moved to Texas.

J. D. Lee returned to his old home at Missionary, was the grandfather of Rev. Smith of Antioch.

J. R. Nealy returned to his old home between _____ and Heidelberg.

Samuel Terrel returned and was state supreme judge.

P. S. Thornton returned to his old home near Heidelberg.

J. B. Lightsey returned and was a writer to newspapers.

James P. Abney returned to Montrose and reared a large family. A son, Rev. J. T. Abney, was a prominent member of the Mississippi Methodist Conference. Another son, R. L. Abney, was mayor of Bay Springs for a number of years.

# April 18, 1957

## HISTORY OF JASPER COUNTY

By J. M. KENNEDY

**Co. K, 27th Mississippi Regiment.**

"Civil War"

(From The Jasper County News, Issue of March 11, 1929.)

This company was mustered into service at Garlandeville in March, 1862.

F. B. Loper, Captain, D. P. English, 1st lieutenant, J. A. McIntosh, 2nd lieutenant, W. W. Hardy, 3rd lieutenant; Henry Bayless, D. M. Comfort, John A. Knox and M. W. Duffe, orderly sergeants. Privates: Cris Alexander, J. D. Alexander, Cab Alexander, Sam Alexander, Henry Addy, Jim Bates, Bush Blackwell, Thos Bender, William Beasly, A. J. Blackwell, George Blackwell, Tom Bender, D. T. Chapman, T. J. Chapman, Thrash Chapman, A. E. Chapman, J. A. Chapman, Billie Booth, Tom Combest, Jim Curry, W. B. Crumpton, Wm Chambliss, Bruce Davis, Elias Davis, Bob Duke, Dan Evans, Wm Hardy, Frank Hardy, James Hargroves, A. Hair, Dr Henry Izard, Henry Jones, W. L. Kelly, Ben Loper, Simps Lay, Jim Loper, Dock Massengale, Russell McInnis, Jack McDaniel, W. L. McIntosh, George McDonald, T. N. Clark, John Curry, Pat Cole, Joe Carthage, Bill Davis, Alonzo Davis, John Dickard, Henry Green, M. M. Hardy, John Hodges, W. L. Holdridge, A. J. Hollingsworth, Will Judge, George Kidd, George Loper, Henry Linder, Jim Lay, John W. McCormick, Dugal McCall, John Middleton, Jim Morgan, Fuller McIntosh, John Miller Neil, Wm Nicholson, Henry Owens, John Plunkett, Bob Plunkett, Tom Peebles, W. A. Pruitt, Bill Robertson, Sebe Robertson, Archy Robertson, Dock Simmons, James Simmons, Ralph Simmons, Wm Sartor, Dock Slone, Joe Sanders, Bill Thompson, Quinsey Thompson, Bill Terry, Mack Walker, Jasper Williams, Nelson Watts, James Wedgworth, Shep Wedgworth, Jim Oliver, John Permenter, Jim Plunkett, Wm Price, Firman Peebles, Harrison Rowzee Robertson, Siman Robertson, Isaiah Rizen, S. V. Simmons, John Simmons, Wash Sartor, John Stringer, Dock Smith, W. D. Thompson, Dan Thompson, Wiley Talor, Jake Thornton, Isaiah Walker, Ben Walker, Rueben Warren, Ewell Watts, Columbus Wedgworth, Tom Walley, John D. Williams, Duncan Stringer, Abe Sims, J. D. Whatley, J. G. Williams, Joe Alexander, W. H. Alexander.

**Comment**

Capt. F. B. Loper returned and was representative of Jasper County, later moved to Newton County.

Dr. Alexander returned and reared a large family and established a postoffice at Baxter. He had four children that were teachers of the county: Will, John, Jula and Julia. He was the father of Mrs Alice Abney and grandfather of Prentiss, and also two members of the legislature, Marzell Alexander and Mildred Cato.

Cab Alexander returned to his old home near Montrose and reared a large family. He was the father of Barr Alexander and Mrs Walter Ware, the grandfather of Sheriff R. C. Alexander, C. B. Alexander and Dr R. D. Pittman, formerly of Bay Springs but now of Jackson.

The Blackwells always lived at Montrose and Randle Hill and two of them have been county superintendents of education: Preston and Arthur.

M. M. Hardy returned and was county assessor for many years.

John W. McCormick returned to his old home at Moss Hill and was president of the board of supervisors for a number of years, also a member of the school board. He was a grandfather of Dr McCormick of M. S. C. W. faculty, Archie McCormick, principal of Bailey High School at Jackson; Mrs Horace Overby, whose husband is superintendent of schools of Jasper County, and Miss Stella McCormick, who is supervisor of Jasper County schools.

Miller Neil returned and lived at Heidelberg and Montrose, was the father of C. F. Neil, who was president of the board of supervisors and member of the county school board; was the grandfather of Rev. J. L. Neil, C. Lamar Neil, former president of Ellisville Junior College; M. L. Neil, former superintendent of Louisville High School (now deceased); G. T. Neil, superintendent of Wilkinson County schools. He was the great grandfather of John Neil, member of the legislature from Jones County, also the famous Dr Neil of Jackson.

W. A. Pruitt returned to his home at Moss Hill. He was the father of Mrs J. W. Abney of Montrose; also of the very popular teacher of the writer, Miss Hattie Pruitt, married to Duncan Burnett, now deceased.

Shep Wedgworth returned and lived at Randle Hill, was the father of R. I. Wedgworth.

Harrison Roberts was captured, took sick and died, and was buried in Arlington Cemetery at Washington, D. C. His grave is well marked, giving name, company and regiment.

The Alexanders originally came from Charlotte, N. C. They first built a log church and named it Charlotte after the King's daughter. A Mrs Jackson who lived nearby was highly incensed about naming the church for the King's daughter. She was a Hutchinson and lived in Scotland about the time England was sending an army to capture it, which he finally did. She and her people could not take this and all came to America. In a short while her husband died and she said that she would not bury him at Charlotte that the Alexanders were uppish, so she with the help of her neighbors dragged his body on a sled ten miles to Waxhaw for burial. The Alexanders, however, made the first move against England with the signing of the Mecklinberg Declarations. The county of which Charlotte is the county site.

**Male Slaves**

(A continuation of "Uncle" Heck's tale about slavery days, from A. J. Brown's history.)

As the writer worked with "Uncle" Heck he had many questions for him and he always had an answer with reasons, whether or not it was true or not. "Uncle" Heck worked mostly around the community and let the family work the crop. His pay was generally molasses, meat, etc. An old hunter lived next door and in the autumn the neighbors would go with him to kill wild hogs in the swamps, carrying a wagon and some on horse backs. The men on horses would ride through the swamps and shoot a hog when seen or sometimes the hogs would chase the dogs back to the wagon when the men on the wagon would take a few shots. They also had hogs in the pen at home, in this way each farmer had plenty of meat, and they would like to dispose of it before summer as the meat would get rancid, as they called it. So, if the Negroes could get some meat and molasses for sweets with potatoes and vegetables, they could live.

One of the questions the writer asked "Uncle" Heck, did the masters cut (castrate) the slaves? In some cases it had to be done, a master who had a few wenches and one male had to do that or sell them or they would inbreed. The wenches did not like for themselves to be sold and would agree to cut them. A cut Negro would bring more money than a bull Negro as the bull Negroes would always be fighting. It was the old mammy's business to keep the wenches with baby. Sometimes the mistress would not nurse her baby and it would be turned over to a wench that had a baby of the same age. (Later years the writer noticed a large tomb in a cemetery, "To My Mammy." I asked about this and they told me that a wealthy man whose mammy died, had placed this tomb to her memory.)

In Tap Roots, the cajen girl classifies women as having rosebuds when young, cabbages later and if the woman has had a lot of children, she has flops. So the mistress sometimes did not desire to nurse too many babies as it might injure the looks of her breasts.

**The Indian Witness**

A few years after the Civil War the court at Paulding had a murder case with only an Indian as a witness. (The writer has heard old men relate this case, one that was on the jury). The jury was empaneled and the Indian was put on the witness stand and told what he saw in a simple manner. The lawyers began to ask him some questions but the Indian would point to the court clerk and say, "Me done told you read him."

The Indian then began to get down from the stand and the judge told him he would have to answer the lawyers' questions. The Indian replied, "Me told it all". The judge told him that he would have to put him in jail if he did not answer the lawyers' questions. The Indian came back with the same answer, "Me told it all". The judge put him in jail and locked the jury up for the balance of the week, but they never could get the Indian to talk more.

**PAULDING IN 1878**

By B. H. Thigpen

(Published in The Jasper County News, Dec. 8, 1932.)

It may seem odd that I can remember so far back. Of course, I was small and in my first breeches, and likely wearing the first hat that I ever owned, given me by my grand-daddy. I have a faint vision of old Paulding in its heyday before the North Eastern, now the Great Southern railroad was built.

When you approach Paulding from Tallahala or Rambo bridge from the west you will see a road leading to the south before you get to Town Creek, near the site of an old water mill. This road leads to the old Pleasant Hill community where George Clayton and other prosperous and unprosperous farmers lived. Leading out south on the same road you come to old Masonic Lodge of the Oak Bowery community, which had a wealthy and highly respected citizenship. Here Judge McCallum had a store and water mill.

Clayton, who at this time ran a country store and plantation, had just bought and installed a steam mill for grinding and ginning cotton. It was something new in the country then. Many had never seen one before. They were afraid to go near it, they thought it might explode. The sputtering of the steam, the revolving of the governors and the blow of the whistle woke up the neighborhood and was the talk and wonder of the day. Lum Risher, a few miles down the road, soon established one and so did Abney a little farther down.

Pleasant Hill was a pleasant neighborhood to live. There lived the Claytons, the Rishers, Betheas, McCormicks, Hartsfields, Bufkins, some of the Thigpens, the Ulmers, the Lightseys, Maxeys, Jones, and Tuckers. John F. McCormick also ran a store there. I forgot who the school teacher was but think it was Henry Hartsfield. Several years before that James K. Thigpen taught there; John L. Bufkin and Miss Ann Patterson taught there before the Civil War. But during the war a man by the name of Johnson, who hated the Yankees and loved Jeff Davis, taught there. Every time he heard of a southern victory he would yell hurrah for Jeff Davis.

(Continued Next Week.)

**April 25, 1957**

## HISTORY OF JASPER COUNTY

By J. M. KENNEDY

Some of the old citizens who lived here then and were too old Ully Buykin, who was a Mexican War Veteran, his father was John, for active duty in the war were; who was among the first settlers of the county. John H. Cook, father-in-law of Clayton, Henry Cook, his brother lived not far off, Cary Patterson, John Lightsey and John Ulmer. Most of these old men and their fathers came mostly from South Carolina, who moved here years before to the rich land of Mississippi to get rich by working their slaves. Some got rich and some didn't. There was also a Caraway and a Bridges family who lived here and among them a Dr. Bridges who moved off and I never heard from him after that.

The physicians who practiced in this community lived either at Paulding or Claiborne, the latter a flourishing village and a whiskey stand. Dr. W. J. Baily was there and practiced. Also a Dr. Dillihay, a dentist, lived there.

Now we will go back to Paulding. The physicians at this time that lived there were Dr. Nunn, Dr. Dozier, Dr. Cotton, Dr. Oliphant, Dr. Walton. Walton was a very popular man and did the lion share of it. Dr. Orr, a hard old drinker, was a dentist. He was mighty rough, blocking and deadening the nerve of a tooth was then unknown. It was said that when he went to pull a person's tooth he would take a drink and give the person a drink and when pulling the tooth would tell the person that it would not hurt and is going to be just like eating cheese.

My parents lived on this road that led to Pleasant Hill, about two miles before you get there at the Ridgeway place. We called it the Jack Rhodes place. This splendid old two story colonial structure was blown down and tumbled in a gully by the storm that blew Lake Como away in 1890.

As I said I was too young to give many details, for it seems to my mind like a vision, a dream, or a picture that one would get from reading a novel, but I remember well the talk of the old folk. My father was then a young man now an old one with a splendid memory and can greatly refreshen and greatly supplement my personal knowledge.

As I went to say I remember Paulding on my first visit there as a thriving, hustling for those times. The streets were crowded with wagons, both mule and ox, saddled neighing horses hitched to the racks. Very few people then were able to own buggies. An automobile was then never dreamed of and a prospect of an airplane was a miracle. I did hear a fellow say to another one day that he heard of a man making him some wings and got on top of the house and tried to fly. Another man said he guessed that he made a greasy spot where he lit. It seems that they had the idea all right.

Yes, the streets of Paulding were crowded with cotton wagons, McKinstry was the chief cotton buyer. Though many people in the fall wagoned to Enterprise, Shubuta and even to Mobile. Greenwood, a Jew, was the largest cotton buyer at Shubuta and Weems at Enterprise, but then Paulding was a big place as large as either Enterprise or Shubuta and they were big places. Paulding and its suburbs extended from town Creek on the west and to the same creek on the South and North to the Jim Foley place, where Dr. Cotton formerly lived and east to beyond the old Chapman place.

Saturday, and especially in the evening would be when the people went to town to swap horses, tell jokes, civil war stories, how they made the Yankees bite the dust about the chickens, bee hives and beeves they would steal while out foraging, how they would be surprised, and how they would retaliate while on picket duty in the war.

In those days and at this time it was the custom for men to go armed. Most every man had a pistol or bowie knife or both. It was considered a part of his personal equipment. It was not against the law, then.

There were many saloons and of course when went to town, and was principally what he went for, he wanted a drink of whiskey and flash to take home. Sometimes they would get drunk, cuss and fight, and some of the devilish fellows would get a scarry fellow and run him home and then laugh about it. But rarely did a man get shot and less so did one get killed, though there has been several men killed at Paulding. One old Chactaw Indian named Joshia killed an Indian by the name of Millitubia there in a drunken row. But that is no worse than at Bay Springs and at other places as I saw a man shot down at the depot and another one killed about a dime. Talking about Indians the country was full of squads of them. Sometimes they would go in droves in single file all dressed in red and showy colors. They would camp out in the woods under trees and make baskets out of cane from the reed brakes, artistically bound, painted, dyed or stained, and sell them for it full of meal or flower, the bigger the basket the more it cost. They were not bad to steal but were very superstitious. When you hired one to work for you he wanted you to lock him up in the crib so he would be safe from his enemies.

I will say a few words about the Negro at this time. It had not been long since the surrender, a little more than a decade. The country was much dissatisfied, unsettled embarrassed, and distressed as now, especially the South which had hardly begun to recuperate from the terrible devastation. Money was scarce, wages low, and necessities were high. No market for home produce and business war stagnated. To add to the misery of the calamity there were hordes of ragged, hungry, homeless and ignorant Negroes in the country with nothing to do, idling, pilfering, insolent to the white people, vainly waiting on the Republican government to make good its unfulfilled promises about the forty acres and the mule.

In fact there were so many in some communities that the whites were besieged. The Ku Klux Klan at this time was disbanded, it had served its purpose. The Negroes then had few schools, if any. None of the colored could read or write, and about half of the whites. What few of the whites had any worthwhile education or any considerable wealth were stuck-up and would not associate with the common run of people. To retrospect what progress has been made in this line and others by both races is incredible.

The lawyers at this time in Paulding were Shannon, Street, Capt. W. H. Hardy, Tom Hardy, and if not at this time, previous, Chapman and Murphy. As to whom the sheriff was I am not certain as Wm. Brame preceded Capt. Moss and I think it was Burkett Lancaster that preceded Brame. Anyway, way back yonder there was a sheriff by that name. It's a pity that the records were burned so that we could have kept the records straight. The same way with chancery clerk. Frank Parker preceded M. G. Turner who was formerly assessor, and if I make not Will Murphy preceded Parker. It was Tom Burton or Tom Whatley that was circuit clerk. Ben Thigpen was probate judge of the county; he had formerly been county treasurer and representative. Along about this time there was a paper published at Paulding but I do not remember the name. It was first published by Thigpen and then by Parker.

Where Jorn McDevitt lives is the old Judge Thigpen place. On down the road where John Henry Dean lives is the old T. J. Bingham place. About a mile northeast is the old Hyde place, later known ts the Brame place, and about a quarter southeast is the Jack Hyde place later known as the Moss or Ellis place.

The greatest mistake that Paulding and the county made was to turn down a railroad offered to them by Capt. Hardy. This took the business and people from Paulding, leaving the clay hills.

**Paulding in 1887**

Paulding was like most all other old towns and cities, it was laid off in squares—the courthouse being in the center and stores and offices facing it. The churches, and school buildings were a little more back or retired.

This was the year that I attended school in the south room of the old S. S. Nicholson Hotel which was burned down sometime this year. No telling how old the building was but has been forty-five years since I attended school there under the tutorship of A. T. Burton, who also kept the county poor. Burton was recognized as one of the county's smartest men as far as intellect was concerned. In Jasper county at that time. But unfortunately his usefulness was greatly impaired on account of too much strong drink. Of course, the old courthouse was there, unpainted, looking very much as it did at this time. The old two-story wooden jail was there with the lower story partly under the ground, which was used as a dungeon.

The old house, later known as the Cope House, I forget the original name (Shannon), but it stood where there is a grove of pecans and live oaks now on the west side. By the way, this grove of Pecan trees was put out by Parson Harmon, the father of Gus, Nolan, Duncan and Mrs. S. S. Cope, and who said he would never live to see them bear but perhaps his grandchildren would. (his grandson is now bishop). Next to the Cope house was the "Green House" in which the Eastern Clarion was published.

A hotel was then run by a Mr. James (Champ), the grandfather of John Robert Davis). The Methodist and Catholic churches were there as they are now; the Presbyterian church on the site of the old school house south of the Mike Hanly place and east of the highway to Vossburg. This building was a two-story brick and was still standing but no services there as all the members had moved away. I attended school in the same building before it burned, taught by G. M. Hull in the session of 1893-4. The Baptist church stood on the west side of the square had already torn down. The old two-story masonic hall stood about where Bob Read's store is. It was sometimes used as a school room, also, as a store by Cope and Brenckinridge (who came from Alabama).

A. J. Benison, lived just south of the jail who worked as a druggist for J. D. McNeil whose store was on the N. E. corner with Hass and Tom Fagan store next, then Hanly, then a building where the Review was published. Miss Duck Chapman was postmistress and the P. O. was inside the courtyard. The first store east of the Methodist hcurch was Mrs. Hannon, sister to Mike Hanly, later it was Dick Benison's drug store, then M. G. Turner, Lon Arledge, S. J. Johnson, who later moved to Jackson, Duncan Burnett, then a goober joint by Jess Brown, Andrew Hare, Sanders Hyde, and Nelson Pickens who was Janitor of the courthouse. Nelson died and Joe Williams is now the janitor. The last building on this street was where Bob Read opened when he went to Paulding, then occupied by Bolivar Ferrell.

**May 2, 1957**

# HISTORY OF JASPER COUNTY

### By J. M. KENNEDY

**PAULDING IN 1887 BY B. H. T.**

The old McKinestry building on the north side was still standing but not occupied. This was sometimes called China street on account of so many china trees. On the northeast corner stood the old tavern with a cellar in it, eating place and at one time a saloon.

The names that I remember Sol Street, Lawyer; M. G. Turner, Chancery Clerk; N. J. Sheeley, Circut Clerk; Monroe Hardy, Assessor; McBay, Treasurer; Quint Heidelberg, Member of the Board from the southeast beat; W. H. Mounger, Sheriff; and Tom Lawless duputy; F. M. Moseley, Superintendent of Education.

About this time people were moving away and Paulding was getting "slim, and slimmer all the time." Now some of the people who live there are; Joe Edwards, G. E. Ellis, Dick Reid, Sr., J. K. Thigpen, Mr. Sherman, the Dailys, O'Flynns, McDevitts, Skehans, Harringtons, Dolans, Carrs, Finegans, Kerlys, Malones, Bergens, Mrs. William Brame, George McKintry, Levi Spencer, Nicholsons.

The doctors there then were Doctors Sam Ferrill, W. T Street, Frank McCormick, and Bufkin. Some of the pupils in school there then were Tom and Will Burton, Bill Brame, Daisy Benison, Sam and Jim Ellis, Mamie and Lizzie Ferrill, Henry Hanly, McKinstry children, Dick Reid's children, Street children, Shelly children, Foster Round, Queen Sherman, myself and two oldest sisters.

**PAULDING— "CONFED"**

By B. H. Thigpen

The Jasper County News.

June 11, 1924

To write old Paulding's tale
From what knowledge that I own,
I attend with great travail;
aniedates before the fathers grown,
But one time in her early youth
It has been said with certain truth,
She was the queen city of the East
And that is renown to say, the least.

Her people then were of noble stock,
While of course they had their faits.
In honor's cause, they were of rock
And of earth were its salt,
But ever since then
She has been shaken by many adverse winds
And of her former self bears scarce a trace,
As if forsaken of God's grace.

Her hills of peb and clay and sand are her indestructable part,
Her brooks and rills still course the land,
Works of nature and not of art;
And will always be
As they flow to the sea,
Up hill toward the topic,
Where the climate is humid and misanthropic.

A courtly land I hear them say
In time long past by,
With no thought of future decay
Under her then pleasant and prosperous sky,
Her virgin wood with music rang
As the doe from its hiding sprang,
Startled by the hunter's horn
and the hound's note forlorn.

The country then was stalked with game,
The wolves, the panthers and cats untame,
Lurked behind the shrub and bush,
And to the huhter's delight extreme
He'd bound across bog and stream,
To pursue the various game
which seemed to be half-tame.

The old town was the rallying ground
Of those who wore the gray,
Of those enthused for glory won
In war's heroic ways,
Above whose soil the stars and bars
Rose in the breeze and streamed afar,
And whose delight it was to see
The emblem of what they thought was free.

The ancient site is still there,
The rallying ground renowned,
The rock, the clay, the hills are there,
The remnants of the sad old town,
But the men who wore the grand old gray
Oh where, oh where, are they,
Beneath the clay, the rocks, the tomb
God bless their spuls, their precious bones.

The soldier boys who were then
In their youthful prime to see
Now like aged trees are thin
Old, broken and in eternity.
This is the way of man
When doing the best he can,
After life's labor then one long sigh
He sickens, suffers, lies down and dies.

---

Excerpts from B. H. Thigpen's

**Southwest Jasper**

Jasper County News,

September 24, 1925

He begins at Grayson Hill in eastern Jasper. The last time the writer was there he could see the smoke-stacks at Stonewall and Quitman.

"In beginning this description I will begin at the old place known as Grayson Hill. This old place was at the tip or edge of a range of uplands running north and south through the county forming a water shed. No doubt this was named for the man who first owned it. Later it was owned by Henry Cook of Heidelberg, afterwards by Cary Bufkin who lived and prospered there as a farmer for several years, then by J. L. Bufkin of Vossburg who put negroes on it but now buildings are gone and nothing there to mark the place. (Descendants of these Bufkins now live at Stringer).

We now go West in the direction of Paulding and come to the Albert Rowell place settled by him in a log two room house and nearby another log house where Jim Thigpen lived and who taught the Phalti school for seevral years. The old hill looks about as it did forty years ago, the long skyline where you could see the rising and the setting of the sun and the beautiful colors of nature on the streams in the springtime when nature was in full bloom it was truly beautiful, in other words it was picturesque. It was here that I experienced a fright that I hope never to again. As I was plowing I began to hear a distant rumbling in the southwest which became louder each time. Even the animals seemed to sense the danger. The howling rage, the firery center or vortex of the storm in all its malignity was enough to sing consternation into the stoutest heart. We knew it was a cyclone, and we became fearful of the impending danger, and fled down the hill into a gully and were saved. The next morning we began to look around and found that Ike Arledge's Sr., where everything was swept away. Also Bill Risher's place, Dr. Krouse. People know nothing about the violence of these tornadoes but those who have experienced them and have lived. Another thing that I remember is that one day I was plowing a mustang horse (wild horse from Texas) and two Swiss came by with a dancing bear, the horse became frightened and ran away.

We now leave Phalti chuch on the right and pass the John Garner place where he has lived for sixty years. Then on to the Jack Hyde place and not far from that old man Hyde's place where later sheriff William Brame lived and after Tom Brame Chancery clerk. Then we pass the Judge Thigpen place and soon down the hill to Town Creek.

Up the hill from Town Creek we first come to the Roundhouse (Sometimes used as a school house. This was across the road from where Lex Brame now lives.).

I will say nothing more about Paulding for she has been cussed and discussed for all her present boneyard of her existing glory. We need not disturb her nor grieve over dead for in her senile age may she rest in peace.

We go now to the wild and wooly West as it was sometimes called in that day, I am not so well acquainted with this section as I was so busy plowing and hoeing to make ends meet and sometimes they did not that I had no time to visit. Going Southwest from Paulding we first come to Town Creek again where there was the old Hardy mill for grinding corn for bread and boating and fishing where sometimes we had a picnic. From here we travel on and come to a high hill called Rocky Mounts with a spring at the foot of it, then the old Cotton place, then the Isham Cook place then the last one before we reach Tallahala Creek is Barfield. Here forty years ago a tornado passed through Tallahala swamp and cut a path through this virgin hardwood as though it had been a reaper through a wheat field. We next come to the Medlin place. This is the site of the Mabel school where I attended my first school with my father as teacher. I remember some of the pupils: Jeffy Massey, Monroe Massey, John Sims, Jim Pittman, Dave Pittman, and others whom I have forgotten. On from here we cross Knute Flupper creek and come to the Brinson place, then Kuykendoll, the Sorrell place and Holders Church, then the old Hayes place a double hewn log place where Bill Morris and the Stockmans lived. Now Rufe Cook Judson Eddins and Sing Scott. We are now in Lake Como where lived Joe Blankinship, Henry Eddins, Frank Roper, George Horn, Marion Yelverton, Ab Denson, Caarley, Will Forest and William Thigpen and others that I have forgotten. The road then turns to left and crosses Tallahoma about a mile below where it now crosses and hits the old highway about B. S. Thigpen's (It now crosses 15 Highway at Murphy's store. It hit the Old Jackson Highway to New Orleans. This road at one time had a telegraph wire from Paulding to New Orleans.)

May 9, 1957

COUNTY NEWS, BAY SPRINGS, MISSISSIPPI         THURSDAY, MAY 9, 1957

# HISTORY OF JASPER COUNTY

By J. M. KENNEDY

**JASPER COUNTY TOWNS by Rowland.**

Acme—"A post town 12 miles west of Paulding." People, Tyner, Massey, Dixon, Pittman, James, Kuykendall, Windham, Brinson, Medlin, Aaron, Cook, Morris, Stockman.

Addine—"A post town 9 miles south of Paulding." People, McLaurin, Risher, Collins, Newell, Lee, Windham, Chambers.

Alto—"A post town 8 miles SW of Paulding." People, Cook, Clayton, Hartsfield, Lightsey, Brady, Bridges, Agnes, Fannie and Carrie Cook were outstanding teachers of Jasper John Hartfield is very prominent in Jackson. Judge Stone Deavours married a Clayton.

Bay Springs—A post town 15 miles S.W. of Paulding on the M. J. & K. C. R. R., population 1900, 46. It has several good stores, two churches, a saw mill, a cotton gin, block and spindle factory—a bank (1904), an excellent school—a fine mineral spring, population 1906, 1000; made a county site in 1906, a new school building, cost $6000. Bay Springs News edited by S. F. Thigpen.

People—Denson, Burnett, Alexander, Stevens, Abney, Hutto, Ryan, Pittman, Boykin, Tedder, Cole, Fail, Cook, Stringer, Myers, Ainsworth, Rogers, Bayless, McKinnon, Burnham, Windham, Haden, Harper, Ford, Horn, Arledge, Hall, Simmons, Brame, Parker, Narro, Martin, Shepard, Phillips, Newcomb, Brown, Eddins, McBay, Evans, McFarland, Thompson, Sims, Jones, Kennedy, Johnston, Blankinship, Mason, Hayes, Harrison, Hendry, Pruitt, Holder, Keys, Russell, Massey, Greene, Yelverton, Huff, Lightsey, Gatewood, Rasberry, Bingham, Bostright, Upton, Smith, Sumrall, Hegwood, Grayson, Mayfield, McLeod, Hinton, Keown, Dear, Jenkins, Sims, Raynor, Lee, Boyd, Bates, Heidelberg, Porter, Houston, Barnett, Grisham.

Cooley—A post hamlet 12 miles S.E. of Paulding. People—Cooley, Thomas, Chisholm, Kennedy, Sanders.

Garlandsville—Oldest town in the county (1833). It had a most inviting site, level and healthy, settled by wealthy planters which gave it importance. Early families were: Watts, Brown, Hodge, Williams, Dillahey, Beard, Cowan, Loyerly, Hamlet and Harris. It sent two companies to the Civil War, headed by Chatfield, and Loper. Little is left to remind one of its former glory. Gen. Grierson passed through Garlandsville in April, 1863, on his way from Decatur to Hazlehurst, captured 1000 prisoners, 1200 horses, 3000 stacks of arms, and inflicted a loss of $4,000,000. People — Williams, Knowles, Weir, Kurr, Shinfessel, Wilson, Keyes, Spann, Moseley, Bostick, Hardy, Ward, Lockridge, Bonner, Harris, Lang, Gibson, Griffith, Dent, Harry, McCrory, Wall.

Hamlet—A post office 16 miles West of Paulding. People—Ainsworth, Rogers, Keys, McLaurin, Holder, Tynes, Sims, Massey, James.

Heidelberg — An incorporated post town 10 miles south of Paulding. Important railroad station, money and express orders, several stores, two large cotton gins, a bank, three churches and a good school, population: 1900 225, in 1906, 400. People — Heidelberg, Clayton, Risher, Abney, Dantzler, McCormick, Morrison, Lyon, Thatch, Burns, Jones, Parker, Weems, James, Cook, Kelly, Cooper, Rowell, Thornton, Wilson, Carr, Huddleston, Ellis, Satcher, Travis. Travis of the latter prominent lawyers in Jackson, the other in Meridian. J. A. Travis is employed by the Mississippi Education Association.

Hero. A post hamlet 14 miles North of Paulding. People—Harris, Wall, Gibson, Ratclif, Tisdale, Boulton, Dolan, Sea, Wyatt.

Hosey. A post hamlet on Nukeshupper Creek, 15 miles S.W. of Paulding. People—Hosey, Blackwell, James, Aarons.

Lake Como. A village 14 miles S.W. of Paulding, 1 mile East of Tallahoma Creek, 4 miles East of Bay Springs. Population, 1900, 50. A site of a high school. People—Thigpen, Yelverton, Blankinship, Rogers, Boulton, Waites, Tyner, Denson, Pittman, Scott, Roper.

Leona. A post office 5 miles south of Paulding. People—Neelly, Wade, Pryor. Post office discontinued, now the site of the East Jasper High School for colored.

Louin. An incorporated post hamlet 16 miles N.W. of Paulding and 4 miles S.W. of Montrose, station on the M. J. & K. C. R. R. It has good general stores, a saw mill, a shingle mill, a church, a good school, a bank (est. 1906,; population 1900, 25; 1906, 300. Named for the postmaster's son, on the old Jackson Highway. In the early days Henry Barber built a log church there and named it Mt Vernon. People—Ishee, Ball, Smith, Bassett, Long, Grayson, Parker, Lightsey, Anderson, Perry, Leech, Land, Boyd, Fanning, Lightsey, Carr, Hankins, Royal, Wilkerson, Wilkins, James, Morgan, Dyess, Wall, Harris, McGee, Tally, Halford, McInnis, Kennedy, Gardner, Lewis, Waldrup, Simmons, Phillips, Dawkins, Jones, Ainsworth, Boutwell, McMullan, Buchanan, Rogers.

Missionary. A hamlet 6 miles N. of Paulding. Post office discontinued. People—Russell, Dolan, Drew, Mask, Green, Kennedy, James, Reed, McDaniel, Harrington, Chatham.

Montrose. A post hamlet on Tallahoma Creek and the M. J. & K. C. R. R., 36 miles S.W. of Meridian and 13 miles from Paulding. It has a money and express office, a bank (est. in 1905), several stores, three churches, the Mississippi Conference Training School, saw mill, cotton gin, Jasper County Review edited by W. W. Moore and J. M. Kennedy, population, 1900, 150; 1906, 500. People—Abney, Pruitt, Alexander, Neill, Burnett, Knott, Hutto, Sharbrough, Lightsey, Hardy, Kennedy, McLaurin, Gammage, James, Sartor, Blackwell, Lightsey, Nix.

Moss. A post office in the southern part of Jasper County on the M. J. & K. C. R. R., two stores, 2 churches, a school. People—Moss, Nicholson, Jones, Legg, Mauldin, Ishee, Stringer, Windham, Bulloch, Stennett, Evans, Horn, Walters, McCord, Pool.

Otoe. A post office on Roaring Creek, 18 miles S.W. Paulding. People—Johnston, Wilson, Alderman, Ishee.

Massengale. A post office 15 miles N.E. of Paulding. Discontinued. People—Massengale, Bogan, Buckley, Richardson, Cross, Baskett, Little, Dyess, Dear, McMillan, Johnson, Gandy, Hamrick.

In the early days, the writer taught school in this community with Judge Sam Whitman. We boarded around, we always had a good bed to sleep on and good food. A small boy who attended school was Claude Cross. A prominent lawyer now in Boston, Mass., and was employed in the famous Hiss case.

Paulding. The Capitol of Jasper County, 33 miles S.W. of Meridian. Vossburg is the nearest railroad station. Heidelberg is the nearest bank. Named for John Paulding. It has two churches, two stores, a cotton gin, a grist mill, and a good school. Population in 1900, 220. People—Read, Brame, Hawkins, McDevitt Bergin, Smith, Carr, Harrington.

Penantly. A post office 9 miles N. of Paulding. People—Foley, Peek, McCormick, Boulton, Risher, Blackwell, Davis, Gandy, Pruitt.

Ras. A post office in central part of Jasper County on Tallahala Creek, also on Three-Chopped-Way. People—Green, Read, Pugh, Brewer, Bankston, Walley, Henry, Evans.

Rose Hill. Formerly Twistwood, which was located on the Finnegan place. It was moved to the site of the Holland Camp Ground in 1889 by Dr Peek and named Rose Hill. Soon a famous high school was established there by very efficient teachers, named Day and Grandberry. It has one church, a cotton gin, 4 stores, fine farming land. People — Chatham, Davis, Lewis, Martin, Cooley, Smith, Avery, Eikes, Dansby, Pruitt, Herrington, Reynolds, Graham, Holyfield, O'Rourke, Finnegan, Workmaster, White, Booth, Porter, Conklin.

Stringer. A post hamlet on M. J. & K. C. R. R., 16 miles S.W. of Paulding and 15 miles N. of Laurel. Bay Springs is the nearest bank, population in 1900, 86; 1906, 150, it has good general stores, a saw mill, cotton gin and a good school. People—McAlpin, Hosey, Stringer, Foley, Price, Johnston, Roberts, Dykes, Reddock, Ford, Ishee, Anderson, Jones, Miller, Clark, Myrick, Timms, Sims, Welborn, Moore.

Vale. A post office 8 miles N.W. of Paulding. People—Harper, McCarty, Brady, Pharish, Buckley, Beason.

Vernon. A post office on Tallahoma Creek, 12 miles S.W. of Paulding. People — Hosey, Risher, Blackwell, Wade, Courtney, Aarons, Myrick.

Verba. A post office in the N.W. of center beat. People — Brady, Smith, Temple, Knotts, Anderson, Loper, Dawkins, Reid, Halford.

Vossburg. A village 10 miles S.E. of Paulding, 20 miles S.W. of Enterprise, money and express office; four stores, one church, a cotton gin.

A good hotel which is noted for mineral water which is shipped to all parts of the United States. At Stafford Springs is a large hotel with all modern conveniences. The Vossburg Lithia Spring is another valuable spring much patronized. People—Lee, Arledge, Williford, Martin, Bounds, Thornton, Chatham, Bennett, Carr, Stafford, Allen, Ellis, McCormick, Barnett.

# HISTORY OF JASPER COUNTY

### By J. M. KENNEDY

**THE SIMPSON TRIAL**

In the eighties and nineties the circuit court was held in the spring and fall and Mayers of Brandon was judge. My father would always say, "Work hard, boys, and get up early with our crops so we can go to court next week." I have just read the life of the famous Dr. Hand of Mississippi State and he said he and other folks would go to court at Paulding to hear the McLaurins plead their cases. People were there from all parts of the county but perhaps the Simpson trial had more people than any on account of one witness.

The house, yard and streets were covered with people and an acre or two behind the stores, where many were trading ohrses.

After Simpson was indicted for murder, he sent for Anse McLaurin, Green Huddleston and Bart Sharbrough and made a deal with them to defend him. The sheriff, Mr. McFarland, had to convey him in a buggy to his home in the southwest corner of the county to get his money. I heard Mr. Mc when he came back. He said Mr. Simpson went down in the reedbreak, near his home, and reached his hand down by a gum tree and pulled out a jar of gold; then he went to the barn and took down some plow gear and knocked out a large peg in a post and pulled a roll of greenbacks. In those days people who had money were in for a lot of trouble and sometimes caused them to lose their lives.

Gossip was all around that men would go to his home, put a rope around his neck and tell him that if he did not tell where his money was—up he would go; they would then pull him up and then let him down and tell him this was the last time he was going up but all would be well if he would tell where his money was. The next crowd would pull a big knife across his throat and tell him that next time it would be cutting if he did not tell about his money.

In 1904 people had sold their timber and most all had money. I was ready to graduate and had no money. I secured an insurance man and came down in the county and we collected nearly $1500 in one day; took dinner with a farmer and he went in the house and counted us out nearly $400. We went to Newton and spent the night, and the insurance man said he was going the other way and for me to carry the money back to Jackson. I caught the four A. M. train into Jackson, arriving there about daylight. I was afraid to leave the station and remained there till I knew that the office was open but in going up there I kept my hand on the money. I took up the business and folks said we were skinning the boys. We went to Louin to work but the boys said they wanted to keep their money at home and were all investing in business.

In a few years a panic came and they lost all, but the insurance folks saved their money. The county had trouble with its money; it was collected in the fall when the farmers sold their cotton. But the robbers came and got their money. Gabe Ellis and Vince Anderson paid the county money from an iron cage.

The Simpson case was set for the second week and it was reported that Newt Knight would be a witness. I had heard so much gossip about him that I was afraid to see him. On the day of the trial the courthouse was jammed; they even the women come to court, the first time that I had seen that. It was reported that he had paid the two big lawyers $1000 each and Sharbrough $250. The trial was long and tedious. Sylvester McLaurin was prosecuting and in his speech he said that the biggest robbery on Simpson was when these lawyers robbed him. Newt at last came to the stand and to my surprise he looked like other men. A Ph.D. from Emory University came in the state last year seeking information on the Simpson trial.

Excerpts from a letter of Mrs. R. L. McLendon, published in The Jasper County News Dec. 1, 1932:

As others are writing about Paulding in the days when she was classed as the "Queen City of the East", I thought I would say my word.

Those were interesting days back when my mother and her sister who were later Mrs. W. H. Arledge and Mrs. C. H. Hyde, and walked the selfsame road from the old Bingham place to Paulding. There were the Shermans, the Nuns, the Cottons, the Terrals, the Soules, the Quaries, the Shannons, the Streets, the Mottons, the Binghams, the Hydes, the Parkers, the Murphys and many others that I have forgotten.

My mother was Cordelia Ann Murphy, daughter of John S. Murphy and Eunice Ann Bingham. He was a lawyer and the first editor of the Eastern Clarion. It was published on the S. B. Cope lot. His father was a prominent lawyer of the state and author of several books. He was buried in the Natchez cemetery. The family was originally from Boston, Mass.

**Statements from the Diary of Chap. A. M. Fikes, of 22rd Alabama Regiment**

We were mustered into service at Montgomery, Ala., Oct. 5th, 1861, and remained in camp there for a short while and then went to Mobile, Ala. for sometime. We were then sent to Tennessee; Chattanooga, Morristown, Knoxville, Clinton and many other towns where we remained for more than a year; then ordered to Jackson, Miss. In a few days we were sent to Warrenton, then to Port Gibson where we intercepted Grant's army about two miles S.W. of Port Gibson at the old Shaifer place, May 1st, 1863.

We were soon back at Baker's Creek and then into Vicksburg May 17th. On the 18th Grant's army charged the Confederate breastworks with great loss. On the 22nd, another charge was made but to no avail. By this time the city was completely surrounded by Federal soldiers who kept up a continual bombardment until July 4th, when the city surrendered.

**Comment**

In 1862, the Federal Gunboats captured all the towns along the Mississippi River up to Vicksburg but failed on Vicksburg. After Grant was successful at Shiloh, Corinth and Memphis he sent Sherman with a large force to capture Vicksburg from the north but this failed. Then Grant with a large fleet of gunboats attempted to capture the city from the river, but soon saw that would not succeed. He then tried to cut a canal across Delta point in order that boats could then pass up and down the river without being molested by the guns on the hills at Vicksburg.

After working at this for a while he decided that he could not do that. He then floated his vessels by Vicksburg and had his soldiers to meet the vessels below Vicksburg. They soon came to Jeff Davis' home where Grant secured the saddle pony of Mrs. Davis and kept it for his own use during the war. They landed at a point opposite Alcorn.

They then proceeded in the direction of Jackson and had small battles at Port Gibson, Raymond, Jackson, Baker Creek which was a hard battle, many of the Confederates were cut off from their lines, captured and carried to Rock Island, Ill., and kept in prison. Grant believed that he could break through the Confederate lines on the east side of the city but the writer has heard a number of men say that all the men that made that charge were killed, some tried to retreat but were killed. They let the wounded and dead lie in the sun for three days. The writer has heard Jasper soldiers and also Fikes that he was preaching in the courthouse one Sunday morning and a cannon ball hit the building.

After the war Fikes settled in this county near Rose Hill. He was pastor of a number of churches in this county. He had twin boys, George and Bob, who were preachers. He has a grandson, Mellon Fikes, who is a preacher in Missouri. He has a daughter still living at Rose Hill, Mrs. Cooley. Mrs. E. A. Martin, who is employed by the county welfare office is his grand-daughter. Many of the Jasper soldiers were in the battle of Vicksburg.

The Bonner house at Garlandsville, noted for its ante-bellum furniture and its historic value, figured during the Civil War, when Federal cavalry, under Gen. Grierson, passed though the state from the Tennessee line, on their way to Baton Rouge. This place also figured during Indian days at the historic Indian crossroads at Garlandsville.

**May 23, 1957**

*COUNTY NEWS, BAY SPRINGS, MISSISSIPPI* — *THURSDAY, MAY 23, 1957*

# HISTORY OF JASPER COUNTY

### By J. M. KENNEDY

**THE OLD ROUND HOUSE**
by B. H. Thigpen
The Jasper County News
November 11, 1932
1889-90

The lamented death of L. L. Denson brings to my mind the old buildings at Paulding when he visited our school, taught in the Old Round House by my father, James K. Thigpen. In the election of 1889, L. L. had defeated Stone Deavours and Al Smith (who was head of the Heidelberg school and brother to Col. John Smith and uncle to Milt Smith) for the office of Superintendent of Education. With him there was beginning to come a regiment of young men in office. W. J. McFarland was elected Sheriff; A. J. Hutto, Chancery Clerk; Tom Brown, Circuit Clerk; McBay, Treasurer, and Monroe Hardy, Assessor (the last two being old confeds. Sometimes before the entire ticket was old confeds). Mike Hanly was supervisor from center beat and Q. C. Heidelberg from the southeast beat.

At this time there only a few high schools in the county which were supported by private subscription. They were: Lake Como, headed by L. L. Denson; Pleasant Hill by Stone Deavours and Brown; Montrose, L. D. McLaurin and a Mr Massey; Rose Hill, Day and Grandberry; Hamlet, by King and Hester. They were of the old type, heavy in mathematics, Greek and Latin. The other schools of the county were one and two teacher schools taught in a log school house with a large fire place in the end and the wood brought in from the woods by the boys. Sometimes there was a rough edge California fashion. Most of the teachers were men. These ran four months and the children attended mostly when their parents did not need them at home for some work. Sometimes there were two months taught in the winter and two in the summer, said by some to be better as they did not need fire and the children were barefooted and therefore made no noise in walking in the building.

The common pastime for people were going to preaching on Sunday, log rollings in the week days and dances on Friday and Saturday night. All families kept whiskey in their homes, even the preachers. They believed that was their own personal business. However there was little drunkness. They believed in temperance but not prohibition.

The children who attended school at that time were: Edwards, McFarland, Copa, O'Flinn, Street, McDevitt, Ellis, Bufkin, Thigpen, McGlauthin, Garner.

Let me get back to the old building. It was on the left as you come up the hill from Town creek accross the Brame place. It was a large two story building with a large brick chimney in the south end. The walls had all kinds of marks on them with some bullet holes said to be fired there by Henry Calhoun when old Parson Henry Jones lived there, a Methodist circuit rider.

### Clippings from the EASTERN CLARION

at Paulding, October 27, 1855

Simeon R. Adams was the editor, said to be the greatest publisher of his day. The paper was called the bed-blanket paper on account of its size, said to be the largest in the state, now said to be one of the largest in the world. A proclamation signed by Governor John J. McRea offered a $200.00 reward for a runaway slave named Jenk who was said to be hiding in the swamps of Jasper County. He had inflicted a gun shot wound on a free white man named Thomas S. Fogg.

Paulding had a great number of lawyers in that day, James J. Shannon, Sol T. Street, George Wood, Wm. T. Powe, John S. Murphy, Henry Calhoun, A. F. Dantzler being among the names that appear.

The coming November election was announced with the following candidates: For Representative, Ben Thigpen and Thos. C. Moffitt; Probate Judge, S. W. Jones and George Ryan; Circuit Clerk and Probate Clerk, Thos. W. Grayson and James A. Chapman; For Sheriff, Sam Parker and John R. Terrall; For Assessor, R. W. Lake, John Rush, Duncan McInnis, Richard Simmons, N. F. Ferguson; For Justice of Peace, center beat, W. T. Powe, L. W. Carroll; For Board of Supervisor, center beat, Robert James (father of Champ James), Isaac Downs; For Surveyor, John W. Jones.

J. Flinn advertised as a "tailor, habit, corset and stay maker" and "warranted a good fit in all cases."

Col. R. H. Henry in his book on editors that I have known says that Adams edited and managed one of the most remarkable papers of his time. He also says that his two sons, Will and Frank, who edited the Enterprise Courier; and a son-in-law, Walter Acker who edited the Paulding Messenger. Frank was also a lawyer. He also says that the editors did deal in personal news as they do now but write on subjects which are interesting to the people using a great number of adjectives.

Below is an example.

The Historical Research Project of Jasper County has located through Mrs. A. B. Hosey, a copy of "The Eastern Clarion" published at Paulding June 28, 1856, S. R. Adams, Editor.

The following Obituary of Edwin Samuel Read found in said issue will be of interest to his posterity.

### OBITUARY

At this place, on the 21st inst. of Pneumonia, MR. EDWIN SAMUEL READ, his 26th year.

The King of Terrors has again visited us, and summoned to his gloomy dominions one of our most esteemed citizens—a man beloved by all who knew him. His kind and benevolent disposition, his mild and unobtrusive manners, and his genuine Christian integrity won for him the love and respect of the whole community. As a fellow townsman his memory is endeared by a thousand pleasing recollections. His death had caused a sad blank in the family circle of which he was wont to be the joy and pride. He leaves behind him a loving wife and three little ones to lament the sad separation. But they have that divine assurance to console them which is far better than any earthly comfort, that God will be a husband unto the widow; yea and a father unto the fatherless to them that put their trust in him. Then, dear companions, repine not,—it is the finger of God, and it is our duty to bow with meekness and submission to the will of him, who doeth all things well; for truly the Lord loveth whom he chasteneth. To his relations and friends sincere sympathy is offered, and that spirit was strongly evidenced by the large concourse of sympathizing friends, of both sexes, that followed his remains to the silent city of the dead. To his sorrowing partner, I would teach the beautiful lines—

Thou art gone to the grave, but we will not deplore thee,
Though sorrow and darkness encompass the tomb;
Thy Savior has passed through its portals before thee,
And the lamp of his life is the guide through the gloom.

Yes, put your trust in that Savior, at whose right hand your departed husband shall live forevermore.

—W. H. M.

### FROM APPOMATTOX TO PAULDING.

April, 1865, by R. J. Lightsey, in Veteran's Story.

(R. J. enlisted in the first company that went out from Paulding, the Jasper Grays, who were soon sent to Virginia, where they remained with Lee for four years.

"When we surrendered, our division commander, Billy Malone formed us all in a square, with him in the center, he gave us his last farewell speech, paying us a glowing tribute. The soldiers were paroled as fast as possible and turned loose to get home the best way we could. We had known nothing but war for four years but the journey home was a "tug of war". No transportation (trains all stopped), no rations, no money, ragged and heartsick, with miles and miles between us and our homes.

"After moving out a few miles from camp, we decided that this road would not do as too many of our boys were ahead of us and they had cleaned up all provisions. There were four of us who decided to make the journey together. We found a new road and after going several miles we came to a home with plenty of grub. The old man marked out a route for us to travel where we could find plenty of food. The people on this route were most all loyal to the Confederates, some would ask us to spend several days and rest but we were anxious to push on home.

"After crossing the Dan River we entered North Carolina, where we found some strong Unionists. We spent one night in this neighborhood and the old man told us that he was glad we got whipped. His wife took up for us and the old man said no more along this line. The next morning we moved on and found the people very friendly through North Carolina, Georgia and Alabama. Before we reached Atlanta we hit a section where Sherman had been and everything was swept clean. Atlanta was in ashes, all railroads were torn up and everything in wreck.

"Reaching West Point, we crossed the Chatahoochie River in canoe and went to Montgomery where we crossed the river on pontoon bridge. From there we went to Selma where we boarded a train the first we had been on since we left Virginia. At Demopolis we crossed the Tombigbee on a steamboat and boarded the train for Meridian and then we met three of our Jasper County friends which made us happy, they were John McCormick, Li Brame and Henry Cook, who were still in the war. John told me about my brother being killed in battle which I had not known. Henry gave me a pair shoes which needed very badly. All Meridian was in ruins Sherman had been there.

"That night three of us boarded the train for Shubuta, arriving there about two A.M. We soon started on our 25 mile journey for home. Up in the day we soon came to the section where we were known and mothers were hailing us to hear from the boys. We were sorry to have tell some mothers that their boy would never come home.

"Ah, it seems but yesterd (this was written in 1899) when I review thrilling days of the sixties but.

"The years have glided onward Since those eventful days,
We've learned to love 'Old Glory' And ever speak its praise.

"The flowers of peace have blossomed
In our sweet southern clime,
North and South have blended
By generous hand of time."

May 30, 1957

# HISTORY OF JASPER COUNTY

By J. M. KENNEDY

Excerpts from the report of J. R. Preston, State Superintendent and L. L. Denson, County Superintendent, 1889-90, 1890-91.

As a whole the condition of the public schools of Jasper county for the past two years has been good, and the progress gratifying. There have been some hindrances, some drawbacks, some clogs, but notwithstanding these, the cause has moved on to a higher plane.

The number of schools in the county was eighty-five. The number of teachers: white, male, 43; female, 35; Colored, male, 27; female, 5. Amount paid to teachers: white, male, $30; female, $22; Colored, male, $20.; female, $18. While the teaching profession of Jasper county is not an exception to the universal law that all tailings are doomed to be imposed upon by some "dead Heads" failures, yet the ability of our teachers is constantly increasing. Out of 88 white teachers last year 46 held first grade licenses, this year 55 held the same and quite a number hold two and three year licenses.

A majority of these teachers are students or graduates of our high schools. While they have not had the advantage of professional training schools (of which we are in very great need), yet they are well founded in the rudiments, and many possess that "natural tact" that needs only practice to make them excellent instructors. They have that professional zeal and manifest that interest in the work that not only impresses the children under their care but extends to the entire community.

Not only their work but their examinations show very marked improvement. A large per cent read educational literature. This spirit seems to be increasing to know more of the great work, more of what others are doing, more of the true methods of teaching.

Jasper can justly boast of the large number of excellent school buildings she has within her borders. Yet she has cause to be log huts in the county. I have ashamed of the large number of asked the county school board to be careful about granting a school to a community unless they furnish an excellent building for the same.

Jasper is justly proud of the large number of high schools in the county. There are six regular high schools in this county, all of which are chartered. The influence of these schools is very marked on our entire people. They are doing a grand work in refining, elevating the ideas of, and developing the manhood and womanhood of our boys and girls. There is no better means of ascertaining the grand work that our schools are doing than to go among the people. Here you find a warm interest in everything pertaining to education. May the good work, under good officers and the guidance of Providence, go on to higher planes of usefulness.

### Jasper Normal High School, Hamlet, Miss.
R. H. Hester, Principal

This school was established in October 1886. It was chartered in October 1890. We have a large school building, 36 by 80 with movable partitions and patent desks. The trustees and patrons have purchased all ordinary apparatus for sciences, manikin, physiological charts, skeleton, globe, chemicals, a complete set and chemical apparatus, lenses, mirrors, gyroscope, prism, etc. Library, 200 volumes. Rhetoric, literature and criticism in English, Algebra, geometry, trigonometry, calculus, book-keeping and surveying in mathetics. Physiology, philosophy, chemistry, botany and geology in sciences. Latin begins with primer, grammar, Caesar, Ovid and Virgil. A high course in music is given. The enrollment first year 80; second year, 124; third, 138; fourth, 144.

The school was controlled by the trustees who were elected by the stockholders. Soon the school had 90 pupils. Course of study, History — Mississippi, United States, Grecian, Roman, English, French and General.

Sciences — Physiology, philosophy, chemistry, geology, botany, and astronomy.

Mathematics—Arithmetic, algebra, geometry, trigonometry, calculus and analytics.

English — Grammar, composition, rhetoric, criticism, essay writing, debating, outlining, and studies of the leading authors.

### Rose Hill Institute
O. Hunt, Principal

The people of Rose Hill, Jasper County have always manifested more than ordinary interest in school affairs (said to have had the first free rural school in the state). In 1862, the present buildings were erected and a charter granted. In 1890, the charter was amended and an act passed that no liquor was to be sold within five miles of the institute building. The campus contained 20 acres of land. Pupils boarded in teacher's homes and in private families. The number of pupils was 150. Miss C. H. Boulton was music teacher and instruction was given in vocal and instrumental.

### Lake Como Institute
L. L. Denson, Pres.

Lake Como Institute was established in 1887, under the present principal. A charter was granted April 27, 1888. We have one large building with music and primary set apart. All is equipped with double automatic desks. Teachers and private homes accommodate the boarders. Capacity 100. The school is located in a healthful place, surrounded by a moral, thrifty community. It is the center of attraction in a growing, thrifty village. The course of study includes: higher English, mathematics, sciences, Latin and Greek. Last year we had 152 students with fifty boarders. Connected with the school are two flourishing literary societies—one for boys and one for girls.

### Montrose High School
L. D. McLaurin, Pres.

The school was established at Montrose in 1884 and chartered in 1888. We have a large L building divided into three rooms by movable partitions and a music room set apart. The school is under the control of the M. E. Church, South. The course of study includes higher English and mathematics. Attention is given to natural science, mental and moral sciences and an interesting literary society. The enrollment last year was 117.

### Pleasant Hill High School
James A. Jourdan, Prin.

The leading citizens of Pleasant Hill community met in 1888 and organized themselves into a stock company to support a high school. They were impressed by normalism and hired Stone Deavours, a normal teacher and a graduate of Iuka Institute as the principal teacher. The school was a success from the beginning. The next year they secured the services of J. E. Brown, now of Cumberland Normal Institute. The next year James A. Jourdan was elected head of the school.

---

### GARLANDSVILLE

Garlandsville is one of the most historical towns in the state. During the French rule of Mississippi Territory, the French came from Mobile, Biloxi and New Orleans to Garlandsville to trade with the Indians. Garlandsville was at all times the capitol of the Sixtowns and a great part of the time, the capitol of the Choctaw nation.

The old books at Jackson give an account of the famous Red Shoes having a difference with the French traders and that he had four of them scalped. Travel in the early days was by horses and some horses swam low and some high. The horses that swam high could carry a passenger or pack of goods across a river without getting them wet. This route from New Orleans to Garlandsville is marked on some old maps at Jackson by Columbia, Williamsburg, Taylorsville, Louin, Montrose to Garlandsville, and on to Nashville. During the War of 1812, Gen. Jackson had an army at New Orleans. He would receive recruits from Tennessee, and the Choctaws who would travel this route to New Orleans.

He would discharge some, some sick and were sent home along this route. We know that Gen. Jackson came this way one time and this route has since been known as the "old military road."

The old Jackson oak at Garlandsville was pushed down last year and burned.

Pushmataha was living at Garlandsville, then later was chief of the Choctaws. During the War of 1812, an Indian chief from the north visited all the Indian chiefs and told them that now was the time to fight the whites who would soon own all their hunting grounds. Pushmataha used great oratory in answer to this chief before the Choctaw council and the council decided in his favor and Pushmataha soon led a force of Choctaws to the aid of Gen. Jackson, who was about to be surrounded by the fierce Creeks. The Creeks had already massacred the people at Fort Mims.

Pushmataha followed Jackson to Florida and on to New Orleans.

Later, Pushmataha secured the grounds for the city of Jackson and where our state capitol now stands. In 1824, Pushmataha visited Gen. Jackson Washington, D. C., where he died and was buried in the Congressional Cemetery with honors.

Garlandsville was one of the gathering places for the Indians to leave for the Indian Territory of which a book has been written, "The Trail of Tears"

The Williamses came to Garlandsville before the Indians left. The place is laid off in lots and streets. The chairman of the building commission for the old courthouse at Paulding lived at Garlandsville, a Mr. Watts. The A. & V. Railroad was first surveyed to pass by Garlandsville, but the merchants at Enterprise made a fight against this because they thought it would cut off their trade from the West, and so the road goes by Newton.

After the capture of Vicksburg Gen. Sherman decided to make his first raid from Jackson to Meridian, and Gen. Grierson with about 2000 men was detached to go south of the A. & V. road. When he approached Garlandsville one of his men was shot. When some of his men came to the old Bonner home, a Negro woman met them and told them that her mistress was upstairs with a small baby and that if they would not burn the home they could use the first floor and that she would be glad to cook for them. They accepted her offer, as they needed a place to treat their wounded soldier and they remained for several days, trying to run down the culprit but never did find him.

The soldier recovered, and when the Blues and Grays met in Washington, D. C. a few years ago for a reunion, this wounded soldier told about the affair at Garlandsville and asked if anyone there knew anything about it. The man who did the shooting arose and said, "I am the man that shot you." It is said that these two men spent most of the time in Washington togther. This was published over the nation The mother of our Rhodes scholar man and president of a California college, Wilson Lyon, was reared at Garlandsville.

# June 6, 1957

*COUNTY NEWS, BAY SPRINGS, MISSISSIPPI — THURSDAY, JUNE 6, 1957*

## HISTORY OF JASPER COUNTY

**By J. M. KENNEDY**

### THE RAILROAD.

In 1903, talk began to go the round that a railroad was to be built through western Jasper. On July 4th, 1904, the first passenger train came to Newton. Large crowds turned out to see the train and soon we had the towns of Mossville, Stringer, Bay Springs, Louin and Montrose. After the timber was cut, companies came and blew out the stumps and so we have fine farming land in western Jasper.

In 1912 the boll weevil hit the county. This took away the main money crop the South had had for years. The condition of the farmer was terrible. Some tried cabbage and potatoes, bought fertilizer, plants, cultivated them, bought lumber and made crates and shipped them on consignment to St. Louis and waited for a check, but instead of a check, a notice came to send a check to help pay the freight.

B. L. Moss worked out a plan and produced a fair crop of cotton, by planting it early and thick. Farmers came from all parts of the South to see the cotton. This with the Republican rule bringing on a panic every few years in order to make the rich richer and the poor poorer, caused the country to be in a terible condition. The people could easily make a living with their year-round garden, but as for money, it could not be made. What they did make, a lot would not put it in a bank. For this reason people would not sell anything they had because they did not know what to do with the money; if they kept it about the house, robbers would get it; if they buried it, it might be lost or found by some one. The writer knew an old man who had gold and had it buried and his neighbors would watch him at night and finally got his money. Another old man had a long shed filled with cotton; when you would see him out or at church, he would be wearing only the clothes that his wife had made him. Robbers would even get the county money after tax paying time. On one occasion the outer door of the safe was blown off and the windows blown out. The money was behind the inner door of the safe. The safe was used for a long time in that condition.

An old lady lived in her log hut, had her chickens, cow, garden and a corn patch. She occasionally sold a calf and eggs for her spending money and lived happily. She had a large tract of timber but would not sell it for this same reason; but her neighbors told her that the timber company was cutting up to her timber and she would have the last chance for selling it. She sold and put the logs of her hut, some between her mattress. Some people came and got the money.

They were disguised, for sure, but as they went out, she told them that she knew who they were and she was going to tell. They went out and came back and blew her brains out on the side of the wall.

Some would risk their money in the bank; said it was better than getting killed; but the least whisper would start a run on the bank. Of course, the bank had the money invested and could not pay off the depositors without notice and so the bank had to close. The employees generally had to leave town as the people were after them with guns. One banker had a run started on him and his bank was in good condition, but as he had paid a lot of money on cotton which could not be shipped on account of box cars which the railroad could not furnish as fast as cotton was bought. He saw what was happening. He locked his safe and told the employees to pay out the money in front; that he was going out and get some more money. He went out, caught a passenger train into Laurel; borrowed by the sackful and hired a railroad engine and came back with it, and told the people to come and get their money. The people came and got their money and in the late afternoon the bank employees were still paying out money and the banker announced that they would keep the bank open so all could get their money. Crocker sacks of money were still in view and the people were still wandering around town with their money in their pockets. Still seeing sacks of money in the bank they began to put their money back in the bank and thus the bank was saved.

Such a condition in any country is terrible. If Franklin D. Roosevelt had not done anything else but make the banks safe, that alone was enough to make him a great man. He changed the financial capitol from Wall Street to Washington, D. C. The first time the money power was made to behave. When he came in office all the gold was gone from the U. S. Treasury. It is said that the millionaires had their boats loaded to sail off to some island and let us fight it out and then come back and buy our property. This is why he had to pass a law, calling all gold in and putting it in the ground in Kentucky.

In 1892, the writer was county superintendent of education and found a private school in this section. I asked them if they had ever received any public funds for their school and they said No. I told them that the township had some money and if they would see the board of supervisors they might receive some. They did, and the board allowed them what was on hand. They had only an elementary school and would send up North for high school work. Now this section is one of the richest oil fields in the state. Plenty of gas one mile down, and oil down two miles. One old woman is left of the old crowd in Jasper County and she has an oil well near her cottage.

Local option law was passed in 1886 and a campaign was put on in 1887 to vote out liquor. Rev. W. C. Black was the speaker favoring it and the election was carried by about 300 votes. The people were talking that the whiskey was gone. The county work was kept up till only a few were left and then the state passed a prohibition law. In 1920 the nation passed one. The writer was present at the national meeting in Washington, D. C. A large hall selected for this meeting and even though it was snowing, the hall was packed, even they said that all could not get in. Bryan was speaking at midnight and I saw people standing up in the rear of the balcony. Each time the people said that the liquor was gone, but it is still here. It is said that in some counties in the state that strong drink has been sold in the open at all times. Sometimes a man would be arrested for selling it and his lawyer would call for a jury and at the close of the trial the jury would retire and bring in a verdict "Not guilty." They say no law is any good unless the local people are willing to enforce it.

In the eighties a tornado hit in the Antioch community and killed a whole family, the Moodies. Some of the family was found hanging in trees. It came at night. No other home was hit.

In 1893, a tornado hit down in Secs. 19, 20, 21, 22, 23 in township three North and range 12 east, and demolished a number of houses, but no one lost his life; one was seriously injured by being crushed under a two-story brick chimney. The storm came about eight o'clock at night and Byrd was not found until the next morning when some one was walking over the debris and heard him groaning. After being on the bed for a month, he was able to be up some. This was an old antebellum home (a very beautiful one), and stood where Highway 15 runs on the hill east of the monastery. The homes destroyed were: Henry Bishop, Pete James, Ross Byrd, Edd Harrington, Bill O'Flynn and the Glover place.

About a month later another tornado began near Lake Como and went east through the county. It came about ten o'clock in the day time. The writer was plowing in a field north of Paulding and after hearing the roar the air was soon filled with all kinds of debris falling. Dr. Joe Thigpen's mother was killed with others being injured. It leveled all homes except the old Thigpen home and the Wiley Jones home east of Tallahala, occupied and owned by F. I. Cook. A Medlin dwelling was picked up and carried three miles across Tallahala Creek. The first one of that year and was only about one-quarter of a mile wide. This one, they claimed, was about four miles wide.

In April, 1920, one began a few miles southwest of Bay Springs and passed through the town, destroying many homes and the main building of the Jasper County Agricultural High School and one of the dormitories, also a music hall, killing about thirty-five people. It passed in the general direction of the Highway 18. At Rose Hill it killed all the family of Longmire Russell, except the baby, O. M. Oates' wife and baby were killed. Ava C. Ritchie the daughter of the county superintendent of education was killed. Sheriff Jim Ellis was killed. This storm came about ten in the morning.

Tornadoes come so quick and do such terrible things and things that are are unaccountable. The scientists do not seems to understand them. The writer has seen where one passed through swamps of oak and hickory and all were laid down in all directions and in all shapes, some torn out by the roots; some twisted off, some broken off. A building torn away and the bed left. Ine one instance, a sick person was on the bed and was left unharmed. Air planes, thought for a long time that they could fly through one of these storms but they have had some terrible crashes along this line. An experienced army pilot passed into a storm cloud a few miles west of here and he and his six men were brought out of the woods in wash tubs. Another, a private plane, attempted to pass through a storm cloud and all four passengers were lost. Last year a passenger plane was leaving Tyler, Texas, and passed into a storm cloud when all were lost but one who fell into a mud hole. The most accepted theory now is that the whirling motion creates a vacuum and the air on the inside of the building tears it into fragments. It has a swift, forward motion, causing flying timbers to be going along its path. A storm pit seems to be the safest place one can be when it happens. They generally move in a northeasterly direction.

In the eighties the Confederate veterans had their first reunion at Paulding. The writer was given a silver dollar and allowed to go. I saw great things that day. The first thing was a tent, into it I went and a man was making tin type pictures. I walked up and demanded one. He told me that I would have to wait until he got through with the people already there. I was afraid they would all be gone before I could get one, but it was not long before he told me to sit in the chair and so I parted with my silver dollar. All at once the Enterprise band started up and began to march. The soldiers fell in line which was very long; all had beards, some very long; one I remember came below his knees. They marched from the Catholic Church to the Presbyterian Church, which was a big two-story brick building, marching almost to the Brame home. There was one of the first phonographs there that day. It had no reproducer at that time and used ear tubes. This was a great day for some time, but soon the ranks were so few that it was abandoned.

## June 13, 1957

# HISTORY OF JASPER COUNTY

### By J. M. KENNEDY

**My Visit To Newt Knight**

Since I had heard so much about Newt Knight and had seen him in the Simpson trial, I decided that I would like to hear his own story. At gatherings and firesides he was accused of all the crimes in the book. At the Simpson trial people said he had not been at Paulding since he came there with a bunch of men during the Civil War, and had carried away all the corn, meat, etc., collected there for the Confederate Army. I liked to hear the stories that the men told from porches in front of the stores in Paulding.

One day, I remember, that the men were laughing at a man, said to be in a crowd to catch Newt. He admitted that they went down in that section and rode up to a house and asked a woman about her husband. She said she did not know where he was but that she could get him if they wanted to see him. They told her that they would like to see him. She went into the house and came out blowing a cow horn and gave it a peculiar sound. Soon horns began to blow all over the community. He said they liked to have run their horses to death getting out of there. An old gentleman then explained that the reason they never could catch him was that he had his women trained to blow signals with horns, and that at first the counties looked after conscription, and that he and his gang were in the corner of four counties, Jasper, Smith, Covington and Jones, and that when one county was after him, he would move over into another, and that three thick swamps converged in that section.

He said that people from north Alabama came and joined him. He said men who were busy getting information on him were murdered at night, naming a prominent man even in Ellisville who was killed one night. He also said that near the close of the war the state decided it would end this business and sent Gen. Lowry, who one time lived in Smith County and married in Jasper County, down with a regiment to take and hang all of them.

When Lowry came into a thick swamp, Knight's men began to fire on them from the thicket; the general had to go back to Jackson with a lot of his men missing.

He also said that the Federal Government furnished him supplies from an outlet on the Gulf. An old soldier present said that when Vicksburg surrendered, Grant called the men from this section, asking about Newt Knight. James Street made fiction out of the affair that he wrote.

After the war, Newt settled on Etahoma Creek, just inside of Jasper County.

I easily found my way to his home and he was very friendly and we talked quite a while before the main subject came up.

He said he served a while in the army but came home and found conditions very bad at home and they had passed the conscription act and had exempt the slave owners who were the men who got the war up and that very few people had slaves, and that slavery was dying out; people were freeing their slaves and paying their way back to Africa for all those who wanted to go; that the preachers up North began to preach against, and women wrote books which caused the common people to begin stealing the slaves by the "underground railway", and the slave owners and Irish could not take this and so they brought on war about a dead issue, making the common people fight it. A damned outrage.

If the common people had turned out and killed the slave owners, we would not have had this terrible war, he continued. They were not any to amount to anything in this part of the state. After that when I would see a line of Confederate soldiers, I would think about what Newt said. "Tricked into it".

**Excerpts from the Life of John N. Waddell, D.D., LL.D.**

Having moved from South Carolina to Green County, Alabama, where with the Rev. Dr. Gray, we had a large cotton farm. Our market was Mobile to which we traveled by boat from Gainsville. In going to Mobile, we would meet farmers from Mississippi. A farmer from Montrose made us an offer on 2500 acres of land at Montrose for our farm in Alabama. We decided to make the exchange. About that time I had to return to South Carolina, concerning my father's estate and in the meantime Dr. Gray was to make the removal to Mississippi.

When I returned I found faces of strangers. I then went to Mobile where Dr. Gray was to meet me, but he was detained for about a week. I spent a lonely time in Mobile during this week. While I was walking the streets something happened which was to concern my future but I did not know then. I saw a news office and went in to while away the lonesome hours and I saw something from Mississippi. The legislature was considering the matter of establishing a university.

After arriving at Montrose I found fertile land but unsatisfactory labour. We built a small log house and organized a Presbyterian church. Then I started my school with nine pupils. The school grew and we soon had to erect a larger log building. The senator from Jasper County, Simeon R. Adams, rode by one day and told me that I was elected trustee of the proposed university. After some years of wrangling the university was opened in 1848.

In the meantime our school kept growing and we were forced to erect a large two-story plank building. The first floor was for church purposes and chapel for the school where we had services morning and evening. The school now had boarders from east Mississippi and west Alabama.

During all this time I had been doing church work. After our church at Montrose had grown, we established a church at Mt. Moriah. I went to Raleigh in Smith County where I had two Presbyterian families, Curry and Campbell, I also went to McFarland.

As the university was to open in 1848, I applied for a teacher appointment and was accepted. I soon made arrangements to move to Oxford where I was to enter a larger field of work as a teacher for a few years and then appointed Chancellor.

### EARLY CHURCHES
**Baptist**

The first Baptist church in Jasper County is said to have been at the Rose Hill cemetery, one mile east on Highway 18, where the Three-Chopped Way connects with 18. The writer, in the early days visited relatives and friends and taught school in the rural sections of Jasper County and heard the stories of old about Henry Barbour and have seen write-ups about him. After burying his grandfather, Abraham, in Anson County, North Carolina, he came as a young preacher with his father, Noah, over the Three-Chopped-Way to Mississippi. As he came to the beautiful stream called Twistwood by the Indians, he remarked, "Such a beautiful stream to be baptized in," and "such a beautiful hill for a church." He persuaded his father to settle near, and was soon enlisting settlers to organize a church. His father, Noah, was at other work and in 1837, he organized the first rural free school in the state, so it is said. It was supported by 16th Section funds. The voting precinct was soon located, called Twistwood, and was at one time the largest in the county. It is now Rose Hill. A post office was soon located called by the same name but was changed to Rose Hill in 1888.

After getting a nice hewn log church with a large membership, he began to visit other communities in Jasper County and later went to Clarke, Smith and Newton Counties. Then the war came on and followed by conscription. He took his four sons and son-in-law and went to war. One of his sons was soon lost and the one was wounded. In the battle of Atlanta, he saw his son-in-law shot to pieces, but was turned away because Gen. Hood was retreating in haste. He wondered what his daughter would do with five small children. His daughter, Stacy, lived at Enterprise and received a telegram that her husband had been killed at Atlanta. She prayed most of the night and it was revealed to her that her husband was alive. She arose early the next morning, sending her second, third and fourth child to Twistwood to be cared for by her sisters, but the older girl would go with her to help care for the young baby and she, with these two was soon at the station to catch the train to Mobile. The town was soon in an uproar and some suggested that she should be stopped by force, that her husband was dead, that the country was full of runaway Negroes and Yankee soldiers; railroads were torn up, the train goes to Mobile but it is stopped and searched by Yankees before it gets to town.

On she went and was able to board a boat up the Alabama River, but the going was tough after leaving the river. She was walking a part of the time; rode Negro ox-cart for a long way. She finally reached Atlanta to find it was burned and the Confederate wounded has been carried away to LaGrange, about one hundred miles away.

She kept on and found her husband and nursed him for a month and brought him home where he lived until 1905.

Henry kept up his work after the war and sold his rich farm and moved to Sylvarena to help Capt. Bill Hardy to establish Baptist academy. He later moved to old Goodhope, five miles south east of Hickory, where he is buried. His seventh generation still lives in Jasper County.

### The Congregational Methodist Church

The Congregational Methodist Church was organized in 1855 by people from Jasper County, H. T. and L. J. Jones, G. W. Todd, who married L. J. Jones' daughter Caroline, now living in New Augusta, Miss. Todd is the grandfather of L. O. Todd, president of Meridian Jr. College, Hunts and Huddlestons. The first church organized was Mulberry in the center of Jasper county. H. T. Jones was pastor until he died. Mt. Zion was second church organized which has always had a large membership. It is located between Union and Decatur. Green Valley and Liberty came next, and also had a large membership. Liberty is located near Stringer and Green Valley is located near Rose Hill. Some of the preachers are: Henry T. Jones, Seaborn Wiley Jones, Bart Huddleston, Fiem Huddleston, W. P. Massey, J. W. Cook, G. W. Ryan, and Hunt.

**June 20, 1957**

# HISTORY OF JASPER COUNTY

### By J. M. KENNEDY

### SENATORS AND REPRESENTATIVES JASPER COUNTY

**Senators:**
- 1836—Oliver C. Dease
- 1840—J. C. Thomas
- 1844—S. R. Adams
- 1848—James McDougald
- 1852—R. N. Hough
- 1859—Robert McLane
- 1865—F. H. Napier
- 1870—Wm. M. Hancock
- 1871—John Watts
- 1874—T. B. Graham
- 1877—H. C. McCabe
- 1878—Asa R. Carter
- 1882—Thomas Keith
- 1884—John F. Smith
- 1888—T. A. Wood
- 1893—W. W. Heidelberg
- 1896—T. A. Wood, D. W. Heidelberg
- 1900—B. W. Sharbrough
- 1904—D. W. Heidelberg
- 1908—Sam Whitman, Jr., Mike Thigpen
- 1912—J. D. Fatherree
- 1916—J. W. White
- 1920—J. D. Fatherree
- 1924—W. B. Thigpen
- 1928—H. F. Case
- 1932—G. N. Brown
- 1936—Edgar Hardee
- 1940—Dr. E. M. Gavin
- 1944—Emmett Buckley
- 1948—J. C. Smith
- 1952—Havis Sartor
- 1956—Jewell G. Smith

**Representatives—**
- 1836—J. C. Thomas
- 1838—Petre Loper
- 1840—L. B. Ellis
- 1842—Peter Loper
- 1844—L. J. Jones
- 1846—John McDonald
- 1848—L. B. Ellis
- 1852—L. J. Jones
- 1854—J. J. Shannon
- 1856—B. Thigpen
- 1858—D. D. McLaurin
- 1859—A. F. Dantzler
- 1861—J. S. Dantzler
- 1865—L. J. Jones
- 1870—Elisha Dansby
- 1872—J. M. Loper
- 1874—A. F. Smith
- 1876—Duncan D. McLaurin
- 1878—A. M. Dozier
- 1880—D. A. Morris
- 1882—Joe Blankinship
- 1884—Sam Whitman
- 1886—B. W. Sharbrough
- 1888—W. W. Heidelberg
- 1890—Sam Whitman
- 1892—M. A. Ryan
- 1896—R. A. Land, N. F. Thigpen
- 1900—E. A. White
- 1904—W. J. McFarland, W. W. Heidelberg
- 1908—M. A. Lewis
- 1912—J. W. White, L. L. Denson
- 1916—H. L. Finch
- 1920—M. L. Alexander, H. L. Finch
- 1924—G. N. Brown
- 1928—C. C. Chatham, W. A. Lewis
- 1932—O. W. Phillips
- 1936—A. M. Cockrell, Edgar Harris
- 1940—Mildred Alexander
- 1944—Dr. T. L. Massey, W. A. Lewis
- 1948—W. O. Peek
- 1952—T. G. Roberts, J. C. Smith
- 1956—J. T. Weems

### A Baseball Game In 1892

In the summer of 1892 with no entertainment except hunting and fishing and sometimes a picnic, the young men at Missionary organized themselves into a baseball club. After practicing awhile with the population of the community looking on, a match game was arranged with Phalti. At that time the population of each place was large as there were no jobs or anything to take people away like it is now. Both places are almost without people now. Missionary was at one time the third largest voting place in the county.

When time came for the game to begin, a large crowd had assembled. The visitors went to the bat with Bill Brame, catcher, and Walter Parker, pitcher. John Alexander was teaching at Phalti and he was on first base. The baseball glove was not known then. The writer remembers a few on the home team:

Mat Reed was catcher, Bob Dease, pitcher, Mike O'Flinn, Mike Harrington, William Davis.

As the game proceeded quite a number of runs were made as the boys could not hold the ball so well with the naked hand. People remarked about Walter's left hand pitching, saying that the boys could not hit it. John Alexander won much praise as he would catch the ball, high or low, and also to either side with his long arms. Some had heard that baseball pitchers were throwing a curve ball but no one believed it; even science did not until it was shown them. With Walter Parker's left hand pitching and John Alexander's catching on the first base, Missionary was badly defeated, but all enjoyed the game.

When you make a public change or change what has been a custom, then you have discord. Neighbors are pitted against each other. The questions get into politics and officers are for and against it. This should be no qualification for an officer. The writer remembers that east of a certain place the people were for the stock law, while the other way they were against it. The result was that after the stock law was passed the people who were against it built a fence around themselves and had everything as as usual. Some farmers did double fencing, a fence around his pasture and a fence around his crop. Fencing was a terrible job in the early days as it was rail splitting and then building was a hard job and took constant watching as the wind was likely to blow it down or fire get out and burn it.

As soon as the town of Bay Springs began to grow, they began to advocate that a courthouse should be at Bay Springs as the majority of the people lived on this side of the county and that Paulding was far east of the center of the county. The Bay Springs News favored it and people would write letters to the papers favoring it. The Review at Montrose was against it, and said that the courthouse at Paulding was paid for and that people had been going to it for seventy-five years and that it would cost more to run two courthouses and that the county was too poor to support two courthouses, and that Bay Springs was within two miles of the Jasper-Smith line. People would write letters to the Review telling why they were against having two courthouses. Soon the matter was in politics and people would vote for an officer as to whether he was for or against two courthouses. A public change must raise a public fuss. Forces were pro and con before the legislature passed the law, and soon the board of supervisors were enjoined from building a courthouse at Bay Springs. Large crowds were attending the court and people were telling the judge they would vote as per his decision. After it was settled, people would vote the same way.

During Bilbo's administration a movement was begun to rid the state of the cattle ticks. Cattle that was produced here became immuned to it when small, but some died and it was claimed by veterinarians that the local cattle was stunted by it. When imported stock was brought into the state the tick fever would kill them. Thus it was argued, that cattle could not be improved unless the tick was obliterated. Vats were built and people were forced to dip their cattle. A public change and so a public fuss. Vats were blown up, law suits against the sheriff, fights, etc. Bilbo ran for Congress in 1919 and was defeated by Paul Johnson. He said the tick beat him.

Names of Jasper Countains appearing in Goodspeed Publication:

**1891**

J. P. Abney, W. W. Abney, J. M. Acker, Joseph Blankinsnip, C. W. Clayton, W. M. Cole, F. L. Cook, J. H. Cook Sr, N. D. Graham, Capt. W. H. Hardy, Capt. Francis Loper, B. F. Moss, John W. McCormick, B. F. Peek, C. W. Tatum, Mart Turner, S. D. Russel, Irve Heidelberg, Tom Heidelberg, Dr. S. G. Louchridge, J. C. Thomas.

Names of Jasper Countains appearing in Roland's History, 1907.

M. Webster Buckley, Dr. C. W. Bufkin, Dr. I. H. C. Cook, Dr. J. D. Donald, J. D. Hardy, W. H. Hardy, M. W. Hyde, Wat E. Jones, Dr. W. E. Peek, E. H. Mounger, Rev. E. H. Mounger, Henry Mounger, A. W. Nobles, B. W. Sharbourgh, T. E. Waldrup.

Jasper names appearing in the "Heart of the South," by Roland 1925:

J. A. Terral, R. W. Heidelberg, G. W. Hosey, W. W. James, J. S. Turner, F. S. Harmon, Green M. Merrill, A. F. McCormick, Enoch D. Travis, Jared C. Windham, A. W. Brunson, C. W. Thigpen, John F. McCormick, Emma Heidelberg Hassel, Stone Deavours, Dr. C. C. Risher, O. F. Moss, R. C. Pugh, Thomas Brand, C. J. Hyde, Henry Mounger, John H. Cook, J. M. Kennedy, F. A. Baucum, Sam H. Terral, W. J. Shoemaker, C. E. Boulton, J. Q. Richie, John Lindsey, Dr. M. W. Waldrup, C. A. Huddleston, Gus Harmon, Chas. Shannon.

Jasper names in Mississippi History, Taylor and Ethridge, 1940: Earl E. Hosey, J. A. Thigpen, E. V. Buckley, R. C. Pugh, G. Bill Hosey, Dr. C. E. Burnham, J. M. Hartfield.

Jasper names in "Men of Spine," by Rand, 1940:

Robert Lowery, Sam Dale, W. H. Hardy, Pushmattaha.

In 1930 the greatest panic hit the country that had ever been. The stock market had a great crash, banks and business houses were closing everywhere, 1931, and 1932, and times getting worse all the time. In 1932 Franklin D. Roosevelt swept the country for President. No jobs, factories closing. As soon as the president was sworn in he called Congress in extra session and closed the banks (the ones that were not closed). He asked Congress to pass a bank insurance law which was done. Certain qualifications were given for a bank to open. The people of the industrial towns were starving. He arranged for exchange of produce. The West was burning corn for fire wood and coal was piled up at the mines and could not be sold. Apples were rotting in sections. Soon all products were moving and it was given to the needy by a committee from the board of supervisors. Soon the people who were in need were getting something to eat. Projects of all kinds were formed and employees were paid by the government. Mississippi could have gotten by because they had no all fear for garden, cows, pigs, chickens, etc. but industrial towns where the factory had closed down, there was no way to live. But still the farmer was not helped much therefore could not pay his taxes, therefore the state and county was bankrupt. The legislature was called together but nobody had any money. They could not sell bonds as the banks were filled with state and county warrants which could not be cashed on account of no money in the treasury. A sales tax was proposed after a month or two of deliberating and was quickly defeated. Later on the bill was brought again and defeated for the second time. The merchants organized and would run trains into Jackson, making parades against the sale tax. They said that the people would go to other states to do their trading, and why should they be made tax collectors?

# HISTORY OF JASPER COUNTY

By J. M. KENNEDY

The writer came in as superintendent of education January 1st, 1932. The school fund was in arrears for the four months of the session of 1931-32, and three months on session of 1930-31. The board of supervisors notified me that no warrant would be honored till all indebtedness was cancelled. The teachers and bus drivers met and notified me that they would mandamus me for their papers. In May, the legislature introduced the sale tax bill for the third time which would be the last time (revenue bills can not be introduced but three times). The bill was passed by one vote. But the state was in such a run-down condition that it took a long time to get the debts cancelled. The farmers had refused to pay taxes and were letting their homes sell for taxes. A national moratorium law was passed on homes. Still for several years it took all the money received to pay on debts. The bank would loan money to the best risks and the majority could receive no loan, some teachers were arrested for not paying their board, small school buses were picked up for debts. I persuaded Mrs Kennedy to loan these teachers and bus drivers money and take an order on their warrants. She did not like to do it, but finally agreed to do so if I would make two copies of the order, one to get the warrant and one to keep. I told her that there was no need for that but she insisted and so the same was done. I had a mix-up with the auditors on a college board. Later I appealed to the state quick for government money and received $17,500 extra money. The auditors were miffed and soon I was checked up short, and the warrants that Mrs Kennedy had received were placed before the grandjury without the order and with an oath from the person made that they did not sign an order. As soon as it was found that Mrs Kennedy had had a copy of the order properly signed it was all over with. I appealed my audit to the state and soon had a signed statement from the state auditor and field auditor that the audit was incorrect. Several auditors were fired.

The sales tax is still in force and has been increased and all the states around us have put on a sales tax. President Roosevelt had a survey made of living conditions in the South and was amazed at the low cost of living. Here was a family of ten children and father and mother whose income in money was six bales of cotton at twenty five dollars a bale would be one hundred fifty dollars. This would make the cost of living in money one dollar and five cents per month per person. He made the statement that he would see after the forgotten man or that he would get a "fair deal". All kinds of projects were started giving people work. In 1926 a bond issue had been granted in Beats Three and Four to build a gravel road through the county, through Montrose, Louin, Bay Springs, Stringer, and the same kind of road by Heidelberg and Vossburg. When I would go out in the county to visit schools I would have to watch the weather, if it began to rain I would not get back. A project was granted to build a road through the county east and west. After it was surveyed the farmers were allowed to cut the right-of-way, then dig up the stumps, then grade the same. This took a long time but it gave the farmers some ready cash. Other road projects were granted and health, and public building. C. C. C. camps were established over the country and farm boys were allowed to enlist in that. Farm loans were granted to farmers and they began to make a better living with their farms. Farmers were encouraged to plant cover crops and crops that would improve the soil. The government gave money to aid schools, to pay teachers and aid in buildings. In 1938, the government gave money to help build roads. With state aid and the government aid Highway 15 was paved through the county in 1938. A highway had already been paved through the southeast corner of the county, making it possible to make most of the county on pavement. Later the state paved Highway 18 through the center of the county. Then the county black topped a number of roads to connect these highways which makes a fair system of highways to all parts of the county. All this work employed a number of people from the county.

About the same time that this work was going on fire protection was begun. In the old days it was the custom to burn off the woods and fields each year; the people thought it would keep fire from breaking out and would kill all insects, snakes, varments, etc. The tree was of no value in the early days but after the timber companies had cut the timber the timber companies began to buy the cutover land to be held for young timber. It is said that the Masonite Co. owns sixty thousand acres of land in this county. The first man to protect his young timber was said to be crazy, but in twenty years he was cutting his timber the second time. So a tax was assessed on timber land to employ fire fighters and high towers was built to over look a large section.

In the old days the children carried a piece of corn bread, biscuit or a potato to school for lunch, then the government offered money and commodities for a lunch room at each school so the children could have warm lunch with milk. More people were employed as lunch room workers. The blind, old age, crippled were all looked after. Each county and state has a welfare board which are busy looking after all these things. It requires a large office force. Then came the B. A. W. I. allowing each town or county to issue bonds and build an industrial plant which employs a large number of people.

The health department has been created and each county and state has a large force employed in this department. In the old days each had to look after his own health. Doctors were few and far between. Some had not been to college. If you had one to come to see you it was mostly guess work; the general proceedure was to have you stick out your tongue and the doctor would say you were billious and give you some calomel, followed by castor oil. The calomel was poisonous. They were helpless in pneumonia, typhoid fever, and croup, the patient with appendicitis, they would say he died with cramp colic. I have known families to lose all their children in a week with croup. They choked to death in a few minutes. The same with pneumonia, I have known the family and friends to close the room and put up sheets around the bed. The patient dies from the lack of oxygen, they were helping the patient to die. I have known numbers of young people with typhoid fever, if they fed them they were liable to die with a hemorrhage and if they did not feed them they would die with weakness when the fever left which was about ninety days. People on the farm generally drank water from a spring or running branch, they thought it was all right if it was clear. I knew a family that all died but one and he did not drink milk, the cow was examined and found to have T. B. I knew a man who had his arm shot off, his family and friends were running after a doctor, when the doctor reached the man he was dead. A string around the stub would have saved him. The same happened with a rattle snake bite. Now all children, teachers and public workers are required to be have a health certificate and be vaccinated. This has done a great deal to stamp out venerial disease in which the history of is terrible. People thought the only thing to be done with T. B. was let them die. Now when found in time it can be arrested or cured Mississippi is said to have the finest T. B. hospital in the world. Counties have to coopeprate with state in health work but some counties unite in a health unit such as Jasper and Smith. Franklin D. did a great work for the south, the first time since the Civil War that the South has had a hand-out. There are now eight Rural Electric offices in the state Laurel, Lorman, Hollandale, Greenwood, Carthage, Clinton, Columbia, Yazoo City. These offices are extending electric line to all the rural section and along with it goes the telephone. The farmer can now have television, telephone, radio, electric light, refrigerators. etc.

### EXECUTIONS

The story goes that an Indian killed one of his race before the Civil War and that he was tried and sentenced to hang. He told the court that he was owing man and that he would like pay him before he died. It is said that the court did not desire hang him anyway and excused him to pay this debt thinking the would see him no more, but in about one year he came back and said that he was ready to be hanged. The sheriff carried out his wish.

During Richard Simmons term of office as sheriff Lew Morgan (a Negro) killed one the Calhoun boys, was tried and hanged.

During the last term of W. McFarland as sheriff a Clayton Negro was hanged for raping Negro woman.

# July 4, 1957

COUNTY NEWS, BAY SPRINGS, MISSISSIPPI — THURSDAY, JULY 4, 1957

## HISTORY OF JASPER COUNTY

### By J. M. KENNEDY

In 1914, Mose Johnson robbed the pay car en route to the Gilchrist-Fordney logging camp which was located near Antioch and killed Fitzpatrick of Laurel and wounded Velma Simmons and a Mr Johnson. Mose took part of the money and left, throwing the other in a stump hole. After doing this, he crossed himself, coming from the stump hole. Gants' bloodhounds were secured by the next morning and they began the chase, going up the railroad except in the town of Louin where he passed only one Negro cabin but came back to the railroad above town. The chase continued to a grade above Montrose where the chase ended. Mose was thought to have caught a north bound freight train about nine o'clock. All prominent people, and the great Gilchrist-Fordney Co. involved, caused great excitment. The company sent a special train for the bodies, but Simmons was so near dead (sixty shots in his face), they did not take him back to Laurel but he was carried to his father's home. He was not dead the next morning and so-they sent the train to Louin after him and he was in the hospital about one month. The affair happened just north of the overhead bridge, between the railroad and Highway 15. There was a station just north of the bridge called Stevens and a railroad ran from there to Fouke Lumber Co., located in the center of the county. Gilchrist-Fordney used this line out to their camp. Fitzpatrick and Robinson came up the P. M. passenger train and Simmons met them with a gasoline car. They did not go very far until they saw a crosstie on the tracks. Simmons got out to remove the tie when he was shot. Fitzpatrick stepped out and was shot in the throat. Robinson ran the other way and was shot in the back but was not injured very much. It was said that there were a thousand people on, the chase and Sheriffs from ten counties. A large reward was offered for his arrest. Two weeks went by and nothing done, but a Negro was seen at Louin going south. A large crowd gathered following him but missed him, but the crowd proceeded on to Stringer when the Negro woman living in the cabin referred to, sent the writer word that this same Negro passed going north. I ran to town which was almost depopulated (all on the chase at Stringer) but I secured two boys and some shot guns and ran to the place where the hounds ran and he came along in about a minute. He had three hundred dollars in gold certificates on him, which was the money that the lumber company paid off with. He came very near being mobbed in town but the passenger train was about due and the sheriff, Henry Jones, was on the train. I was very glad to get him off my hands. The sheriff had to slip him off to Jackson to keep him from being mobbed. He was tried and hanged. He was hanged in the hollow in front of the courthouse and there was an enormous crowd there. People came and camped the night before; the railroad ran special trains. It got into the newspapers even in the North and the result was that a law was passed not to allow public hangings.

While R. C. Alexander was sheriff a Negro by the name of Newell killed a Mr Sims in the southern part of the couity and was electrocuted in the courthouse. Since then a law has been passed to put them to death in a gas chamber at Parchman.

### Jasper Singing Convention

In about the year 1897, G. W. Evans, W. T. Grayson, George Stockman, J. M. Massey, C. W. Green, R. G. Read and possibly others, met at High Smith Methodist Church, now known as Read's Chapel, and organized the Jasper County Singing Convention. Three of these are still living: W. T. Grayson (now dead) C. W. Green, and R. G. Read They drew up rules and regulations by which to be governed by, and agreed to meet every fifth Sunday. W. T. Grayson was elected president; J. M. Massey, secretary. Those serving as president since are C. W. Green, R. G. Read, C. W. Evans, J. W. French, Byron Hendry, F. D. Hindman, Charlie Phillips, T. L. Wilkins, S. O. Haden, Lemon HadHen and Ott Buckley.

(By C. W. Green.)

The writer always enjoyed attending the singing convention and I am sure they did a great good. It is the only art that we carry to the next world, as we speak of the angels singing. The writer roomed next door to the chaplain of the penitentiary and he spoke of his services as doing the singing himself, and you know a convict can not sing. We are made better by singing or hearing singing.

### Frank L. Stanton on Old Hymns

There's lots of music in them—
the hymns of long ago,
And when some gray-haired brother sings the ones I used to know
I sorter want to take a hand—I think of days gone by—
"On Jordan's stormy banks I stand and cast a wistful eye".
There's lots of music in them—
Those dear sweet hymns of old,
With visions bright of lands of light, shining streets of gold;
And I hear them singing—singing where memory dreaming stands,
"From Greenland's icy mountains to India's coral strands".

And so I love the good old hymns
and when my time shall come—
Before the light has left me and my singing lips are dumb—
If I can hear 'em sing them then,
I'll pass without a sigh
To "Canaan's fair and happy land where my possessions lie".

### Schools

As we have said, the only schools we had before the Civil War were private with one exception and that was near Rose Hill, where they had the first rural public school in the state which was financed with Sixteen Section school funds. Noah Barbour was president of the board.

Minutes of the board were furnished us by Miss Myra Pruitte, who is the dauhter of our only "Forty-niner". This was a leather bound book, written with ink and goose quill and was turned in to the chancery clerk.

During and after the Civil War there was practically no schools. Mississippi had no provision for public schools but by the constitution of 1870 a four months school was provided for. Richard Simmons was appointed county superintendent. No interest was shown in schools and Richard was elected sheriff and Col. O. C. Dease was made superintendent. A Negro was state superintendent Dease's daughter, Pinny, taught in the old log church at Missionary. Other teachers began to show up in the county: M. Oates from Alabama; Tom Thaggard, Tom Watly, Jim McDevitt, Jim Peacock, Ras Caston, Hattie Pruitt, Ollie Gray, etc. In the eighties and nineties the Texas "fever" hit the county and great numbers of people migrated to Texas. My father and mother even tried it, with ten other families but hit the swamps beyond Vicksburg in a rainy season. There were no bridges and they had to do a lot of winding, trying to find a ferry; they swam a lot of the bayous and there were a lot of wild animals which kept the women scared about their babies. One told that her baby was on a quilt while she was doing her wash. She heard the baby crying and tried to finish her wash, and when she did, she looked and saw an alligator going in the water with her baby. They reached the hills beyond the Ouachita and my father found a cousin and there they spent a year and then they returned home, but could not buy the old home back and did not have the money to buy another.

The old log church decayed and fell down, and so we had no school or church. On one side were the Irish Catholics and on the other, a bunch of gangsters. I had heard of their pranks at the old church, putting a sharp peg under the old preacher's saddle, fights, etc. They were committing all sorts of crimes in the community, mostly disappointing girls in marriage. I remember we had company and people always carried their dogs with them when visiting as the only means of travel were horse back and wagon. Several men went by in a lope and for sure, the dogs took after them, when pistols began to fire. My mother had us to move inside as she said they soon would be coming back. A short while after this happened the gang met at the double branches between Paulding and Missionary, and began to fight and then to shoot. For a long time there was a case in court called the double-branch battle by Judge Mayers, but he could never try the case as those that were able to get away, were never heard of any more.

Some time after this there was talk that they were going to build a log school house which was finally done. Time had passed for my brother and I to go to school. I did not want to go any way as I had heard that the teacher whipped the children. I had heard my father and mother talking about sending us to school but our mother had been teaching us as she was reared in Enterprise where they had a good school. The school ran two months as the patrons said the children had to work (this being in the summer).

Jim Peacock was the first teacher, then Miss Murphy, Ras Caston, Hattie Pruitt, T. J. Abney (who later became a preacher), Ollie Gray, F. M. Mosely, P. L. Blackwell, Bettie Jones, etc. We did not progress very much as only four months and so many classes. We were classed by readers. Col. O. C. Dease (was our neighbor) had the teachers go to his home where he asked them oral questions and then gave them license if he thought they deserved it. State Superintendent J. R. Preston (1886-96) introduced written examinations at the county site.

Most of my teachers were from Montrose and I had the opportunity of attending commencement there. I thought if I could pass the teachers' examination and teach I could go to school at Montrose. I asked Miss Jones about it and she told me I could if I would study. I thought if that was the only thing that stood in my way that I could make it. Some of the books I had not studied at school, but I bought them and would carry my books to the field with me. I was present at the next examination and A. A. Kincannon, who said that he was going to raise the scholarship of the teachers by giving harder examinations. There were thirty-five teachers present, some college graduates, some old teachers. After Dease the superintendents were F. M. Mosely, A. N. W. Smith, L. L. Denson and S. F. Thigpen. T. A. Massey was the superintendent and he was in favor of more stringent examinations. They graded the hardest subject; my grade was 93 and four others made in 50; all the others were out which caused a big fuss

July 11, 1957

COUNTY NEWS, BAY SPRINGS, MISSISSIPPI — THURSDAY, JULY 11, 1957

# HISTORY OF JASPER COUNTY

### By J. M. KENNEDY

**THE WRITER BEGINS TO TEACH**

I secured a school for that fall, but found that they had not had a school for two years; that the boys had run off the teachers. The Irish had trained me in boxing and boxing, so I did not think I could be run off, but we had a lot of "acting around" there when the school began, getting my color at the beginning and they might have got me if it had not been for a dog that followed me to school and he joined in and did good. I taught the school out and built a plank building and taught a second term there. I then began to attend school at Montrose.

It had been hard earned money that I had made for this schooling and so I was assigned only four subjects and so I asked the old professor one day if he was charging me three dollars per month and only gave me four subjects. In a few days I had nine subjects and was teaching one subject. I did the same thing at Millsaps. I had decided that I wanted to teach school and that a teacher should have a great store of knowledge. I also wanted to get good returns for my money. I had some of the professors in the classroom by daylight. When graduation time came, the president of the school called me in the office and told me that I was entitled to all the degrees that … gave but that the faculty had voted that I could have only one and that they would let me choose that one. After that I was attending school or teaching each summer. I have credits from seven different colleges.

P. L. Blackwell was county superintendent from 1900 to 1904 and the county schools were graded during that time. W. J. Shoemaker was superintendent from 1904 to 1908, when the separate districts came into use whereupon a tax was assessed for paying teachers. This gave teachers their first guaranteed salary for eight months.

**START CONSOLIDATING SCHOOLS**

About this time the Jasper County Agricultural High School was organized at Bay Springs. These schools were organized in most all counties of the state. They were first advocated by W. H. Smith, who some called "Corn Club" Smith. He advocated the dropping of so much ancient language and substituting agriculture for boys and home science for girls. Boys and girls each had a dormitory and pupils were entered from all parts of the county, free of tuition. The school was to have a farm, cows, chickens, hogs, etc. They could bring farm produce from home to pay for their board. A number of boys and girls had jobs to pay their board. This was a great school as many boys and girls received an education. Some of these institutions later became junior colleges which caused Mississippi to lead the nation in junior colleges.

From 1908 to 1916, L. R. Massey was superintendent, when consolidation appeared on the scene at Mossville, which started a long and hard fight. School board meetings were stormy. Pupils were transported by wagons which was not satisfactory. Boys were to push the wagon out of mud holes. One day, in one instance, they refused; the farmer unhitched his horses and went home. The movement, however, was growing over the state, but all agreed that the roads were the greatest obstacle. The consolidated school law permitted a rural district to put on a tax on the district and to issue bonds for buildings and teachers' homes. The result was that the consolidated school had better buildings, better equipment and better teachers. All farmers adjoining the consolidated district could petition the school board to annex them to the consolidated district which weakened the rural district all the time.

C. E. Watkins was superintendent from 1916 to 1920. The World War was going on at that time and people were distressed about their boys leaving and so little progress was made, however some was made.

J. Q. Ritchie was superintendent from 1920 to 1928. Times were good and the county issued bonds for roads and the road from Laurel to Meridian was completed, passing through the southeastern part of the county. A road tax was collected by the sheriff. Progress was made along all lines. The Agricultural High School reached its height during this period; graduating 42 pupils one year and having one of the largest teachers' normals in the state. Although there was some fighting over consolidation. A story is told that Ritchie appointed a popular Baptist preacher on his school board. The minister felt highly honored about his appointment; he came out at the first board meeting with his long tailed coat and high collar and there was a large consolidated petition before the board. It was reported that there was no opposition, and that it would be a great move for better schools. All voted yea and went out for lunch. As they returned to the courthouse they saw a crowd and the sheriff in the crowd. There was a small district in the consolidated district that only one man had signed and who did not confide in the other patrons of the rural district. One person of his rural district had been present when the vote was taken to consolidate. He had mounted his horse and reported to the patrons of the rural district that their school was gone. All were soon at the courthouse and had a fight with the one signer. When the preacher came in, one of the patrons pushed him against the wall and said, "Dawn, you preach to us on Sunday and take our school away from us on Monday." The preacher went into the office and told the superintendent that this was no place for a preacher, and resigned and went home.

L. R. Massey came into office for the third term to which no one had ever been elected. The panic hit the country and the schools in four years were about a hundred thousand in debt.

J. M. Kennedy served from 1932 to 1940. Schools were in debt and practically no income from taxes was available as the people were letting their property sell for its taxes. The sale tax was at last passed after a fight of nearly five months. The government was giving aid in paying teachers' and office aid; lunch rooms were adopted. A two hundred thousand dollar school building program was put on with the aid of the government. By more consolidation, the county was made into ten districts; Montrose, Louin, Bay Springs, Stringer, Mossville, Heidelberg, Paulding, Ras, Antioch, Rose Hill and Penantly. All were good buildings, well equipped with teachers' home and gym. The Jasper County News made a special education issue, giving pictures and write-ups of each school; the county was declared the representative county of the state.

Excerpts from a letter:

Matherville, Miss., 5-8-39

Dear Mr. Kennedy:

I am working on a master's thesis at Peabody College on "The Need for More and Efficient Supervision in Mississippi". Your county was selected by Mr. Clyde V. McKee of the Department of Education as the representative county.

Sincerely,

Grace Mauldin.

W. C. Grayson was superintendent from 1940 to 1944; A. B. Blackwell from 1944 to 1948; D. T. Horn from 1948 to 1952, and W. C. Grayson for a second term from 1952 to 1956. During these terms progress and consolidation continued until now the state educational survey has recommended that only two schools should be in the county: Bay Springs and Heidelberg.

Old clipping about the schools: Jasper County News June 24, 1954: Edd Shoemaker brought us a copy of an old program of an entertainment staged at the Lake Como Normal many years ago. Date 1897, Feb. 19. Reading—C. T. Shoemaker, Historical; Essay, Emma Arledge. All is not Gold that Glitters; Recitation, Lemma McIntosh, prose; Reading, Nettie Brown, humorous; Recitation, Agnes Cook, dialogue; Essay, Gerrie Thigpen, history of the Bible; Essay, B. H. Thigpen, Paddle Your Own Canoe; Recitation, Lee Horn, poetry; Reading, Nannie Thigpen; Oration, J. D. Jenkins. Punctuality; Current Events, Myrtle McIntosh; Music, Fannie Cook.

Debate—Affirmative—
W. W. Jackson, Joe Thigpen, Erastus Elzy.

Negative—S. W. Compton, C. E. Waites, J. W. Myrick.

Question—Resolve—That Foreign Emigration (immigration) should be restricted.

Picture of Antioch school, 1904, published in Jasper County News Jan. 28, 1954. Top row: Edd Phillips, Charlie Phillips, James Sims, Randolph Sims, Lon Williams, Ferman Gregory, Fred Burton, Andrew Phillips, Moselle Williams, Malisse Gregory, Fannie Blackwell, Emma Phillips, Ora McNeil, Isadore Waites.

Second row: Sallis Sims, Ella Hendry, Lottie Shoemaker, Annie Williams, Peggy Ervin, Billie Sims, Luther Montgomery, Bobbie Richardson, Dave Hendry, M. A. Thigpen (teacher).

Third row: Sims Boy, Alice Williams, Claude Williams, Jossie Shoemaker, Maude Richardson, Emma Shoemaker, Mollie Shoemaker, Emma Raynor. Fourth row: Lucius Waites, Esmarada Hendry, Grady Hendry, Walter Cole, Charlie Cole, Steve Sims, Ollie Shoemaker, Addie Phillips, Pearl Phillips, Effie Sims, Phillips girl, Bonnie Hendry, Florence Down, Ella Shoemaker (teacher). Bottom row: James Gregory, Chester Williams, Thad Waites, Walter Downs, Lee Shoemaker, Beckie McNeil.

The writer attended his first state meeting of the teachers' association in 1901, with P. L. Blackwell, superintendent, and J. L. Neill. I have attended ever since, with exception of the two years in World War I. Nothing more do I enjoy attending. In 1910, I was on the program with the subject: "Present Day Problems in Education", this meeting being held in Meridian. The meetings then were shifted from city to city, going to the city that would make the best offer as to entertainment. Now the association is so large that no city is able to entertain it but Jackson. At first the membership dues were two dollars, now they are ten dollars. In 1917, I was elected vice president. They later offered to elect me president, but I told them no as that was a big man's job.

July 18, 1957

COUNTY NEWS, BAY SPRINGS, MISSISSIPPI      THURSDAY, JULY 18, 1957.

# HISTORY OF JASPER COUNTY

### By J. M. KENNEDY

In 1925, I was elected director of the state teachers association for three years and we did two outstanding things for the teachers: adopted a group insurance policy for the teachers, and built the home on President Street (Jackson), for the teachers and officers. The insurance policy was said to be the cheapest insurance policy in the United States. The annual premium was only seven dollars which not only included death benefit but total disability also. The writer and wife went on the road for this policy in 1928-29-30. She had been on the Educational Survey of the state schools in 1926. We enjoyed visiting the schools very much. I was also a member of the National Education Association for most of the time and was a member of one of its committees part of the time.

Copy from old records at Jackson-Advance, Nov. 1934:

### REPORTS FROM SCHOOLS.

The schools of Jasper County have improved more in the last few years than perhaps any schools in the state. The good work is due mostly to the work of County Supt. J. Q. Ritchie, who was re-elected last summer by the largest vote ever given a man for re-election to that office. He has increased the school term to seven months on the same levy. The county is almost covered with taxing districts. There are three Smith-Hughes Vocational schools and four accredited high schools.

The County Agricultural High School, under the careful management of J. M. Kennedy, has been rebuilt after being destroyed by a tornado and the school is now caring for more than a hundred boarding pupils.

### Advance of December, 1934

G. C. Hamilton remains at Louin for the second term making improvements. W. E. Johnson is making Stringer the largest school in the county. It is now a Smith-Hughes school with S. N. Boyd, an A. & M. man, is in charge of vocational work. The district has been enlarged. M. C. Bennett is still at Mossville where he has been for more than 20 years. He broke the "ice" in Jasper County and established the first successful consolidated school. W. L. McGahey, an A. & M. graduate, is head of the Claiborne Consolidated school and we hear good reports from him. Maud Williams is at Heidelberg and we expect good reports from him. Rev. J. T. McClellan is at Montrose for his second term and he has a new dormitory for his boarders. There are some new faces on the A. H. S. faculty: J. Simmons, A.M., of Mississippi College, 1914; G. L. Neill, A. & M., 1917; Mrs. Fannie Oates and Jean Robert of France. J. M. Kennedy is on his fifth year as superintendent and forty-two were graduated last year. J. M. Watkins, who has been on the A. H. S. faculty for two years, is now head of Rose Hill Consolidated school with a new building and a teachers' home. Walter Shoemaker is head of the Fellowship Consolidated school. He attended school at A. & M. College. L. R. Massey is at Ted Consolidated school and we have heard good reports from there.

From the old records of the Mississippi Education Association the oldest record found was, in 1901, State meeting held at Jackson. Supt. P. L. Blackwell, J. L. Neill and J. M. Kennedy attended. Kennedy was assistant secretary.

### M. E. A. Attendance—Jackson, 1905.

R. J. Beaver, Bay Springs; Fannie Cook, Bay Springs; W. R. Flanagan, Pine Valley; Ola Foley, Rose Hill; Minnie Ford, Claiborne; Addie Johnston, Hickory Grove; Eliza Jones, Baxter; Edna Jones, Oak Bowery; J. M. Kennedy, Montrose; Minnie Killam, Fellowship; Lois McAlpin, Otoc; Waldo Moore, Montrose; Daisy Russell, Montrose; W. J. Shoemaker, county superintendent; J. E. Wilson, Hickory Grove.

### 1907, Gulfport

Carrie Cook, Alto; L. T. Dyess, New Providence; Ola Foley, Red Hill; May Hadden, Bay Springs; W. S. Huddleston, Bay Springs; Eliza Jones, Heidelberg; J. M. Kennedy, Montrose; Pearl Killam, Dear; Louise McGee (Learned), Baxter; Eva and M. McWilliams (Daleville), Turnerville; Clayton Neill, Bay Springs; Lamar Neill, Millsaps; R. C. Pugh, High Smith; Miss M. Richardson, Hero; J. Q. Ritchie, Pendleton; Emma Shoemaker, Tallahala; W. J. Shoemaker, county superintendent; Mr. and Mrs. S. L. Stringer, Louin.

### 1909—Jackson

Carrie Cook, Porto Rico; L. R. Massey, county superintendent; J. H. Newcomb, Mulberry; J. Q. Ritchie, Homewood; S. L. Stringer, Louin; J. M. Kennedy, Union (Newton County); W. J. Shoemaker, Bay Springs.

### 1910—Meridian

Bertha Abney, Montrose; Claude Bridges, Bay Springs; Hattye Cheek, Baxter; Carrie Cook, Waldrup; Myrtle Dear, Montrose; Addie Denson, Bay Springs; Minnie Ford, Bay Springs; Annie Gray, Montrose; B. F. Hardy, Moss; W. S. Huddleston, Bay Springs; J. M. Kennedy, Shubuta (on program; Present Day Problems in Education); Mittie and Julia Kennedy, Montrose; Bessie Louchridge, Garlandsville; Belva and L. R. Massey, Bay Springs; Lois McAlpin, Stringer; Stella McLaurin, Montrose; Ruby Neill, Montrose; Dollie Richardson, Bay Springs; W. C. Rogers, Bay Springs; Mr. and Mrs. S. L. Stringer, Louin; Zula Thigpen, Lake Como; Ida Travis, Heidelberg; C. E. Watkins, Rose Hill.

### 1911—Columbus

B. F. Hughes, Bay Springs; Rolfe Hunt, Montrose; J. M. Kennedy, Louin (elected vice president); J. S. Rushing, Louin; C. E. Watkins, county superintendent, Bay Springs.

### 1925—Jackson

J. M. Kennedy, Bay Springs; elected director of M. E. A. for three years; J. Q. Ritchie, Bay Springs, county superintendent; L. T. Neill, Bay Springs.

### Advance—February, 1935

A large picture of the new building at Stringer and write-up of school. Faculty: J. E. Sansing, superintendent; Ruby Lee Aycock, Winnie Cook, Jewel Grafton, Ethel Harper, Opal Ishee, Z. C. Ishee, H. G. Merrell, Mary K. Price, G. E. Stewart, Inez Stewart, Gertrude Suggs, Berta Mae Touchstone, Ira Turner, Irene Whichard.

### From International Encyclopedia:

Perhaps the greatest man teaching in Jasper County was Gen. James A. Smith, who came to Paulding after the Civil War and taught school and, later marrying Calanthy Calhoun. He afterwards moved to Jackson and became state superintendent of education, in the eighties. He succeeded Gen. Hood after losing the battles of Atlanta and Stone River. It was said that he came to Paulding under the influence of Capt. Bill Hardy.

## CENTENNIAL CELEBRATION OF JASPER COUNTY

Excerpts from The Jasper County News, 1933.

In July, 1933, the Rotary Club appointed the following committee to work up this celebration for Jasper County: J. M. Kennedy, C. B. McDonald, E. U. Parker, W. J. Shoemaker and B. W. Johnston. The Improvement Club met and appointed Mesdames J. J. Denson, S. M. Hinton and O. M. Oates on the same committee.

On the day set for the celebration, October 27th, 1933, a large crowd gathered in Bay Springs and the morning program was carried out in the public school auditorium as follows: W. J. Shoemaker gave a brief history of the schools of the county. Mr. J. M. Massey spoke for his father, Mr. James Massey, who exhibited some old papers concerning the history of the county. Mr. A. J. Benison of Laurel and a long-time citizen of Paulding, told of some early history of Paulding. The Rev. R. L. Campbell, pastor of the Macon Presbyterian Church, and a native of the county, spoke about the progress of the county. How the saying "Mighty Men of Jasper", came about was told by Judge Whitman.

The Rev. W. B. Jones of Magnolia, but a native of the county, gave a short history of the Methodist Church. Then Hon. T. C. McCallum, a former mayor of Laurel, Representative of Jones County and a native of Jasper County, made the address of the day.

The afternoon program began with the town and county officials leading the parade, coming next about 25 Choctaw Indians, followed by Antioch school representing the early settlers; Rose Hill, early schools and customs. Stringer came next portraying slavery days; next came Louin, showing Colonial and Civil War times. Paulding gave an example of the square dance. Reconstruction Days were shown by Mossville. Montrose, the Oxford of Jasper County, stressed education. General progress in education was shown by Heidelberg.

Many antiques were on exhibit in the city hall.

Excerpts from The Jasper County News, November 2, 1933:

### SPEAKERS CONTRAST THE PRESENT WITH PAST.

Jasper County fittingly celebrated the close of a century of its history, a history replete with many incidents that, too, were a part of the life of the nation. A great throng was in Bay Springs Friday afternoon to witness the pageant that depicted stirring scenes of a bygone day. The day was an epoch in the history of the county. When some person of the next generation will write the history of the county, he will be enabled to tell those living in that day that their forefathers celebrated the first century of their county's age in a noble manner. High lights of history-making epochs were vividly told by costumes, by floats, by earnest men and women who sought to recall the past in honor of a noble history.

A number of speakers were listened attentively to Friday morning in the grammar school auditorium, as each speaker told something of the early days of the county. J. M. Kennedy, master of ceremonies, announced the first speaker of the day. W. J. Shoemaker, former editor of The Jasper County News, and one time superintendent of schools of Jasper County. Mr. Shoemaker gave a brief history of the schools of the county. His address is published elsewhere in this issue. J. M. Massey of Waldrup, spoke in behalf of his father, James Massey, who, because of infirmities of age (he is 94 years of age), could not be present. Mr. Massey showed old tax receipts, one indicated the school tax was 10 cents and the tax for the poor amounted to 30 cents. At this stage of the program, Mr. A. J. Benison, a former respected citizen of Paulding, Jasper County, but who now resides in Laurel, was requested to come forward and speak.

Mr. Benison told an interesting bit of news that few of the present generation know. Many years ago, when the early settlers wished to build a new court house at Paulding there were some who opposed the move. Not to be outdone, the proponents of the idea paid an old Negro to fire the log structure. The remuneration for the deed being a quart of ten-cent whiskey.

(To be Continued)

**July 25, 1957**

*COUNTY NEWS, BAY SPRINGS, MISSISSIPPI* — THURSDAY, JULY 25, 1957

# HISTORY OF JASPER COUNTY

### By J. M. KENNEDY

Dr. R. L. Campbell, Presbyterian minister who resides at Macon was introduced. Dr. Campbell contrasted the past with the present and declared how glad he was that tax payers were called upon nowadays to pay more than a ten-cent tax for the education of the children. He told how pleased it made him when two railroads came through the county. Dr. Campbell was born and reared in the eastern part of Jasper County.

How the epithet, "Mighty Men of Jasper" originated was told by Judge Sam Whitman, who, while not a native of the county, has spent the greater part of his life here. United States Senator Henry S. Foote came to Paulding to speak. Senator Foote was a rabid opponent of session, loudly exclaiming, "Is there a man in Jasper county who wants this?" "Yes by G— I do" was shot back at the Senator by Bryan Morris, a highly esteemed Jasper countain. "Almighty God! Hear that, ye mighty men of Jasper" shouted Senator Foote.

Judge Whitman, a staunch Democrat of the old school, told the children present in the audience to always respect and honor the memory of their forefathers and the issue that brought on the War between the States.

Something not on the announced program was a song, "How Firm A Foundation," sung by the audience followed the reading of each verse by Rev. Thompson who was requested to do so by J. M. Massey, one of the leading figures in county singing conventions.

Rev. W. B. Jones, Methodist minister of Magnolia, gave a sketch of the history of the Methodist churches of the county touching also upon the other two large denominations of the county, the Baptist and Presbyterian churches. The county furnished 29 ministers of the Methodist faith, declared the Rev. Jones.

Chairman Kennedy introduced State Senator Torrey G. McCallum former Jasper countain who now resides in Laurel. Senator Torrey was the feature speaker of the occasion. His address dealt mostly with the changing social system, stating that it is impossible to get something for nothing. He said the nation was drawing away from the individualistic state and now the mass movement had taken place. He feared the greatest foes of the nation were not outside it but the vices lay within. Easy living was one of the foes he characterized as being most insidious. Every man has not got his price, said Mr. McCallum. People must not lose confidence in their fellow man, he declared.

"Chords that thrill with greatest pleasure,
Vibrate chords of deepest woe."

A tribute to the hardihood of the pioneers, brought forth the admonition that the virtues should be remembered by their descendants. "Plant a tree in the next century for someone else," concluded the speaker.

Mr. Kennedy gave a brief sketch of some high lights in the county's progress: White people first came to the county in 1818. In 1828, missionaries from Massachusetts settled in Jasper County at the site now known as Missionary from the fact that the missionaries stopped there. There were large plantations in the eastern section of the county where many wealthy slave owners resided. In 1880, the Northeastern Railroad came through the southeastern tip of the county.

### EXHIBITION OF ANTIQUES

Taking advantage of the Centennial, many persons who have heirlooms, old relics and antiques in their possession, brought them along Friday and placed them on display in the city hall.

This was in charge of Miss Lodell Rasberry, Grace Currie and Mrs. J. J. Denson. A miniature farm had been built, showing how the people lived a hundred years ago. While right beside it was a model of the modern farm. The contrast was too obvious to need explanation.

The manual training department of Stringer school had on display several articles of wood made by the students. L. T. Simmons of Louin had on display a Dutch oven said to be over 200 years of age, being brought from Scotland when the Simmons' ancestors came across. Mr. Matt Stringer had an old-fashioned dinner horn about six feet in length of a very great age.

There was a Bible printed over a hundred years ago. The book had been presented to Abiah Robertson in Abbeville District, South Carolina, for attendance on Sunday school in 1835.

The Mississippi Power Company had a modern kitchen fixed up with all the latest electrical appliances. This was quite a contrast to the old-time way of preparing food.

A candle mould, a wood bread tray, made by a slave 154 years ago, an old doll, 80 years old, many old cooking utensils and household effects of great age were on exhibit.

In the department allotted to the exhibition of needlecraft were quilts, one 85 years of age, Mrs. S. L. Ryan, Mrs. W. B. Pruitt, Mrs. R. R. Rogers, Sr., Miss Sue Ann Blackwell Mrs. R. W. Ainsworth, Mrs. H. A. Hinton, Mrs. W. O. Mason, Mrs. B. W. Johnston, Mrs. H. D. Myers, Mrs. C. W. Cheek, Mrs. Van Sanders exhibited many and varied lines of needle work, either in the heavier things such as quilts or the finer work as embroidery and lace.

A quilt depicting the stirring life of the last century was on exhibition and had won honorable mention at the Chicago World's Fair and was made by Mrs. Ethel McLeod Carter. Other heirloom dahlias, grown by Mrs. W. H. Alexander, were displayed.

Marion Ryan and Reuben Hall and Julia K. Thigpen had their works of art on view.

Henry McKay had a very old musket. There were also documents, heirlooms which had become priceless to families which had had those things handed down through generations. There was one a land grant, signed by Franklin Pierce, president of the United States. It was dated 1854.

An immense clock, known to have been a hundred years old, and thought to have been much older, was displayed by R. L. Abney.

Gilchrist-Fordney Company of Laurel had a fine display of their lumbering operations.

The idea of fittingly celebrating the hundredth anniversary of the county's history originated with the Rotary Club. A committee from this organization was appointed and also the Woman's Improvement Club appointed a committee, headed by Mrs. S. C. Hinton to work in collaboration with the other committee. The whole affair was a success and a fine spirit of congeniality ought to come, for the whole county enjoys an honorable history, and a great future lies ahead.

### FRIDAY'S BIG CENTENNIAL PARADE

The great crowd of people which thronged the streets of Bay Springs Friday, was only exceeded one other time. It is estimated that there were from four to six thousand people on the streets.

The line of march of the big parade, showing the epochs in the history of the county, commenced at the street between the Methodist and Presbyterian Churches and moved east, turning south in front of the postoffice, then passing through the street north of the court house to make the circle once again.

The parade was led by Sheriff J. C. Basset, Mayor D. L. Fail and Marshal J. B. Vanderslice. These officers were mounted on well-groomed horses. Following them closely were the supervisors of the county in an automobile. Then came the real original settlers of the county, a group of Choctaw Indians in their beads, gay colors and passive looks. These first settlers were afoot. There were probably twenty-five of them including their children.

The days of slavery were graphically portrayed by the Stringer school. There were some in the crowd whose memory might have carried them back to that period in the life of the county, but to the big majority, it was purely a fact of history.

Louin school tried itself in depicting colonial days and Civil War times. A log cabin atop a truck showed country life in the long ago. They even had a "coon" holding a live possum by the tail. The "Bonnie Blue Flag", with a detachment of boys armed with muskets following, brought the War Between the States to mind.

Pioneer days were recalled by the Antioch school. An old wagon loaded with a man, armed with his trusty musket and having his family, with three or four ragged urchins following, made the day of long treks by wagon, through the forests and over streams, real.

Reconstruction Days with its ordeals was vividly portrayed by Moselle. Two white-robed figures surrounded by a group of men brought to mind a dark period in the history of the United States, a period that leaves a dark blot on history's pages. The Ku Klux saved the South from the Carpet Baggers and the lash of an unbridled age, just released from all confines without a knowledge between the difference of license and liberty.

Old Paulding demonstrated to the satisfaction of all that there are people who yet know how to perform the square dance. The crowds didn't give the dancers much opportunity to demonstrate the art as they would have, but kept crowding in and finally the dancers had to give up their place to the next school.

Rose Hill pupils were the fashion book for the last century, styles change as well as times, and perhaps the present generation will go back to the long ago and resurrect styles of that day. The world has done a lot of queer things lately.

Montrose, the Oxford of Jasper County, stressed education. It was stated that in one class of nine at one period during the life of Montrose school, there were seven who went out of the class and became ministers. Supt. McClue briefly told the high spots in the history of the school.

Heidelberg school gave a graphic illustration of the present method, including advanced stages in the educational field. The whole courses of study in a modern school were developed.

Contrasts between the old and new were vividly illustrated by an ox-drawn cart on which Negroes were seated carding cotton after one of their fellows had picked the seed from it. An old T-Model Ford car contrasted greatly with a spick and span late model Chevrolet car. A large cotton truck with 22 bales on which were seated the King and Queen of the day. R. H. Hancock and Miss Kathleen Carter, made up the different method of transportation.

The highway crew had a scene showing the difference of hard work with pick and shovel to the later methods of machine and trucks.

The old-style buggy with its riggings were driven by an elderly gentleman and his frau. All these marked the tremendous gap between old methods and new ones.

The local stave mill gave an interesting illustration by having a truck loaded with nearly 16,000 pounds of stave bolts, followed by a truck on which men were actively engaged in processing the staves.

The cheese plant had an admirable display of its manufactured product. A large drawing of a cow impressed the mind with the possibilities for dairy development.

Brooms company and the plant each had floats advertising their respective businesses. Other businesses ought to have been in the procession.

A delapidated old wagon which reposed an "injured" man was followed by Alexander Hardware's latest Ford ambulance, a thing of beauty and comfort. In the ambulance lay "emergency" case, with doctor and nurse in attendance.

Uncle Sam's rural letter carriers followed this and brought up the rear of the parade. It quite a leap from the old ways handling mail to the present quick and intelligent manner in which the mail is expedited.

**August 1, 1957**

# HISTORY OF JASPER COUNTY

**By J. M. KENNEDY**

Excerpts from History of Methodism in Jasper County, by Dr. George Jones in The Jasper County News, beginning August 16, 1934.

The Jasper County territory was in the Leaf River circuit in the eighteen-twenties but no report of any work done as the Indians had their mission at Missionary. In the early days the division of the church seemed to be by rivers as they had no other to mark them off. The circuit rider would pass through sometimes but there were no roads or bridges. It is said that people came into Jasper territory before the county was formed.

The oldest churches in the county are given as follows: Paulding, Garlandsville, Pleasant Hill, Mount Zion and Holders. The date that Hopewell changed from Methodist Protestant to Methodist Episcopal. (The records at Jackson say that John McCormick organized Hopewell church as soon as he settled in the county which was in 1833). The names of the early Congregational churches are as follows: Magnolia, Oak Bowery, Liberty, Smyrna, Mulberry, and Green Valley. He says that this sect was very strong in the early days. (Should have been as the church was organized mostly by Jasper Countians. In contacting some of the leaders of this sect they claim that the church was organized by L. J. Jones, Henry Jones, G. W. Todd, B. M. Huddleston, Hunt, etc. and that the first church was Mulberry in 1853, the next year Liberty and Green Valley.)

With the changes in the county, roads, railroads, etc., the following churches have died: Missionary, Rawls Chapel, Porto Rico, Fonks, Hickory Grove which gave its life to Rose Hill, Price Chapel which gave its life to Montrose, Mt. Zion which gave its life to Bay Springs. It seems then that the oldest Methodist churches in the county are Paulding, Garlandsville and Holders which is said to have had 79 members in 1835. Rev. E. B. Strickland seems to be the great builder in the early days. Paulding circuit was organized in 1837.

Today (1934) there are sixteen churches in Jasper County and are as follows: Bay Springs, Camp Allen, Garlandsville, Heidelberg, Holders, Homewood, Hopewell, Louin, Montrose, Paulding, Philadelphia, Pleasant Grove, Reads Chapel, Rose Hill, Stringer and Vossburg. These are served by four pastors. Some names that were on the early rolls are still found there: Abney, Blackwell, Brame, Burnett, Burton, Chatham, Clayton, Cook, Dantzler, Davis, Dawkins, Dent, Foley, Fowler, French, Gammage, Gillon, Heidelberg, Hinton, Holder, Holyfield, Jones, Kennedy, Lewis, Lightsey, McCormick, McLaurin, ison, Neil, Porter, Pruitt, Read, Risher, Stringer, Stockman, Thompson, Tatum, Terrell, Travis, Ulmer, Wall, Williams.

Paulding soon became the "Queen City" of the East and was not only made a circuit but a district. Names familiar to the county were R. J. Jones Sr., R. J. Jones Jr. and Kenneth Jones as pastors and presiding elders. In 1872, Rev. Holland became pastor and soon organized a camp ground near Rose Hill school which was already becoming famous over the eastern part of the state. The camp ground was named in honor of its founder, Holland. It soon had a large attendance; one account gives two thousand present in one day. In 1886, a church was organized there but services were still held at Hickory Grove. In 1884, Dr. Peek was appointed post master at the nearby post office, Twistwood, and he succeeded in getting moved to Rose Hill with the name changed to Rose Hill. Rev. Hawkins followed Holland and sent his children to Rose Hill school which resulted in moving the parsonage to Rose Hill. Paulding still remained as head of the district for a short time. The early rolls give the names of Lightsey, Cope, Benison, Vick, Chapman, Ferguson, Edwards, Green, Herrington, Sherman and Nobles, Sharbrough, Brown, Harmon, McGinnis, Alridge, Hinton, Chatham, James, Kennedy, Halford. Later rolls give the names of Nicholson, Brame, Duckett, McFarland, Foley, Cochran, Rowell, Parker, Round, Kelly, Edwards, Traylor, McClelland, Sanders, Combest, Heidelberg, Jones, Windham, Tatum, Street, Hudson, Read, Scott. Rev. Henry Jones, a local Congregational preacher was a great help to the church, also Dr. J. W. Harmon, two of his sons, Nolan and Gus became valuable members of the Mississippi Conference. (Nolan, the father of the new bishop.) Rev. Joe T. Nicholson was a native of Paulding. (A new history of Long Beach church just came out, stating the Rev. Joe Nicholson in 1884 rode a horse from Handsboro and started the church in a goat house.) A partial list of the Sunday school superintendents are G. G. Cope, S. S. Cope, C. C. Tatum, E. J. Parker, M. E. Cochran, H. F. Round, J. E. Foley, C. C. Street, Mrs. R. H. Read. Some of the stewards were J. S. Kennedy, T. Q. Brame, E. J. Parker, G. S. Harmon, C. C. Tatum, J. E. B. Traylor, J. E. Foley, H. E. Porter, R. H. Read, Lex Brame.

Some of the names on the roll of the old Hickory Grove church were: Hicks, Cooley, Caston, Lewis, Smith, Davis, Combest, Holyfields and Whites. The new church at Rose Hill soon grew to 190 members in 1898. Some of the names were: Fowler, Cooley, Combest, Davis, French, Graham, Holyfield, Cook, Lewis, Porter, Reynolds, Smith, Sumaker, White, Hicks, Fikes, Avery, Braddock, Bentley, Pruitt, Land, Aycock, Harris, Logan, Traylor, Hosey, Eddin, Starling, Keheay, Moody, Merrill, Chatham, Danaby and Winstead. Stewards: J. A. Porter, W. B. Lewis, O. F. Peck, J. R. Davis, R. W. Lewis, B. F. Lewis, W. T. Booth, J. W. White, S. B. Avery, J. A. Davis, M. H. Holyfield, C. P. Hicks, C. M. Davis, J. N. Davis, W. C. Lewis, M. W. Porter, J. E. B. Traylor, C. A. Cooley, W. A. Lewis, T. F. Graham, W. P. Pruitt, H. A. Porter, Mrs. Katie Smith, C. E. Chatham, J. W. Smith, D. H. Davis, E. Y. Porter and C. C. Chatham.

The Holland Camp Ground at Rose Hill was described as follows: The tabernacle was built in the center of a ten acre lot with logs stood on the end and the campers were in tents on three sides of tabernacle 4 deep. Room between them all, large enough to drive a wagon. Sometimes there were as many as fifty tents. The first year lights were fires built on scaffolds but after the first year oil lamps were used. Scaffolds with pine straw on them were used for beds. Cooking was done by fires built on scaffolds. Services were 8 A.M., 11 A.M., 3 P.M., and 7 P.M. A number of preachers were always present. Bishop DuBose, A. M. Little and Joe T. Nicholson were licensed to preach there in 1876. No meeting was held in 1878 as that was the year of yellow fever most all over the state; most of the people of Lake died from it.

The Pleasant Grove church was organized in the early days of the county by the Moulds and Loveys. Some of the Sunday school superintendents are: A. W. Atwood, W. R. Moulds, W. W. McPherson, Lee Ulmer, Jeff Moulds, E. B. Murray, W. W. Murray, Mrs. R. C. Ulmer, C. B. Ulmer and Noel Ulmer (now a preacher). Stewards are: D. M. Lovett, J. C. Murray, W. B. Lewis, Roland Ulmer, E. B. Murray, W. W. Murray, John W. Moulds, Seamon McKinnon, J. E. Tisdale, H. J. Moulds, W. B. Moulds and Noel Ulmer. For a number of years A. W. Atwood and W. W. McPherson were licensed exhorters. It was their duty to hold prayer meetings and exhortation when there was an opportunity directed by the pastor. Today (1934) there are about one hundred twenty-five members who are Atwood, Boutwell, Cooley, Coker, Davis, Hutto, Hicks, Lewis, Lovett, McCarty, Murray, Moulds, McKinnon, McNeil, McPherson, Nelson, Scruggs, Sims, Rogers, Ulmer, Booth, Herrington, Lyle, Parks, White, Arthur, Speed, Graham, Parker, Bailey, Tisdale, Harper, Braddock, Sanders, Caraway, Dolan, Castale, McLean and Hart. Three ministers are buried in the cemetery: A. Y. Armistrong, A. M. Fikes and Jeff Moulds. The church has furnished the conference with four ministers: Robert and George Fikes, Noel Ulmer, A. A. Sims and D. W. Ulmer.

Hopewood was organized in 1911 by Rev. W. H. Lane with the enrollment of nine families as follows: Lewis, Cooley, Braddock, Lovett, McKinnon, later members Oliver, Simmons, Bently, Hutto, Boutwell, Pierce, Herrington, Hicks, Caraway, Sisson, Sims, McPherson and Reeves. Sunday school superintendents, D. A. McKinnon, O. F. Cooley, W. B. Lewis, N. J. Blackmon, L. N. Boutwell, and T. G. Lewis. A local man, E. H. Cooley, also G. R. Fikes and David Ulmer were licensed to preach.

Hopewell church was founded more than a hundred years ago (this was written in 1935) about the time of the organization of the county. The McCormicks were the principal spirits in its organization. On Sunday, April 30th, 1933, the church celebrated its centennial celebration with a large crowd present. Preachers present were S. C. Moody, pastor, H. R. McKee, M. L. Burton, W. B. Jones, J. T. Abney and the writer. W. B. Jones had his father's notebook which stated that he held the quarterly conference there in 1840, Saturday, Aug. 11. The writer was related to four former pastors and two presiding elders.

Early members were Ratcliffe, McCormick, Pruitt, Loper, Risher, Boulton, Foley, Seay, Aycock, Maske, Davis, Sims, Underwood, Pharis, Ethridge, Harrison, Boyd, Evans, Ogburn, Scott, Dr. Peck, Dr. Tatum, McDonald, Reed, Fowler, Owen, Linder, Hardy, Dease, Weir, and Wyatt. Stewards are Dr. Peek, J. M. Risher, J. W. McCormick, W. E. Foley, O. C. Boulton, J. O. McCormick Sr., C. E. Boulton, W. O. McCormick, J. E. Foley, J. O. McCormick Jr., Peter Barrett, Will Pruitt, O. A. Boulton and F. F. McCormick Jr. Sunday school superintendents were: F. F. McCormick Sr., J. M. Risher, W. E. Foley, C. M. Foley, C. J. Ogburn, J. O. McCormick, J. O. McCormick Jr., and Fred Davis.

Read Chapel seems to have had several names. In 1894, R. Bradley came out from Montrose and preached in High Smith lo, school house, as also did his successor, M. L. White. At one time services were held at Gridley another time in Ras school house. The first organization contained the names of James C. Brewer, Lou C. Brewer, Louisa Elizabeth Read, Mary E. Pugh, Sallie Brewer, Lula A. Read, Ada Read and Katie N. Read. Later added were Mary M. Brewer, Maudie T. Reid, Lou C. Read, Susie L. Read, Luther E. Read, Rufus W. Read, Ida Alford, and Mary Alford. Other names added are: Harper, James, Hayden, Haira, Moulds, Lee, Dawkins, Baucum, Morris, Froshour, Eddieman. The trustees are: G. D. L. E. and W. M. Read. Stewards were the same.

# August 8, 1957

## HISTORY OF JASPER COUNTY

### By J. M. KENNEDY

**Excerpts from History of Methodism in Jasper County, by Dr. George Jones, from The Jasper County News, beginning August 16, 1934.**

Rawls Chapel was organized in 1890 by B. H. Rawls. The first names are: Aaron, Whatley, Hardy, Braddock, Jordan, James and Reed. The church was not long lived and only some graves are where the church stood.

Louin—The Methodists invaded Louin in 1906, when Rev. A. M. Broadfoot held a meeting there and afterwards services were held in the school building until 1913, when S. J. Tally, Billy Boykin, Dave Lightsey and John Carr built a church there. Some of the first members were: Lightsey, Tally, Williams, Stockman, Lecke, Hankins, Smith, Kennedy, Foster, Perry, Holder, Armour, Morgan, McPherson, Perkins, Hindman, Sheppard, Read, Ratliff, Simmons, DuPree, Harris, McGee, Dawkins, Swann, Doolittle, Long, Eddleman, McMurry, Edwards, Holman, Speed, Cook, McKithen, Shell, Brady, Strother, Montgomery, Gooson, O'Sullivan, Jones, Matthews, Wedgeworth, Milan, Holyfield, Foley, Geter, Land, Martin, Jordan, Walker, Shoemaker, McCrory, Carlton, Cooper and Hollingworth.

Sunday school superintendents: W. H. Boykin, P. L. Blackwell, H. A. Kennedy and C. B. Holder.

**Camp Allen.** The first camp of Gilchrist-Fordney Co. was Seven Springs, near Antioch. Next place was McNeil, not far distant. The next camp was Camp Three, west of Bay Springs, then Dushau, near Louin; then Camp Allen, 1931.

At Seven Springs, Miss Nona Stanly, a public school teacher, organized a Sunday school which was kept going till the company disbanded. The superintendents were: W. M. Meeks, Wiley Knight, A. H. Waldrup, Ollie Barnett, R. L. Jourdan, W. M. Chronister, Percy Barnett. Stewards: Dr. L. Golden, Mrs. J. B. Mustin, Ollie Barnett, A. L. Yeager, Wm Chronister, and A. L. Griffin. Names on the roll: Hankins, Cook, Clark, Hester, Brogan, Curtin, Blackledge, Mustin, Usery, Warren, Brown, Knox, Riley, Staples, Walters, Rowell, Stanly, Meeks, McAfee, Golden, Baucum, Childress, Hancock, Green, Rawson, Jordan, Mosely. The writer held a very fine vacation Bible school at Camp Allen and was assisted by Mrs. L. Walter, Miss Minnie Lee Waldrup, Miss Nona Nestor, Miss Elise Chronister, Miss Gladys Barnett and Miss Waites.

**Mt. Zion.** No date is given as when this church was organized, but perhaps is one of the oldest in the county. It was very large and influential as it had one of the high schools of the county. It is said that the building is still standing but being used as a barn. It gave its life to Bay Springs. List of members are Holder, Hinton, McBay, Thompson, Fail, Stringer, Rogers, McLaurin, Hankins, Little, Cook, Crowder, Williams, Hall, Ducksworth, Brown, Yelverton, Land, Toshenberger, Ford, Hill, Summers, Keown, Ishee, Gregory, Jones, Armour.

**Bay Springs.** The first church work at Bay Springs was done by W. F. Thompson, who was appointed by Mt. Zion church to conduct a Sunday school which he did and served after the church at Bay Springs was organized; served a long time after and then was followed by R. L. Abney, J. M. Watkins and then by D. T. Burnett. Members at Bay Springs were as follows: Hinton, McBay, Thompson, Stringer, Holder, Hall, Keown, Tyner, Jobes, Smith, Burnett, Horn, Boykin, Massey, Rasberry, Brame, Abney, Brown, Jordan, Shamlee, Roper, Windham, Yelverton, Alexander, Thigpen, Cole, Wilson, Ryan, Bullard, Pittman, Myers, Cheek, Blakeney, Herrington, Hayes, Pruitt, Lewis, Mason, Terral, Parker, Fail, Dempsey, Harper, Crisler, Dyess, Boyd, Deen, Bunch, Evans, Upton, Leveatt, Cook, Flurry, Whitman, Kennedy, Nelson, Durr, Maske, McCormick, Poole, Barnett, Germany, Bishop, Dixon, Pertuitt, Denson. The building has gone from a small plank building building to a large brick building. Bay Springs Methodist Church had four local preachers: C. E. Boulton, Parvin Hankins, Warren Ware and M. K. Miller.

**Stringer.** The Stringer Methodist church was organized in 1910 with Geo. A. Dykes, Lemma McIntosh, Marion McIntosh, Jerry Dixon, W. F. Hopkins, Ben J. Moss, J. E. Evans. Stewards: O. P. Foley, J. G. Moore, Ben J. Moss, J. E. Evans, F. S. Ford, W. C. Mabry, J. G. Holder, Mrs. H. H. Denson, Mrs. J. G. Moore, Hollis Price.

**Bethlehem.** George Jones did not seem to know where the above church was located. He quoted an old divine, who said he thought it was near Moss Hill. (This church was located on a very old highway of the county, running from Newton to Paulding, on the hill after crossing McVey creek. There was a story about this church that was spread over half of the county. A young man, from another community, went to this church one day and asked a young lady, if he could walk her home, and she said, "No". The people called it a "kick" or slight to him—a disgrace to any young man. To her surprise, he was back the next "preaching day" and he asked her the same question, and received the same answer. The third preaching day, the girl slipped out of the back door and ran home alone. The young man came with her brother for lunch. This went on for some time when she "gave in" and married him.)

"Bill and Alex Under, and Tatums were the main members of this church. The Traylors and Buckleys lived nearby but were members of the Baptist church.

**Montrose.** Montrose was named for James Montrose, a Scotchman. The first settled was Jacob Blackwell, the grandfather of Wash Blackwell. His name, with several other Blackwells, appear on the Jasper County tax list of 1834. Rev. E. W. Strickland, the church builder, built a Methodist church at Montrose before 1840 but it seems that the Methodists were "smothered" by the coming of Drs. Gray and Waddell and the building of Waddell's school. Waddell secured the Pickens plantation (some say 25,000 acres) and a number of settlers. The Methodists later built a church at Price chapel.

Dr. Waddell left for the University in 1948, and Dr. Gray soon after left for Vicksburg. The school, however, ran for some time, even during the War between the States. An old soldier states that as they left for war, the lady teacher, Miss Kate Kennedy, daughter of Dr. Kennedy from Rose Hill, came out on the second story porch and addressed them.

Montrose Academy soon became famous in east Mississippi and west Alabama, and therefore soon brought other settlers besides the Waddell-Gray delegation. Robert Lowrey attended school there and married a Gammage (Marie). Other settlers there included the Burnetts, Wedgeworth, Campbells, Harts, Alexanders, Dawkins, Hardys, Barnes, Dukes, Gammages, Gains, Selbys, Neills, Burtons, Harrisons, Abneys, Huttos and Lightseys. In 1857, a Methodist church was organized and called Price Chapel after pastor. R. J. Jones, presiding elder. The church was built by Miller Neill, grandfather of Rev. J. L. Neill. The church was located south of town near the J. P. Abney home (now owned by Gordez Neill.

In 1864, W. P. Massey of Oakland, Miss., came to Montrose and organized a high school, and in 1908, it was adopted as the Brandon District High School. The school prospered and later became the Mississippi Conference Training School and continued till 1926. At one time the school had 75 boarders and it is said that 40 preachers were educated there. Most of this time it did college work which was accredited at the state colleges. After Massey's coming, people began to talk for a new church in town, which was completed on the present lot in 1893.

**Philadelphia.** The origin of the church is not known but it was the home church of R. J. Jones, Sr. and W. R. Benge was the donor of the land. R. J. Jones Sr. was pastor in 1853. He lived on the hill as you enter Heidelberg from the west. He was the father-in-law of Rev. B. M. Huddleston and the father of R. J. Jr., K. A. and W. B. Jones, all preachers.

W. B. Jones is the oldest living graduate of Millsaps College. All of his children have graduated there, and one, George, has had a D.D. degree conferred on him and is now the editor of a church journal in Nashville, Tenn. Most of his grandchildren have graduated there, as have a number of other relatives who completed their education there. He attended the last Annual Conference at Jackson, 1957.) A number of the old citizens were members of this church, such as Abney, Risher, Heidelberg, Travis, Thornton, McFarland, Bethea, Hinton, Lyon, Morrison, Clayton, Hartfield, Hudson, and Cook. R. H. Jones, a son of R. J. Sr. has the oldest marked grave in the cemetery, 1862. R. J. Sr. is also buried here, 1872, and also Rev. C. C. Evans, 1930. After the coming of the railroad in 1882, the church was torn down and rebuilt about where the Confederate monument now stands. With the establishment of the town of Heidelberg, the church became known as Heidelberg church. Later, the citizens west and northwest organized and located the church on its present location, it is said that the membership of the church is the Lightseys and their kin. The same thing is said about the voting precinct recently (1957) located there. The church is now a station (1957).

**Missionary.** The church was built in 1892, by R. F. Witt. (This was the second church on the lot. The first was a log building and used as a school house. Penny Dease and Tom Thaggard taught school there but it had fallen down before this). It was a beautiful lot situated in the fork of the road leading to Hickory and the old Indian road leading to Garlandsville. It had a beautiful pine grove in the front. Across the old Indian road was the Indian mission cemetery). It was always very small on account of Catholics on one side and Rose Hill and Hopewell on the other. The stewards were A. Lewis, W. T. Ulmer and J. S. Kennedy. Sunday school superintendents were J. M. Kennedy, W. T. Ulmer and Mrs. S. D. Russell. Members were James, Ulmer, Kennedy, Green, Maske, McDaniel, Halford, Pharis, Underwood, Jackson, Logan, Rogers, Boyd, Chatham, Edwards, Dolan.

**Holders.** The deed for Holders was given by Major Waldrup and wife, Rebecca Waldrup, on Aug. 21st, 1854. Major Waldrup was the grandfather of Rev. F. Waldrup (Baptist) of Louin and A. H. Waldrup of Camp Allen. The church, however, existed before that date. This deed named Spius Dixon, Daniel W. McMillion, John McMillion, J. Daniel McMillion, and Rev. R. J. Jones, trustees. The deed was filed for record in October. James A. Chapman, clerk, and Edward Terral, attessor. This deed is being kept by Mrs. J. E. Pittman. Sunday school superintendents were, John Dixon, A. R. Brinson, J. W. Tucker, T. J. Dixon, W. P. Foley, C. E. Boulton, J. B. Vanderslice, Mrs. B. L. Fail and J. E. Pittman. Names on the rolls are: Dixon, Stockman, Holder, Page, Vanderslice, Cook, Pittman, Tyner, Aaron, Thigpen, Hosey, Ballard, Brinson, Evans, Downs, Roper, Braddock, Massey, Morgan, Lee, Smith, Stewart, Lewis, Lovett, James, Kuykendall, Little, Windham, Waldrup, McGrew, Bolton, and Sims. The church was said to be named for Willis Holder, who died in 1846.

# August 15, 1957

## HISTORY OF JASPER COUNTY

By J. M. KENNEDY

Excerpts from History of Methodism in Jasper County, by Dr. George Jones, from The Jasper County News, beginning August 16, 1934.

Vossburg. The town of Vossburg grew after the coming of the Northeastern Railroad in 1882. It was the nearest railroad station to the county site — Paulding — which was a great aid in building the town. The deed is dated July 6th, 1884, with W. J. Heidelberg, R. J. McLeod, A. Johnston, W. P. Mauldin, J. A. Price, E. W. Stafford and James McGowan as trustees. J. S. Turner and Dr. C. W. Bufkin as witnesses and was filed the next month for record with M. G. Turner as clerk. Sunday school superintendents were, E. W. Stafford, M. H. Turner Sr., M. H. Jr., W. L. Yates and W. S. Rowell. Names on the rolls were: Bufkin, Hyde, Bingham, Brown, Hamblin, Byrd, Stokes, Terrall, Bogan, Frazell, Denny, Conner, Raynor, Peel, Sheely, Bondurant, Bradly, Chatham, Barksdale, Downer, Holcombs, Carter, Allgood, Middleton, Foote, Sullivan, Jones, Weems, Kelley, Wimberly, Gray, Self, Blackwell, Bridger, Brashire, McCouch, Tyner, Myrick, Lightsey, Spires, Hinton, Webb, Harisfield, Thornton, Utsey.

Garlandville. The records show that the Alabama Conference had appointments at Garlandville in 1823. This was seven years before the Indians agreed to move and ten years before the county was organized. Even Pushmataha, chief of the Choctaws, lived at Garlandville then. However, the one hundredth celebration was not held till October 25th, 1935. Miss Kate Williams, great grand-daughter of "Grandma" Williams, who named the town, gave the welcome address. Rev. H. G. Hawkins, a former pastor, and now presiding elder of the Vicksburg District, gave a very able address of a hundred years of Methodism.

Rev. W. B. Jones, secretary of the Mississippi Conference and whose father, R. J. Jones, was pastor of the church in 1835 and later presiding elder. Bishop Dobbs was the speaker of the day. During the afternoon, Rev. George Jones, the pastor, gave a brief history of the church. Rev. W. W. Moore and Rev. M. L. White spoke of their former pastorate at Garlandville. Mr. B. B. Davis of Waynesboro, grandson of "Grandma" Williams, spoke very affectionately of his grandmother and other relatives of the church. Mr. C. C. Evans, his sister and brother came with him to the celebration.

Mr. Dan Harry, the oldest person in Garlandville, and who has lived here all his life, read a paper on the history of the town and the Presbyterian Church. Mr. Wad Weir was presented as the oldest member of the church and Miss Virginia Dent was presented as the longest time as a member. Mrs. C. M. Knowles gave a write up of the Missionary Society. Besides the ministers already mentioned were: Rev. W. M. Williams, of Magee; H. J. Moore, Decatur; J. L. Smith, Newton; J. A. Smith, Meridian; J. W. Thompson, and T. Barton West, of Bay Springs; G. A. Broadus, Rose Hill; H. C. Castle, Magee; D. W. Ulmer, Taylorsville; J. W. Sells, Forest, and J. H. Jolly, Jackson.

Prominent laymen present were: Mr. and Mrs. Brooks, Tupelo; Bob and Frank Gibson, Newton; P. L. Blackwell, Newton; O. C. Hull, Lawrence; W. C. Mabry, Newton; G. M. McLendon, Newton; R. C. Pugh, Taylorsville; L. D. McLaurin, Montrose; O. M. Abney, Montrose; H. A. Kennedy, Louin; R. L. Abney, J. M. Kennedy and E. F. Pruitt, Bay Springs; George Todd, Union; Mrs. A. B. Colt, Enterprise; Mrs. C. M. Crossly, Newton.

### BAPTIST CHURCHES

The writer has asked a number of people, including two ministers to write about the Baptist churches but no response. I have visited the Baptist book store in Jackson and still no success. Evelyn Barbour of Vicksburg has a history of the Barbours from North Carolina to Mississippi and without a doubt Twistwood was the first Baptist church in the county. One of the old Lewises told me he helped the Barbours build the church just after the formation of the county. It seems to be the only church built without a nail. This church was the voting place for Rose Hill community until a few years back. The site of this church is now the Rose Hill cemetery where the Three - Chopped Way enters Highway 18.

The next church, according to record seems to be Randle Hill, located about four miles northeast of Montrose. Virgil Randle is named as one of the first settlers of the county, and so the church was named for him which for a long time was prosperous community and one of the voting places of the county. A few of the names are: Blackwell, Pippin, Leslie, Lay, Wedgeworth, Parker, Hardy, McCord, Fortson, Cheek and Coker.

Fellowship has been said to be one of the most stable and prosperous rural communities in the county. The date goes back to the early days of the county and has lately gotten so large that they have two churches now, Old and New Fellowship. Names are as follows: Buckley, Little, McMillan, Massengale, Bogan, Massey, Harris, Dyess, Hamrick, Stamper, Dear, Gandy, Johnson, Cross, Killam, Richardson, Basket. This community includes all the northeast corner of the county.

Concord was one of the early churches and was located near where the Tioch colored school is located, but later was moved to Penantly. People connected with this church were, Gandy, Seay, Harris, Crawford, Wall, Coker.

Mt. Pisgah, most of the people called it Pisgah, was located in the northwest corner of Township 3 Range 12, was one of the early churches of the county and at one time it was a very large church. The writer attended an association there in the early nineties and the crowd was so large that they held services in the large church and a large L. school building at the same time. I remember seeing the old preachers together: N. L. Clark (for whom Clark College was named), Jackson Smith, John Halford, John Simmons, George Boyd and Tom Waldrup. Henry Barbour was dead but his wife was there. There was a cemetery down the hill from the church but Jud Traylor asked to be buried just off the pulpit and his wish was granted, and now there is a good sized cemetery at that place. Names of the people were: McCarty, Harper, Buckley, Barnett, Beason, Pharis, Perry, Clark. Now only one white family lives there, all other are Negroes.

Antioch is the largest, and has been, rural church, in the county. Its history goes back more than a hundred years, and has been a voting place all these years and has always been a very large precinct. It is located in the southwest part of Beat One. In the old days when they had the "merry-go-round" in political years when they had a picnic at every voting place and some time where they had no voting place, Antioch was always at the head of the list. The day before the date named for Antioch picnic, yearlings, goats, sheep and hogs were butchered and the peach and apple trees were stripped, all getting ready for the big day. All over the county candidates and people were moving on to Antioch community to spend the night before so that they would be on hand early. If there was a family that did not have company they felt "slighted" some spent the second night. When time came for speaking to start the hill was covered with people. Lemonade stands each had their candidates that they were crying out for. The people of the county who did not go were soon contacting those that had to find out about the political situation.

The post office at that place was Turnerville. Names of some of the people were: Waites, Phillips, Montgomery, Bishop, Green, James, Shoemaker, Smith, Gregory, Windham, Jourdan, Sims, McCarty, Wood, Fail, McLaurin, Rainer, Mosely, Aaron, Evans, Richardson, Lee, Hare, Massey, Ervin.

### JASPER'S FORTY NINER
(A sketch of the life of Arch Pruitt was given the writer by his son, Charles Henry Pruitt.)

The Pruitt family lived in Noxubee County, Miss., when Arch became a young man. The M. & O. Railroad was being built and sometimes he would talk with a man from St. Louis that knew of the gold field in California. Sometimes he would get a newspaper with a glowing account of the gold field. He saw a man from Jackson who said that people were going from there by way of New Orleans. He had a young friend who was willing to make the trip with him. They secured enough money as they thought necessary to make the trip and caught a way to Jackson where they boarded the train for New Orleans. There they found that most of those going to the field were going by way of Panama by a vessel cross the isthmus and then board a vessel to San Francisco. They decided to take this route, caught a sailing ship to San Francisco which took them four months. When there was no wind the vessel could not go and when the wind was from the wrong direction, the going was very slow and they stopped at each town for trading. They arrived at San Francisco with a fair crowd, going to the gold field.

They gathered together and pledged to protect each other and decided on what arms and ammunition they would carry as they had heard that there was a lot of robbing and killing in the gold field. They decided on Mercer County as the first place to go. The going was not always smooth but they did fairly well the first few years, but after the Civil War had been going on about two years they heard it whispered that California might conscript everybody and make them fight for the Union. The Southern boys did not like this, and so they had heard of a gold field in British Columbia and so a crowd decided to try and make it to this field. They went overland by pack mules but found that this field was not so good as California.

So after the war was over they went back to California by steamer. After staying there for a few more years they began to get homesick and had quite a bit of money. They could always trade their bullion for money and so the scheme for caring for their money on the way home was to get large denomination bills and sew some in the linings of their coats, some in their socks and some inside pockets of their trousers. They decided to go back the same way that they came out: there, but when they arrived at Panama they found no boat to New Orleans. They took one to New York and went from there to St. Louis and down the M. & O. to Macon.

When Pruitt went to his old home he found strangers there. They told him that his people had moved to Jasper County but that they did not know what part of Jasper they were in. He went back to Macon and took the train for Enterprise.

He noticed a lot of brick making and people building brick stores and new homes being built and was told that Gen. Sherman had burned all stores and homes and that they were building new ones. He went to the traders camp and found some Jasper people and they told him that they had heard of some Pruitts north of Missionary and that came to old Three-Chopped Way by Missionary and that he could ride back with them to Missionary.

As soon as he arrived at Missionary he began to travel north and came to a home and asked about the Pruitts. The woman was Mrs. Kit Reed, his sister. He soon bought eleven hundred acres of black land which included a home site on Moss Hill (said to be one of the most beautiful places in east Mississippi) and there lived the balance of his days. His daughter, Myra, still lives on the same place.

**August 22, 1957**

# HISTORY OF JASPER COUNTY

### By J. M. KENNEDY

**PESTLE ROCK—WATER MILLS**

The Indians used what was called the pestle rock to crush their corn and wheat for making bread. The pestle rock was a bowl-shaped rock (flint) and a round-headed rock to fit in the bowl part, where the corn or wheat was placed. The corn or wheat was pounded in this manner until it was fit to make bread. This rock was also used for making fire.

Before the days of matches people kept plenty of ashes in the large fireplace to cover up the fire at night or when not in use. Dry oak was used for this purpose. After it was burning well, the oak was covered in ashes and would last all night. Sometimes it would go out and then the people would have to go to their neighbors for fire if they did not have a pestle rock. There was an old saying, when one made a short visit the people would ask did you come for fire. Some of the mountaineers have bragged that their fire had not been out in a hundred years.

As soon as Jasper County was settled water mills were soon built. They were called water mills because they used water power to turn the mill. It was evident that the mill had to be built on a stream that had a large and constant flow of water and even then it was necessary to construct a large dam in order to hold a supply of water in reserve.

Montrose and Louin had the Gardner mill on the stream that bears that name just before it enters Tallahoma. Garlandsville and Hero used the mill just over the line in Newton County, to the rear of Mt Vernon church, known as the Morris mill. Missionary had two mills, the Green and Morris mills on Goodwater Creek. Paulding had two on Town Creek, Round and McDougal mills, the last one was run by Julius Heidelberg in its last days. Phalti had the McGlouthin mill, later Cook, then Garner, and then Elkins. The southern part of the county had Andrews mill near Corinth church. J. C. Andrews was detailed during the Civil War to run his mill when he had water to grind corn for the soldiers. The Jackson Daily News had a picture and write-up of the mill and Andrews in 1937.

Albritton mill was west of Stringer on Roaring Creek. It was a voting place for the southwest beat for a long time. Keys mill was just west of Bay Springs which served this part of the county.

Bounds water mill, located three miles southeast of Vossburg is more than a hundred years old and is still in use.

Cotton in the early days was ginned by horse power. The gin house was large and had stalls which you would have to go and engage and place your cotton there to await its time for ginning. They only ginned about two bales a day. They had a high press with long levers to which horses were hitched to press the cotton in bales. Steam power came into the county in the eighties. The writer remembers picking cotton late in the afternoon with brothers, sisters and some Negro children and Henry Read (Bob's father) had finished installing his steam mill and gin and was blowing his steam loud and long to let the people know that he was ready to grind corn and gin cotton. We listened with wide opened eyes, and after listening a while, a Negro boy cried out that it was coming that way. Soon the cotton patch had no pickers.

The country was very quiet save for the jay bird, woodpeckers, cow bells, the coon and fox hunters and at eleven-thirty, dinner horns. In event of distress, you were supposed to blow your dinner horn a long time if you needed help. We heard the dinner horn one day at ten o'clock, blowing a long time. Soon the road was sounding with horses' heels; old man Glover had plowed to near that time and had reached his porch and fell dead.

**SPECIAL TAX FOR NEGRO SCHOOLS.**

Jasper was the first county in the state to levy a special tax for Negro schools. This was done in 1936, which led to the establishment of an agricultural high school for Negroes. The colored boys and girls could take their potatoes, eggs, butter, etc., to the dormitory and attend an accredited high school in the county for the first time in their lives. Before that time they had to go to Laurel or Meridian for this service.

The school was located in the northeast beat, near Penantly, and they secured the largest C. W. A. project in the state up to that time. P. H. Easom took up the work and it soon spread to all parts of the state. Hinds County bought Utica Institute from some northern church and put on a levy to support it. It is now one of the largest Negro schools in the state. Jones County put on a special levy for Negroes even though they had a very few in the county. They now have a large Smith-Hughes school for Negroes. Since then large consolidated schools have been established for Negroes; Cottage Hill, Bay Springs, Shady Grove, Leona, etc.

One of the former teachers of Jasper is now president of the Colored State Teachers' Association, Grantham. Excerpts from his speech were printed in most of the daily papers.

**BAPTIST CHURCHES**

Palestine. We have already spoken of Rev. Jackson Smith being the father of Smithtown. He also organized Palestine which has been a strong church with a large cemetery. At the recent funeral of R. A. Smith the large brick church would not hold half of the attendants. In digging a grave there a few years ago, they dug into another grave and found a tintype picture which was still recognizable. Since the early days it has been the voting place in the northwestern part of Beat One. Some of the people were: Smith, Brady, Knotts, Anderson, Parker, Rainer, Temple, Blackledge.

Montrose. In the early days the Baptist church stood just east of Montrose on the Paulding road where the old Jackson Highway crossed it, running northeast by Dr. Smith, E. Sumrall and G. T. Neill to Highway 15 at Richmond James. The name of this church was Liberty. After the railroad passed through Montrose the church was moved to town. Some of the names connected with this church were: James, Sumrall, Knotts, Neill, Alexander, Bayless.

Union Seminary. The writer was riding with Bill Morris one day near Union Seminary and he called my attention to an old reedbrake farm and said that Wade Crawford preached at Union Seminary in the early days, and that Wade told this, how to lay it off as he (Wade) had a reedbrake farm near Enterprise. Wade also has a law suit listed in the Supreme Court records in 1848. So, if Wade Crawford is right, it must be an old one. It is situated about three miles northeast of Mossville. Some of the names in this section are: Windham, Graham, Williams, Hardy, Ulmer, Poor, Currie, Childers, Hosey, Evans, McSwain.

Phalti Church. Soon after the organization of the county Phalti church was organized. It was located on the northern side of Beat 5 and was made a voting precinct. After the church was discontinued the precinct was moved to a nearby water mill and named Cook's Mill.

Down the hill from the church was a large gushing spring which caused the property later to be bought and beautiful lakes were made and cottages built for a recreation place.

A story is told that at the election of 1876, the whites had a row and began to shoot but somehow the bullet always hit a Negro. At one time this was a strong community with such names as Arledge, Rogers, Parker, Cook, Thigpen, Berry (Maj.), Garner, Bingham, Gough, Noble, Smith and Johnson.

Shady Grove. This church was organized in 1845. This church at first was very strong but by the coming of the railroad, members went to Heidelberg. It is located near the famous Stafford Springs. Early names were Bounds, Allen, Ellis, Thomas, Heidelberg, Sanders, Thornton and Cooley.

Louin. In the early days, Henry Barbour went to the Louin community and organized a church and the name that was given it was Mt. Vernon. A small log house was built. In 1897, the community had enough children to have two teachers in the school — Will Simmons, son of the Rev. John Simmons, and Miss Nora Smith. They were soon married. Will became superintendent of education and a member of the legislature from Smith County and later went to Pearl River County where he taught and reared a large family.

With the coming of the railroad some of the members advocating joining the Baptist State Convention, part opposed it and a division was made in the church and thus another Baptist church. Some of the early names were: Grayson, Parker, Boyd, Smith, Ainsworth, Simmons, Ritchie, Ball, Bassett, Ishee, James, Jones, Brown, Buchanan

**August 29, 1957**

# HISTORY OF JASPER COUNTY

By J. M. KENNEDY

### BAPTIST CHURCHES
(Continued)

Ebeneezer was one of the first churches in the county as it was the churches of old Claiborne, one of the first voting places and still is. Some of the names in the cemetery are: Travis, Herrington, Thornton, Cook, Wheeler, Brady, Donald, McCurty.

Corinth. Corinth is located in the southern part of the county on the east side of Talahalla near the old Anders mill site. It dates back before the Civil War and is still a strong church. Some of the names are Patrick, Myrick, Ulmer, Robinson, McCurty, Andrews, Wheeler.

Enon Church was organized about 1874 and was first located on the east side of Talahalla but later moved to the present site in the southern part of Beat One. It is supported by Cook Waldrup, Stockman, Massey, Medlin, Windham, Lee, Hair.

Eden is in the southwest part of the county and is surrounded by Williams, Ruffin, Gunter, Price, Massey, Elzey, Grissom.

Mossville and Stringer churches were organized with the coming of the railroad.

Bay Springs churches are similar to the history of Louin churches with the exception that it does not date so far back as the first Baptist in the Bay Springs community as old Nebo in Smith County. Later a church was located on the hill in the western part of town and later the same division came about as at Louin. Both are very strong churches.

The Primitive Baptists still have a church south of Louin, Bethel, and Bthlehem, east of Lake Como, and Providence near the Smith County line.

### Shady Grove Baptist Church
Jasper County, Mississippi

Shady Grove Church was established as a Campbelite Baptist Church by William C. Bownds (or Bounds) and his brother, Rev. John Bownds and others in the community about 1845. The church was used as a community house as well as a church until about 1890. Mr. A. A. Allen taught school in the church.

William C. Bownds' daughter Araminta, was buried in the Shady Grovge cemetery in 1847.

In 1867, Mrs. John Chapman Bownds, the former Mary A. Donald wrote:

"It looks like the age of darkness is coming over us. Almost all of those who in former days were our guides and instructors in the way of religion are the ones to be the most afflicted and taken away from us. Brother Thigher has been suffering with a complaint in his eyes for several months. It was thought for some time that he would go blind but I hear he is getting a little better Brother Heslip has quit preaching on account of a complaint in his head. I understand that Brother Sumnall has quit preaching in order to make a support for his family. Brother West too, I suppose, has nearly quit only hear home. He has to work to support his family. I do not know what will become of us. We have had some good meetings at Shady Grove. There were over two hundred members, white and black, but the whites have separated from the blacks. There were so many black members scattered over the country that the white members would not look after them and it was thought best to divide. Brother Ferrall preaches for us on the third Sunday and Saturday before. He also has the care of Ebenezer and Beaverdam Churches."

John Chapman Bownds, son of William C. Bownds, was licensed to preach in the fall of 1866, by the Shady Grove Church, but died before he was able to fill that place.

Mary A. Donald Bownds, in a letter written Dec. 2, 1867, says:

"The Sabbath school scholars and everybody else that wanted to, met at Shady Grove and had their Bible Day. All of the scholars had nice appropriate pieces on the scriptures, some committed their pieces to memory, and some read them. It was surely a nice thing. They all behaved so nice and everything was so quiet and calm. I wanted all of my folks to be there and enjoy it too. The Sabbath school has been going on all the fall and had very good attendance. Had a big crowd for dinner and then another crowd came in for the evening and had a big sing. Some of the girls caught beaux. Shady Grove Church called Bro. Hall to serve them again next year. Brother Hall with others held a meeting awhile back at Vossburg and got six members: a Mr. Bynum, young Allen Morris, Ida and Asa Voss, Henry's wife, Jenia Heidelberg, all for baptism."

January, 1890—

"It is becoming very fashionable to take buggy rides on Sunday afternoon. Nearly everyone has buggies: Mr. Walker, Mr. Odom, John Cooley, Wm. Ellis, Billy Herrington, Bud McDonald, Jeff and Sam, your Uncle Austin (Bowndes), Mr. Arrington. When we go to church on Sunday it looks like everybody comes in buggies. Several come from Heidelberg and Vossburg."

From a letter by Mrs. Bowndes to her son, Joe (Tobe), who became a minister:

"Tobe, you asked me what I thought about you going to school to Brother Martin. It might be a good thing for you. He could give you instructions in the Bible. He had a piece in the last Standard that was a very good piece. He is sincere in his belief. The crowd at the Association was Mr. Obe Robinson, Cousin Dick, Brother Turner and a Brother Tolbert, a teacher of the Indians, Brother Thigpen, Clark Shows, Willie Thigpen and Brother Hall.

"If you had been at the Association you could have taken the Colportage work. Brother Clark on Monday called on anyone in the house who was an upright man to take the Colportage work. No one responded to the call. They made up some money to start one the next meeting of the board. That will be the first Sunday in December. Theodore says if you would be here then you could get it if you would write to them soon. Brother Hall had to go to his appointment at Quitman on Saturday and Sunday. He left the note with Brother Bush and he read it in the meeting but you not being present they couldn't proceed."

Mrs. Bowndes writing November 11, 1899:

"The great Sam Jones has been at Meridian. They were to give him a thousand dollars to come there. Some talked like he put the Meridian folks down pretty low and then told them if he hadn't stripped the feathers off they to meet him at the door after dismissal and he would finish the job."

---

This information was furnished me by Mr. P. W. Merrill, who was born in Jasper County 1866, and letters from my grandmother Mary A. Donald (Mrs. John Chapman Bownds). I am anxious to exchange genealogical information.

Lennie Bownds Allen,
(Mrs. Lamar Allen, Jr.)
7120 Dalewood Lane
Dallas, Texas.

September 5, 1957

JASPER COUNTY NEWS, BAY SPRINGS, MISSISSIPPI — THURSDAY, SEPT. 5, 1957

# HISTORY OF JASPER COUNTY

By J. M. KENNEDY

**THE BAPTISTS**
(Continued)

In the early days the only requirement to be licensed to preach was that he was called to preach. This gave plenty of preachers and they went out and preached under bush arbours, goat houses, homes, school houses etc. The writer remembers that when a small boy he was sitting one night at the edge of a bush arbour, the lights poor, and all at once a man came from the dark crawling on his allfours. I was very much frightened as I thought the Baptists were changing into cows. It was explained to me later that this man had fever which caused his legs below his knees to wither and this was the only way he could get about. The old people remembered him as Tommy McCarthy. Rev. George Boyd was conducting the meeting.

In 1920 when the writer was in Washington, D. C., it was announced in the daily papers that the Southern Baptist Convention would meet in Washington and that the meeting would be held in the Billy Sunday Tabernacle. Bill Upshaw told them that the building would not hold the Baptists, that they would think that the "ground was alive with Baptist" when they came to town. Sure enough when the meeting opened the building would not seat all; one old brother with his saddle bags arrived in union station and asked where the meeting was held was pointed to it near by; he walked up to the building and noticed a large crowd, attempted to walk in when he was caught by a Negro policeman and told that all seats were filled. He walked back to the station and caught the next train home, saying that the Baptists had turned to D-yankees.

The people of Jasper should remember Bill Upshaw. He fell on a wagon and broke his back when only eighteen. After he was treated for some time the doctors told that they could do nothing for him and that he could never walk. He began to ask the young people to come to see him and would beg them not to do as he had done, wasting his time frolicking when young"... He would write to the junior department of the Atlanta Constitution. He asked the readers to send him a dime so that he could build on to his bedroom so that his visitors could have room. The writer sent his dime. Later a plaster of paris jacket was found to enable him to sit erect, but he could not use his legs very much on account of the injury of his spine. He secured a rolling chair and sold books to send himself to school. He became a lecturer and an editor and was elected to Congress. When he was a lecturer he came to Bay Springs in 1908 to lecture to a teachers' Normal. The writer came down and found him at the Lewis hotel. After talking for about one hour, I told him that I wanted to run down to the swimming pool before we went to the school building; to my surprise he told me that he desired to go too. He had to be helped in the water but could handle himself then. He was then using two crutches to walk. I enjoyed his lecture very much. I was teaching in a normal at Louisville in 1910 and he came there to lecture. We were to carry our daughter to a certain school in Washington to deliver a recitation which she had delivered at her school closing and so started early to go by and see Bill. We had just heard of his arrival at Washington. After talking for awhile we told him that we had to go to a certain school in the city and he said that he had to go to that school to deliver the commencement address, so we all went together. When he was in Congress for the second term he arose one day and told them that he was very much concerned about a large majority of its members in regard to strong drink and that he thought that a man so honored should not be guilty of such a thing, they began to boo him and he reached down and pulled a list and told them that he would read the names of some patrons of a certain place in Washington, they adjourned. The next year it is said that the whiskey interest sent enough money to Georgia to have him defeated. In 1923 the writer had him at Bay Springs for a week. He spoke not only at Bay Springs but in a number of rural schools. He always had a large and cheering crowd.

Do not think that the above is off the subject as Bill was a great Baptist. All these things have paid off and now the Baptist claim 52% of the population of the state. Mississippi College has a greater attendance than Millsaps even though it is backed by the great city of Jackson, and plenty of money. When the writer was County Superintendent of Education, I was the only graduate of Millsaps while Mississippi College had more than 20.

Holiness. This sect has a church east of Antioch and a very strong church at Mossville, headed by Rev. Mathews. They are sometimes listed as the Church of God.

Presbyterians. We have given the early history of the Presbyterian church at Montrose and glad to say that it is still in existance.

The church at Garlandsville is perhaps older than the one at Montrose but we were unable to get any history about it except that Dr. Harry was a big donator to the endowment of Chamberlain-Hunt Academy.

Pisgah was founded in 1845 and still in existance. Some of the peole connected with it are: Collins, Benge, Abney, Risher, Bolding McLaurin, Lee, Windham, McCallum, Chambers. In later years a church has been organized at Heidelberg, McFarland and New Liberty.

We were glad to receive the article writen by Mrs. Allen of Dallas, Texas, about Shady Grove church in last week's issue. We have received a clipping from a Georgia paper from Mrs Lula Mae Grimsley, of Monrose, Louisiana, stating that the first Congregational Methodist church in Mississippi was organized in 1853, in the home of Rev. Henry T. Jones, who lived at Oak Bowery 10 miles south of Paulding. The writer remembers this building which stood near the home of Singleton Risher and consisted of two stories, first floor for preaching and the second for Oak Bowery Masonic Lodge. Glad to get this clipping. We shall be glad for anyone to send in history that we have not had or any correction but must sent it in at once.

*End of Articles*

# Paulding, Mississippi - Queen City of the East

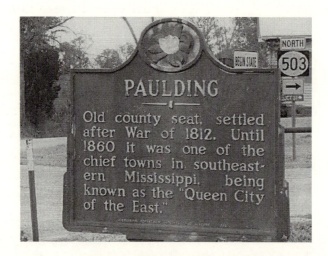

Of all the Jasper County, Mississippi locations that I have attempted to research and write about, Paulding has proven to be one of the most difficult. Although it is was once a major commercial location within the new Mississippi territory, fate and circumstance led it down a path to physical and historical obscurity.

Paulding was settled about 1833 and named for a local resident. John Paulding, a Revolutionary War hero. It became a major hub of commerce, situated at an intersection of the few major roads that existed in those early days. Paulding also became the seat of Jasper County and boasted a brick courthouse of considerable stature. It is reported that the bricks used in it's construction were manufactured on-site by negro slaves.

There are numerous mentions in the period writings of local authors regarding the legal proceedings that took place at the courthouse in Paulding. For example, the J.M. Kennedy articles included in this book reference the activities at Paulding numerous times.

Following the War Between the States, Paulding was bypassed by the chosen railroad route and soon fell prey to economic hardship. Nearby, the cities of Bay Springs and Vossburg began to grow and flourish.

On September 10, 1932, the historic courthouse at Paulding burned. There are numerous rumors regarding how and why the fire started, but none, to my knowledge that were ever proven. Sadly, many irreplaceable historic records of Jasper County were lost, a situation that has served to make the efforts of many researchers difficult or impossible.

*Based upon the remaining records, verbal descriptions, and the Federal Architecture style employed during the time period for other Mississippi courthouses, this photograph is likely representative of the original Jasper County courthouse.*

Today, there is little remaining of Paulding and it bears the distinction of being the only unincorporated county seat within the state of Mississippi. Out of respect, I assume, this distinction is maintained.

Included here are some 1932 newspaper clippings regarding the loss of the Paulding courthouse and some additional Paulding history.

(Continued on Page Thirteen)

## Courthouse At Paulding Built By Slaves, Burns

BAY SPRINGS, Sept. 10 — When fire destroyed the old courthouse at Paulding at an early hour this morning one of the oldest landmarks of east Mississippi went into oblivion. Built in 1837 the old building had witnessed many forensic battles between southern notables.

It was at Paulding the old Clarion which many years afterward was moved to Jackson and subsequently became the present Clarion-Ledger, espoused the cause of Jefferson Davis, who afterwards become United States senator and for years was a great legal light in Mississippi.

The fire was discovered about three o'clock by the parish priest who sounded an alarm. However, when residents of the little hamlet got to the building nothing save two typewriters, a few books and the board of supervisors' minute book were saved. Valuable records which can never be replaced were destroyed as were the contents of the 11-ton safe which is said to have had its doors open at the time the fire was raging.

The safe had been locked the night before with what record books could be stored in it. It also was said by persons who first got to the fire that the blaze started at the north end of the building and the doors on the sides of the hall were burning fiercely. The building was built of brick made by slave labor.

Paulding many years ago was one of the largest towns in this section of the south known as the Queen City of the east. It is said to have ranked third in point of population at one time, New Orleans, Mobile and Paulding the most populous towns of that period.

Beginning sometime after the War Between the States Paulding dwindled into a mere hamlet with one general store building and the courthouse. It was the only one in the county until the second judicial district was created in 1906 and a few residences besides Catholic and Methodist churches and the high school are all that remain.

It is the concensus of opinion that the fire was of incendiary origin but for what reasons the courthouse was destroyed is a mystery that is baffling to officials as well as the general public. There was no insurance carried on the courthouse.

## Historic Paulding Made Deserted Village as Old Courthouse Burns

(By The Associated Press)
Paulding, Miss., Sept. 10. — Fire destroyed one old building here, today and made this historic town a deserted village.

It was a courthouse—a musty thing that clung precariously together by the grace of gravity and around which Mississippians gathered to discuss the atrocity of the Alamo when that massacre was fresh in the minds of Americans.

Jasper county invested its fortune in the red brick structure in 1837 and folks came from over all South Mississippi to water their horses at its trough and gaze at its two-storied magnificence.

Fire early today destroyed it and all records and equipment except a few books.

There was no fire department in Paulding. In fact, there is nothing left in Paulding except some tumbled down mansions, some shady burial grounds and an aloof pride. It is a village that a railroad dodged and in its declining years it changed from a bustling little city to a drowsy hamlet where hogs rooted in the streets and darkies whittled soft pine around the "co'tehouse."

A hundred years ago Paulding was the center of activity in these parts. All wagon roads led here. Irish settlers came from the old country, built their little chapel and with their fists and brains fought their way to leadership of Mississippi affairs. They intermarried with the old families of Jasper and together they made Paulding a city.

Then came the railroad. The town divided over the wisdom of granting a right of way and the railroad, anxious to lay its tracks from Meridian to New Orleans, ducked Paulding and built through Vossburg. Paulding didn't care much then—after all the noise of those chubby little engines frightened fine horses

Continued on Page Two

## Courthouse Fires Mount

### PORTION OF JASPER RECORDS SAFE

## Mississippi's Total 29

Not all of Jasper county's valued records went up in smoke when the historic Paulding courthouse burned Saturday, Dr. R. N. Whitfield of the state bureau of vital statistics revealed here Monday.

Dr. Whitfield said the state bureau had obtained 5080 records of white marriages occurring in the county between October, 1867, and January 1, 1926, in its campaign to collect statistics for the period prior to the bureau's founding in 1925. The records were obtained March 21, 1930, he said.

Dr. Whitfield said the bureau had collected back records in excess of 200,000 dating back as far as 1802 in one county—Adams.

Commenting on the Paulding fire, Dr. Whitfield said courthouse blazes have been the greatest source of loss to valued paper. Files in his office disclosed that more than one-third of Mississippi's courthouses at one time or another have been wholly or partially destroyed by fire, with total loss of records reported in many instances.

The bureau files, although incomplete, revealed that twenty-nine of the state's courthouses have been burned. The list, with date of fires, follows:

Attala, 1896; Bolivar, 1881; Calhoun, 1922; Choctaw, 1878; Clarke, 1853; Coahoma, late in the 1940's; Covington, 1905; Perry, 1805; Franklin, 1876; Holmes, 1894; Jasper, 1932; Jefferson, 1903; Jones, 1867; Kemper, 1912; Lauderdale, 1963; Lawrence, 1932; Lincoln, 1890 and 1893; Newton, 1919; Pike, 1882; Rankin, 1924; Scott, twice since 1880; Simpson, 1844 and 1872; Tallahatchie, 1909; Tishomingo, 1887; Union, 1880; Wayne, 1879 and 1892.

Others for which dates were not available were: Alcorn, Lee and Montgomery.

## ANCIENT MISSISSIPPI COURTHOUSE BURNS

BAY SPRINGS, Miss., Sept. 10. —(UP)—The 95-year-old courthouse at Paulding, one of the two county seats of Jasper county, was destroyed by fire today, together with all its records. The courthouse was built in 1837. Origin of the blaze was unknown.

## HISTORIC PAULDING COURTHOUSE BURNS

### Continued from Page One

and the smoke was bad on the damask of the manors.

So Paulding started dying. The first blow came when Bay Springs was made a county seat, and the county had two capitals. Business drifted away and so did the families until only the courthouse and post-office remained. Sometimes the judge and lawyers would drive over from the river at Vossburg and hold court, but they usually would go to some nearby town for the nights.

The courthouse had big iron stars on its sides and the voices of Mississippi's great have been heard in its corridors.

There gathered the heads of the families in those days when America was quickening to news that South Carolina had left the Union. Jasper county was to instruct its delegate to the secession convention. Neighboring Jones county had voted against secession and all the South was watching this strategic county.

The men parked their gold-headed canes against the courthouse's walls and roared so the crowd outside heard—"Jasper county goes for secession."

### SUPERVISORS' BOOK SAVED FROM FIRE

(Special to The Times-Picayune)
Bay Springs, Miss., Sept. 10.—The courthouse at Paulding was the oldest brick building in this section of Mississippi. Only the present minute books of the board of supervisors and a few other small books were saved in the fire which destroyed it today, according to reports to officers here.

Deputy Clerk Lex Brame, son of T. Q. Brame, chancery clerk, who resides in Paulding, said a negro woman living near by reported having seen a car drive to the building 30 minutes before the fire was discovered and then drive away. Brame reached the building too late to save any records except the books mentioned. He says the vaults and the doors were open then, but that he had closed and locked them last night.

The jail, a brick building, and the postoffice, a frame structure, in the square with the courthouse, were saved.

The courthouse had two stories, the upper being used as a courtroom and the lower floor for county officers' offices.

A visit to present day Paulding will not reveal any hints to it's previous glory. Only a few traces of the old architecture remain, one of which are the ruins of the original jail that remains near the site of the old courthouse. One antiquated general store building remains but has adapted a convenience store format once inside.

*The remains of the old jail*

*Interior of the jail and the lone cage cell*

*Photo of the old Jasper County Jail, taken in 1969 by Sheriff Tom R. Green*

*The old general store building*

Records show that a few Catholic missionaries came to the Choctaw Indian territory several years before the land was taken over by the US Government and opened for settlement. In later years there was a sizable migration of Irish immigrants into Mississippi who were almost exclusively of the Catholic faith. This is evidenced by the early formation of the St. Michael Church and the many Irish sir names etched on the markers in the adjoining cemetery.

*The present day Saint Michael Church building*

*Saint Michael Cemetery*

*A sample of the 1st generation Irish settlers who found their final resting place in Paulding.*

# St. Michaels prepares for 140th anniversary

The second oldest Roman Catholic church in Mississippi will celebrate its 140 anniversary next Sunday.

St. Michaels was established approximately 31 years after Paulding was settled some time after the War of 1812.

Both share a rich history which is firmly rooted in the history of Paulding.

On September 26 Holy Eucharist will begin the anniversary celebration, with the Most Reverend Joseph B. Bunini, Bishop of the Catholic Diocese celebrant at the service.

The present church was dedicated on March 2, 1945 after a fire destroyed St. Michaels on July 3, 1942. The new brick structure was built with money from parishoners, an insurance settlement and a donation from the Extension Society.

The original structure had been the first parish church to be built in Mississippi with the exception of St. Mary's Cathedral in Natchez.

Not only were prominent Jasper names members of the church, including Col. Oliver Dease and James J. Shannon, editor of the Eastern Clarion (later the Clarion Ledger,) but the members and priest were actively involved in the War Between the States.

The Jasper Greys left Paulding in April 1861, under the leadership of Captain James Shannon, Bishop elder appointed Father Boheme as chaplain in 1862. He died on July 27, 1862 on the field of battle and was buried in Richmond.

In 1899 the annual report stated that Hattiesburg, Ellisville and Laurel were at that time missions attached to Paulding. There was a parish school located near the church from 1859 to 1978. Another school, St. Josephs, located north of Paulding operated from 1874 to 1877.

The Cistercian Monastery of Our Lady of Geroval was dedicated on September 9, 1935, which was through Father Dogny's contact with the Monks during his schooling in France. Upon Father Dogny's death, the Cistercian Monks were placed in charge of St. Michaels.

Twenty seven daughters of the St. Michaels parish have entered the religious life along with a parishioner who became a religious brother.

The celebration Sunday will combine the past with the future. A picnic lunch will be held on the church lawn following the morning service. Honored guests for the day will include Bishop Brunini and seven daughters of the parish who are members of the Sisters of Mercy.

*Newspaper clip dated 9/22/82*

# Davisville and Old Salem

In the infancy of Jasper County, a limited network of roads existed. Most of these intersected at the city of Paulding, then referred to as the Queen City of the East. Early Mississippi maps, published in the 1850 time frame, list the sizable community named Davisville. Davisville was located approximately 10 miles to the southeast of Paulding and was situated on the main road that led toward Waynesboro, MS and Mobile, AL. Early land patents support the notion that the Davisville community was centered north east of the present day intersection between the Vossburg/Paulding Road and Interstate 59.

How this community came to be know as Davisville is unknown, but it is reasonable to assume that it may have been named after Hosea Davis. Davis settled in the area on an unknown date, later securing the title a 40 acre parcel during January of 1841. While the founding date of Davisville is unknown, the community likely predates 1833. This claim is supported by the Edward Young Terrall Sr. grave that lies within the Old Salem Cemetery. Following, and likely before, the 1830 Treaty of Dancing Rabbit, settlers began to move into the Choctaw Territory. Many of these people built cabins and made land improvements before they had any legal claim to the land. Naturally, this caused a great deal of grief for some who fell victim to land speculators who sought out developed lands and purchase it from the government when legal sale began during January of 1841. Subsequent settlers appear to have favored the same area as Hosea Davis and secured lands in or near Section 26, Township 2 N, Range 13 E. Most likely, this choice corresponded with the availability of water. Most of these people purchased small plots of 40 to 80 acres, indicating that the community was mostly comprised of small sustenance farmers.

From official U.S. Post Office records, we know that a post office was established at Davisville on January 4, 1852. A stage coach stop, a general store, and at least one community church, Salem Baptist (Old Salem Baptist), also existed. Land patents for the area also support that, Drury Allen Morris, owner of the general store and the Davisville postmaster, May 1, 1857 until December 7, 1871, lived near the location of the remaining Old Salem Cemetery. Records also confirm that Morris served as the Representative from Jasper County in the Mississippi State Legislature during the 1880 – 1882 sessions.

*A portrait of Drury Allen Morris. It was among the possessions of Lillian Morris Hays, daughter of Samuel Jackson Morris (Grandson of D.A. Morris) and Fannie Eddins Morris. During her life, Lillian conveyed that her Great Grandfather, Drury Allen Morris, lived in Jasper County Mississippi, served as the postmaster of Davisville, owned and operated a general store, was a 32nd degree Mason, and served as a Representative in the State Legislature. He was of the Baptist faith and married Phebe Terral. She also stated that Drury and Phebe are buried within the Old Salem Cemetery. (Their graves are unmarked).*

In the death of Drury Allen Morris, of Jasper county, one of the landmarks of the state of Mississippi has passed away. He was one of the pioneers of Jasper county, and was the first to whom a marriage license was issued in the county, but his name will live forever as the instigator of an oratorical bon-mot that will never fall into disuse in his state. About fifty years ago, when Henry S. Foote and John J. McRae were stumping the state for and against secession and for the governorship, Mr. Foote, who was one of the most distinguished orators of that time, often meeting the wonderful Prentiss on the busting and twice on the field of honor, asked in loud tones and a theatrical manner, in a speech at Paulding, "Is there in this vast assembly, any man so unpatriotic, and so lost to every sense of propriety, as to wish to dissolve this g-l-o-r-i-o-u-s union?" "Yes, by ---, here is one!" replied Mr. Morris, rising from his seat and striking his breast with his clenched fist. "Mighty God! Men of Jasper! Do you hear that!" Mr. Morris lived to be nearly ninety years of age, but it was not long enough to see the old exclamation forgotten, and the "Mighty men of Jasper" have been heard from at every state convention since that time.

*[From the Daily Herald (Biloxi, Mississippi), dated April 15, 1904]*

In researching the community of Davisville, the author made the assumption that Salem Baptist Church was likely near the geographic center of the community. Because the cemetery lies within a stone's throw from the present day Vossburg/Paulding road (CR-119), it was assumed that the road remains near it's original location. Using a section map of Jasper county, he made the further assumption that, due to the limited transportation means of those days, the size of the community likely encompassed no more than a two mile radius from the church. Referring to the following map, this equates to sixteen sections of land, the center falling at the Old Salem Church and cemetery.

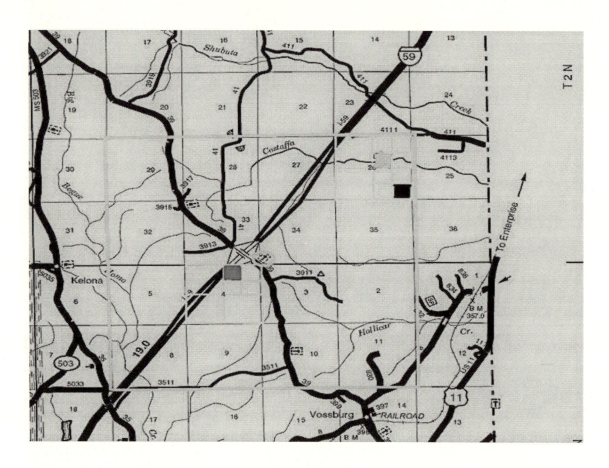

*Color Codes:*

*Light Gray Box = The Hosea Davis Homestead*

*Black Box = The William Eddins Homestead*

*Dark Gray Box = The Drury Allen Morris Homestead*

By searching the records of the original land patents issued for these sixteen sections, we can piece together the names of the families who settled within the community of Davisville. Many of these names are familiar to present day residents and appear on the few stone grave markers that remain within the cemetery. The following records correspond to the land sections described in the above map.

| View Image | Patentee Name | State | County | Issue Date | Land Office | Doc. Nr. | Accession/Serial Nr. |
|---|---|---|---|---|---|---|---|
| 📄 | BARKSDALE, NATHAN | MS | Jasper | 9/20/1873 | Jackson | 86 | MS2320___076 |
| 📄 | GRANT, GREEN W | MS | Jasper | 1/5/1841 | Augusta | 6228 | MS0730___310 |
| 📄 | HERNDON, THOMAS H | MS | Jasper | 1/5/1841 | Augusta | 6228 | MS0730___310 |
| 📄 | NELSON, JERRY | MS | Jasper | 11/10/1882 | Jackson | 1977 | MS2350___355 |
| 📄 | PROCTOR, FARR | MS | Jasper | 1/5/1841 | Augusta | 3974 | MS0690___340 |
| 📄 | WEST, CHARLES M | MS | Jasper | 8/9/1897 | Jackson | 15873 | MS0910___300 |

Residents of Section 29, Township 2, Range 13 E

| View Image | Patentee Name | State | County | Issue Date | Land Office | Doc. Nr. | Accession/Serial Nr. |
|---|---|---|---|---|---|---|---|
| 📄 | FARR, ALFRED | MS | Jasper | 1/5/1841 | Augusta | 4335 | MS0700___176 |
| 📄 | FARR, ALFRED | MS | Jasper | 1/5/1841 | Augusta | 5965 | MS0730___236 |
| 📄 | GRANT, GREEN W | MS | Jasper | 1/5/1841 | Augusta | 6230 | MS0740___026 |
| 📄 | HERNDON, THOMAS H | MS | Jasper | 1/5/1841 | Augusta | 6230 | MS0740___026 |
| 📄 | HODGES, ISHAM | MS | Jasper | 1/5/1841 | Augusta | 3653 | MS0690___041 |
| 📄 | REID, ELLE | MS | Jasper | 5/2/1859 | Augusta | 9664 | MS0800___315 |
| 📄 | REID, ELLE | MS | Jasper | 5/2/1859 | Augusta | 9823 | MS0800___419 |

Residents of Section 28, Township 2, Range 13 E

| View Image | Patentee Name | State | County | Issue Date | Land Office | Doc. Nr. | Accession/Serial Nr. |
|---|---|---|---|---|---|---|---|
| 📄 | CARAWAY, EDWIN S | MS | Jasper | 1/5/1841 | Augusta | 684 | MS0630___155 |
| 📄 | CHERRY, WILLIAM P | MS | Jasper | 1/5/1841 | Augusta | 4982 | MS0710___277 |
| 📄 | COLEMAN, THOMAS J | MS | Jasper | 1/5/1841 | Augusta | 6557 | MS0740___322 |
| 📄 | FARR, ALFRED | MS | Jasper | 1/5/1841 | Augusta | 6153 | MS0730___424 |
| 📄 | FATHEREE, JOHN | MS | Jasper | 1/5/1841 | Augusta | 4997 | MS0710___292 |
| 📄 | FATHEREE, WILLIAM | MS | Jasper | 1/5/1841 | Augusta | 6357 | MS0740___139 |

Residents of Section 27, Township 2, Range 13 E

| View Image | Patentee Name | State | County | Issue Date | Land Office | Doc. Nr. | Accession/Serial Nr. |
|---|---|---|---|---|---|---|---|
| 📄 | DAVIS, HOSEA | MS | Jasper | 1/5/1841 | Augusta | 5823 | MS0730___100 |
| 📄 | EDDINGS, WILLIAM | MS | Jasper | 5/2/1859 | Augusta | 9972 | MS0810___022 |
| 📄 | EDDINS, WILLIAM | MS | Jasper | 5/2/1859 | Augusta | 9491 | MS0800___172 |
| 📄 | HESLIP, THOMAS B | MS | Jasper | 11/10/1859 | Augusta | 13968 | MS0870___137 |
| 📄 | HODGES, CHARLES | MS | Jasper | 3/15/1854 | Augusta | 9158 | MS0790___336 |
| 📄 | MORRIS, WILLIAM | MS | Jasper | 1/5/1841 | Augusta | 3834 | MS0690___209 |
| 📄 | RISHER, JOHN | MS | Jasper | 3/15/1854 | Augusta | 9220 | MS0790___392 |
| 📄 | RISHER, JOHN | MS | Jasper | 4/2/1860 | Augusta | 9971 | MS0870___242 |
| 📄 | TERRAL, THOMAS | MS | Jasper | 1/5/1841 | Augusta | 1261 | MS0640___221 |
| 📄 | TERRALL, EDWARD | MS | Jasper | 1/5/1841 | Augusta | 5821 | MS0730___098 |
| 📄 | TERRELL, EDWARD Y | MS | Jasper | 1/5/1841 | Augusta | 670 | MS0630___141 |
| 📄 | TERRELL, EDWARD Y | MS | Jasper | 1/5/1841 | Augusta | 671 | MS0630___142 |

Residents of Section 26, Township 2, Range 13 E

| View Image | Patentee Name | State | County | Issue Date | Land Office | Doc. Nr. | Accession/Serial Nr. |
|---|---|---|---|---|---|---|---|
| 📄 | **GRANT, GREEN W** | MS | Jasper | 1/5/1841 | Augusta | 6233 | MS0740__.029 |
| 📄 | **GRIMES, ELDRED C** | MS | Jasper | 4/2/1860 | Augusta | 14742 | MS0880__.335 |
| 📄 | **HERNDON, THOMAS H** | MS | Jasper | 1/5/1841 | Augusta | 6233 | MS0740__.029 |
| 📄 | **MADISON, HENRY E** | MS | Jasper | 10/23/1959 | Augusta | 09832 | 1200587 |
| 📄 | **ROWELL, DAVID H** | MS | Jasper | 4/2/1860 | Augusta | 14741 | MS0880__.334 |
| 📄 | **TERRELL, WILLIAM B** | MS | Jasper | 5/2/1859 | Augusta | 13560 | MS0850__.400 |

Residents of Section 32, Township 2, Range 13 E

| View Image | Patentee Name | State | County | Issue Date | Land Office | Doc. Nr. | Accession/Serial Nr. |
|---|---|---|---|---|---|---|---|
| 📄 | **GRANT, GREEN W** | MS | Jasper | 1/5/1841 | Augusta | 6229 | MS0730__.311 |
| 📄 | **HERNDON, THOMAS H** | MS | Jasper | 1/5/1841 | Augusta | 6229 | MS0730__.311 |
| 📄 | **MORRIS, WILLIAM** | MS | Jasper | 1/5/1841 | Augusta | 3714 | MS0690__.101 |
| 📄 | **MORRIS, WILLIAM** | MS | Jasper | 1/5/1841 | Augusta | 3835 | MS0690__.210 |

Residents of Section 33, Township 2, Range 13 E

| View Image | Patentee Name | State | County | Issue Date | Land Office | Doc. Nr. | Accession/Serial Nr. |
|---|---|---|---|---|---|---|---|
| 📄 | **GRANT, GREEN W** | MS | Jasper | 1/5/1841 | Augusta | 6231 | MS0740__.027 |
| 📄 | **HERNDON, THOMAS H** | MS | Jasper | 1/5/1841 | Augusta | 6231 | MS0740__.027 |
| 📄 | **TERRAL, JOSHUA** | MS | Jasper | 11/10/1859 | Augusta | 12913 | MS0860__.339 |
| 📄 | **TERRAL, JOSHUA** | MS | Jasper | 1/5/1841 | Augusta | 2662 | MS0670__.093 |
| 📄 | **TERRAL, JOSHUA** | MS | Jasper | 1/5/1841 | Augusta | 5703 | MS0720__.482 |

Residents of Section 34, Township 2, Range 13 E

| View Image | Patentee Name | State | County | Issue Date | Land Office | Doc. Nr. | Accession/Serial Nr. |
|---|---|---|---|---|---|---|---|
| 📄 | **MCKENZIE, DAVID R** | MS | Jasper | 5/6/1879 | Jackson | 976 | MS2330__.228 |
| 📄 | **TERRAL, JOSHUA** | MS | Jasper | 1/5/1841 | Augusta | 5704 | MS0720__.483 |
| 📄 | **TERRELL, JOSHUA** | MS | Jasper | 1/5/1841 | Augusta | 2884 | MS0670__.298 |
| 📄 | **TERRELL, JOSHUA** | MS | Jasper | 1/5/1841 | Augusta | 672 | MS0630__.143 |

Residents of Section 35, Township 2, Range 13 E

| View Image | Patentee Name | State | County | Issue Date | Land Office | Doc. Nr. | Accession/Serial Nr. |
|---|---|---|---|---|---|---|---|
| 📄 | **MADISON, HENRY E** | MS | Jasper | 10/23/1959 | Augusta | 09832 | 1200587 |
| 📄 | **NEALEY, EADY** | MS | Jasper | 4/2/1860 | Augusta | 10272 | MS0870__.251 |

Residents of Section 5, Township 1, Range 13 E

| View Image | Patentee Name | State | County | Issue Date | Land Office | Doc. Nr. | Accession/Serial Nr. |
|---|---|---|---|---|---|---|---|
| | GRANT, GREEN W | MS | Jasper | 1/5/1841 | Augusta | 6320 | MS0740__.106 |
| | HEIDLEBURG, SAMUEL C | MS | Jasper | 1/5/1841 | Augusta | 3647 | MS0690__.035 |
| | HERNDON, THOMAS H | MS | Jasper | 1/5/1841 | Augusta | 6320 | MS0740__.106 |
| | KILLIN, BENJAMIN F | MS | Jasper | 1/5/1841 | Augusta | 3658 | MS0690__.045 |
| | MORRIS, DRURY A | MS | Jasper | 3/15/1854 | Augusta | 9026 | MS0790__.217 |
| | MORRIS, WILLIAM | MS | Jasper | 1/5/1841 | Augusta | 3713 | MS0690__.100 |
| | MORRIS, WILLIAM | MS | Jasper | 1/5/1841 | Augusta | 5926 | MS0730__.198 |
| | RICH, DAVID | MS | Jasper | 1/5/1841 | Augusta | 3646 | MS0690__.034 |
| | RICH, DAVID E | MS | Jasper | 1/5/1841 | Augusta | 3728 | MS0690__.112 |
| | TERRELL, JAMES S | MS | Jasper | 1/5/1841 | Augusta | 753 | MS0630__.223 |
| | THOMAS, STEPHEN T | MS | Jasper | 1/5/1841 | Augusta | 6008 | MS0730__.279 |

Residents of Section 4, Township 1, Range 13 E

| View Image | Patentee Name | State | County | Issue Date | Land Office | Doc. Nr. | Accession/Serial Nr. |
|---|---|---|---|---|---|---|---|
| | TERRAL, JAMES S | MS | Jasper | 1/5/1841 | Augusta | 3733 | MS0690__.117 |
| | TERRAL, JAMES S | MS | Jasper | 1/5/1841 | Augusta | 6009 | MS0730__.280 |
| | TERRAL, PHEBE | MS | Jasper | 1/5/1841 | Augusta | 4243 | MS0700__.097 |
| | TERRAL, PHEBE | MS | Jasper | 1/5/1841 | Augusta | 5157 | MS0710__.450 |
| | TERRALL, JAMES | MS | Jasper | 1/5/1841 | Augusta | 4704 | MS0710__.011 |

Residents of Section 3, Township 1, Range 13 E

| View Image | Patentee Name | State | County | Issue Date | Land Office | Doc. Nr. | Accession/Serial Nr. |
|---|---|---|---|---|---|---|---|
| | JOURNAGAN, ROBERT D | MS | Jasper | 5/2/1859 | Augusta | 10770 | MS0820__.120 |
| | MCGEHEE, EDWIN F | MS | Jasper | 1/5/1841 | Augusta | 5810 | MS0730__.087 |
| | RODGERS, REDDICK | MS | Jasper | 1/5/1841 | Augusta | 3661 | MS0690__.048 |
| | RODGERS, RICHERSON R | MS | Jasper | 3/15/1854 | Augusta | 9013 | MS0790__.205 |
| | TERRAL, JOHN | MS | Jasper | 1/5/1841 | Augusta | 5156 | MS0710__.449 |
| | TERRAL, JOSHUA | MS | Jasper | 5/2/1859 | Augusta | 10016 | MS0810__.056 |
| | TERRAL, JOSHUA | MS | Jasper | 3/15/1854 | Augusta | 8936 | MS0790__.145 |
| | TERRAL, JOSHUA | MS | Jasper | 5/2/1859 | Augusta | 9975 | MS0810__.024 |
| | TERRAL, SAMUEL | MS | Jasper | 3/15/1854 | Augusta | 9025 | MS0790__.216 |
| | TERRAL, SAMUEL | MS | Jasper | 3/15/1854 | Augusta | 9219 | MS0790__.391 |
| | TERRAL, WILLIAM B | MS | Jasper | 3/15/1854 | Augusta | 9218 | MS0790__.390 |

Residents of Section 2, Township 1, Range 13 E

| View Image | Patentee Name | State | County | Issue Date | Land Office | Doc. Nr. | Accession/Serial Nr. |
|---|---|---|---|---|---|---|---|
| | GRAVES, RALPH | MS | Jasper | 1/5/1841 | Augusta | 4788 | MS0710__.090 |
| | MYLES, LEVIN | MS | Jasper | 1/5/1841 | Augusta | 887 | MS0630__.353 |
| | SCOTT, WILLIAM S | MS | Jasper | 1/5/1841 | Augusta | 4788 | MS0710__.090 |

Residents of Section 8, Township 1, Range 13 E

| View Image | Patentee Name | State | County | Issue Date | Land Office | Doc. Nr. | Accession/Serial Nr. |
|---|---|---|---|---|---|---|---|
| | GRAVES, RALPH | MS | Jasper | 1/5/1841 | Augusta | 4788 | MS0710__.090 |
| | HEDELBERG, SAMUEL C | MS | Jasper | 1/5/1841 | Augusta | 2450 | MS0660__.390 |
| | HEDELBERG, SAMUEL C | MS | Jasper | 1/5/1841 | Augusta | 3037 | MS0670__.440 |
| | HEIDLEBURG, SAMUEL | MS | Jasper | 1/5/1841 | Augusta | 2094 | MS0660__.044 |
| | KILLIN, BENJAMIN F | MS | Jasper | 1/5/1841 | Augusta | 3783 | MS0690__.160 |
| | SCOTT, WILLIAM S | MS | Jasper | 1/5/1841 | Augusta | 4788 | MS0710__.090 |
| | THOMAS, JOHN C | MS | Jasper | 1/5/1841 | Augusta | 1554 | MS0650__.010 |
| | THOMAS, JOHN C | MS | Jasper | 1/5/1841 | Augusta | 3010 | MS0670__.413 |
| | THOMAS, JOHN C | MS | Jasper | 1/5/1841 | Augusta | 3011 | MS0670__.414 |
| | THOMAS, JOHN C | MS | Jasper | 1/5/1841 | Augusta | 3290 | MS0680__.186 |
| | THOMAS, JOHN C | MS | Jasper | 1/5/1841 | Augusta | 755 | MS0630__.225 |

Residents of Section 9, Township 1, Range 13 E

| View Image | Patentee Name | State | County | Issue Date | Land Office | Doc. Nr. | Accession/Serial Nr. |
|---|---|---|---|---|---|---|---|
| | MACGEHEE, WILLIAM | MS | Jasper | 1/5/1841 | Augusta | 1944 | MS0650__.394 |
| | RODGERS, MANIN M | MS | Jasper | 5/9/1854 | Augusta | 8967 | MS0790__.164 |
| | ROGERS, REDDICK | MS | Jasper | 1/5/1841 | Augusta | 754 | MS0630__.224 |
| | ROGERS, REDICK | MS | Jasper | 1/5/1841 | Augusta | 2897 | MS0670__.308 |
| | ROGERS, RICHARD M | MS | Jasper | 1/5/1841 | Augusta | 5882 | MS0730__.156 |
| | TERRAL, JAMES S | MS | Jasper | 1/5/1841 | Augusta | 3009 | MS0670__.412 |
| | TERRAL, JAMES S | MS | Jasper | 1/5/1841 | Augusta | 3178 | MS0680__.077 |
| | TERRAL, JAMES S | MS | Jasper | 1/5/1841 | Augusta | 3644 | MS0690__.032 |
| | TERRELL, JAMES S | MS | Jasper | 1/5/1841 | Augusta | 632 | MS0630__.103 |

Residents of Section 10, Township 1, Range 13 E

| View Image | Patentee Name | State | County | Issue Date | Land Office | Doc. Nr. | Accession/ Serial Nr. |
|---|---|---|---|---|---|---|---|
| | BOUNDS, WILLIAM C | MS | Jasper | 1/5/1841 | Augusta | 5195 | MS0710__.487 |
| | MACGEHEE, OLIVIA | MS | Jasper | 1/5/1841 | Augusta | 3338 | MS0680__.234 |
| | MACGEHEE, WILLIAM | MS | Jasper | 1/5/1841 | Augusta | 1943 | MS0650__.393 |
| | MACGEHEE, WILLIAM | MS | Jasper | 1/5/1841 | Augusta | 3337 | MS0680__.233 |
| | NEWMAN, THOMAS S | MS | Jasper | 1/5/1841 | Augusta | 5215 | MS0720__.005 |
| | NEWMAN, THOMAS S | MS | Jasper | 1/5/1841 | Augusta | 5355 | MS0720__.144 |
| | SANDEL, HENRY | MS | Jasper | 1/5/1841 | Augusta | 5355 | MS0720__.144 |

Residents of Section 11, Township 1, Range 13 E

On February, 27th, 1878, Terrall Smith, was appointed to serve as the last postmaster of the Davisville Post Office. It was discontinued at an unknown date, most likely when the post office was opened at nearby Vossburg on April, 17th, 1882. Nowadays, aside from the unmarked cemetery, any obvious evidence of the community has vanished. Similar to the fate of Paulding, Davisville faded into obscurity when it was bypassed by the railroad. In contrast, Vossburg, with the benfit of a rail service, began to grow and flourish.

*Based upon word of mouth recollections, the Old Salem Baptist Church was located near the center of the western boundary of the remaining cemetery. This sketch of the old church, now gone, is based upon the childhood memory of Jesse Trotter and his elder brother who grew up in the Salem Community. According to WPA community records research, it is likely that this building was also the location of the Salem Church School.*

The Old Salem cemetery contains many "unmarked" graves. I purposely use these quotation marks. Based upon careful probing, we know that a multitude of native stone markers were placed. One must remember that the times of this cemetery fell among the worst economic period for those who lived in the south. Post-war survival for most was harsh, at best. Unless you were rich, and most of these people were not, you likely received a native stone or a wooden marker when you died.

The author learned that his Great-Great Grandparents, William and Martha Jane Hardee Eddins once lived in the Davisville community and that they are interred in Old Salem. Thanks to a bit of luck, oral family recollections, and the efforts of a cousin (B.E.), we were able to identify the proximity of their graves. William and his eldest son, William Abner, were identified to be confederate veterans and we have since marked their graves with an appropriate stone. As a result, Old Salem and the community once know as Davisville has become a significant landmark in our personal family history.

## Confederate Veterans Buried in Old Salem Cemetery

### Vossburg Mississippi

William Eddins-----Pvt. Company H, 27th Miss. Inf. C.S.A.
Jasper Blues

James K. Thigpen-------Company K, 37th, Miss. Inf. C.S.A.
Jasper Guards

James D. Lee--------Company K, 37th, Miss. Inf. C.S.A.
Jasper Guards

William H. Mounger----Company H, 37th, Miss. Inf. C.S.A.
Jasper Guards

James W. Risher----Company H, 27th, Miss. Inf. C.S.A.
Jasper Blues

H. W. Browder-------Al. Light Artillery, Lee's Battery C.S.A.

Gable E. Ellis----Pvt. Company F, 16th Miss. Inf. Reg. C.S.A.
Jasper Grays

M. Dallas Parker---Ms. 9th, Cav. Company G. C.S.A.

Felix V. Kelley-----Pvt. Company H, 37th Miss. Inf. C.S.A.
Jasper Guards

Four (4) Unkown

### "REVOLUTIONARY WAR SOLDIER"
Edward Young Terrall Sr.-------Pvt. SC. Militia "RevolutionarWar"

Edward Young Terrall is the only known Revolutionary War veteran buried in Jasper County. Interesting is fact that the four unknown Civil War veterans mentioned in the above list are reported to be Union soldiers killed in a skirmish with local Confederate troupes. This action coincided with the time frame of General Sherman's march of destruction across Mississippi.

# Bay Springs

Just like a plant, a small community needs some fertilizer to help it grow and thrive. In the case of Bay Springs, the fertilizer came in the form of a railroad. Where towns such as Paulding and Davisville had shown signs of prosperity, both began a slow demise when bypassed by this critical means of transportation. Whereas Paulding was the original county seat, the growth of Bay Springs eventually justified a split of the title. Until this day, the county maintains courthouses in both locations.

Bay Springs was named for a artesian spring, once surrounded by bay trees, located in the western district of the city. Like many rural communities, Bay Springs began it's life as a hub for the lumber industry. The abundance of old growth forest served to feed several sawmills in the area and the introduction of the railroad served as a catalyst for employment and growth. On September 12, 1901 a community plat was filed with the county by a local timber merchant, L.L. Denson. The plan encompassed a total of 173 acres and included commercial and residential districts.

With good transportation and steady employment, Bay Springs and it's residents thrived. Soon, several modern conveniences found their way into the fabric of daily life. A central water system, telephones, and a electrical grid was available throughout the town. Over the years, many new buildings, factories, businesses, banks, churches, and schools were built.

Administration Building, Jasper County A. H. S., Bay Springs, Miss.

Old Courthouse

Downtown District

Rail Depot

1928 THIRD GRADE CLASS OLD BAY SPRINGS SCHOOL HOUSE -- (First row) Orell McBay, Tressie Boyd, Addie Odean Pittman, Margaret Aldridge, Wilma Yelverton, unknown, Ila Kay Lowe, Mary Ruth Hull, Melba Bailey, Lolene Pittman, Mary McFarland. (Second row) Max Ainsworth, Herman Thigpen, A. G. Myers, Ava Lee Knotts, Ruby Windham, Pink Edward Lewis, James Terry, J. J. Jenkins, (teacher) Lois Nichols. (Third row) Dan Lee, Merkel Vanderslice, Jack Pittman, F. C. Smith, Mark Massey, Joe Thigpen, Roland Herrington. Melba Waites, not pictured. This was first year the Lake Como School moved to Bay Springs. *Submitted by Merkel Vanderslice*

# Garlandsville

Garlandsville, a town of significant historical importance, is located south of Newton near the Newton/Jasper County line. The Choctaw name for the community is unknown but it once served as the capitol of the Choctaw Nation. The famous Choctaw Chief, Pushmataha, was a prominent resident.

The fist known European settler was John H. Ward, who operated an inn owned by John Garland. Garland was a resident of mixed Indian and European blood. Later, Garland gave the property to Ward's wife. Out of gratitude, she named the area, Garlandsville.

The Wards improved the property and operated the inn for a number of years. Several important government officials lodged at the facility while negotiating the demise and relocation of the Choctaw Nation to Oklahoma. The inn also served as a stagecoach station and the local post office.

European settlers, taking advantage of the lands acquired by the Federal Government, continued to move into the area, establishing farms and businesses. During 1855, when the rail line from Jackson to Meridian was routed through Newton rather than Garlandsville, many of the businesses and residents of the town moved. A limited amount of lumber and farming industries remained, but Garlandsville failed to grow and ultimately faded.

GARLANDSVILLE SCHOOL -1922 ~ 1923

# Greerson's Raid on Garlandsville

*The Yanks came calling and got more than they asked for.*

## Garlandville Folks Fought To Stop Grierson's Raiders

(Editor's Note: A Bay Springs man, Pat Arinder, has submitted the following account of an historical Civil War event which occurred near Bay Springs. Mr. Arinder notes his references as "Grierson's Raid" by D. Alexander Brown, University of Illinois Press. We thank him for the following article.)

By Pat Arinder

When Colonel Grierson reigned his horse to a stop a few hundred yards from the outskirts of Garlandville, he was surprised to see such a bourgeois group of armed citizens prepared to meet his brigade of mounted yankee calvary. In almost eight days of raiding behind the Confederate lines this was his first time to be in a position where he faced a group of home guard militia.

There were shopkeepers and old men armed with shotguns and a few young boys armed with muzzle loaders and pistols all waiting behind their quickly prepared barricade.

The townsfolks of Garlandville had received the news of the Yankee raiders only a short time previous when a messenger from Newton Station galloped into town and began telling of the destruction of the railroad at Newton and that about 1,000 Yankees were now headed south toward Garlandville. This information threw the populace into a frenzy of activity. The war had never been this close to home. Always the news was of battles at far away places like Corinth or the impending fight for Vicksburg. Now there was a large force of Yankee calvary riding toward their town.

At the beginning of the war most of the young men had left the area and gone to join the Confederate Army. This left only the young and aged men to carry on the activities of the town.

As the news of the impending raid spread, the women and children were taken to places of safety in the wooded area surrounding the town. Simultaneously the militia quickly began to construct a barricade across the road at the north end of town. As the barricade was being completed the vanguard of the Yankee calvary came into view down the road.

Colonel Grierson had begun his cavalry raid at LaGrange, Tennessee, eight days earlier on Friday, April 17, 1863. His main purpose was to create confusion behind the Confederate lines and to destroy the Vicksburg railroad at Newton Station if possible. This railroad was a vital supply and communication link for the Confederate Army at Vicksburg. Also, General Grant was about to begin his assault on the rear of Vicksburg and Grierson's raid was to be a diversion for the Confederate forces guarding Vicksburg.

Grierson had quickly struck at several villages and towns in North and Central Mississippi. His actions were so elusive and movements so rapid that often no warning came before he struck. He had destroyed Confederate property, cut telegraph lines and captured several Confederate soldiers.

This action had not gone unnoticed however. General Pemberton, the commander of Confederate forces in Mississippi, had detached all available calvary units in various parts of the State to attempt to trap and destroy the Yankee raiders. Since the Yankees were not following any definite route and due to poor communications between the Confederate forces, no progress had been made in stopping Grierson. Usually the Confederate forces were almost a half day behind the raiders.

Now as Grierson looked over the barricade, guarding the road to Garlandville he knew this was his first real challenge to his force. He had only a few hours earlier destroyed the railroad and two trains at Newton without even firing a shot. Now he could see that there would probably be bloodshed here at Garlandville.

Grierson quickly surveyed the situation and saw that there only a few poorly armed defenders behind the barricade. He felt confident that his superior force could easily overtake the defenders. On hearing the order to charge, the Yankees galloped at full speed toward the barricade with their sabers waving. The dust from almost 500 horses and smoke from the the Yankees' carbines was a fearful sight for the defenders but they met the charge bravely.

When the lead element of calvary was within range the handful of defenders let go with their first and only volley of shot and shell. One raider was critically wounded and a horse fell dead under another raider. Before the defenders had time to reload the raiders' swept through the town. Confusion and fear gripped the defenders and they ran for their lives. Several were captured before they could reach safety.

Grierson disarmed them and reprimanded them for their resistance. Also, he ordered his men to search the homes for food and supplies. The raiders helped themselves to any stores and goods that they found.

Grierson knew that they could not afford to stay in Garlandville long since his action at Newton Station surely would have Confederate forces even more determined to capture him. Even though it was almost dark he ordered his men to mount their horses and prepare to ride. He followed the road southwestward to Montrose and passed through that village stopping about midnight. Convinced that he was out of danger, at least for the night, he halted his column on the plantation of C. M. Bender, approximately two miles west of Montrose. There his men camped for the night.

The next morning the raiders departed on the road toward Pineville after they had looted Mr. Bender's smokehouse and stolen all of his mules. Within an hour the rear guard crossed the Jasper County Line leaving the citizens of the County somewhat shaken but otherwise unharmed.

# Rose Hill

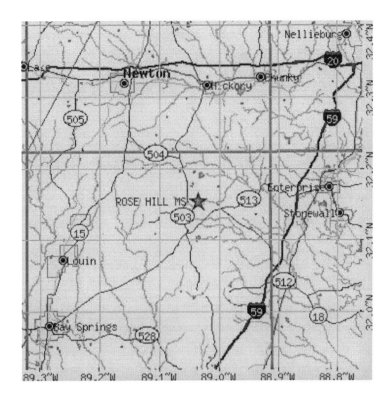

A few photos related to Rose Hill Schools and early businesses. The area is best known for it's productive farming land. Prior to the Civil War, two educational academies, male and female, were located in this community. It is also reported to be the birthplace of the first white child to be born in Jasper County.

Where have all the horses gone? The wagons and carriages in Rose Hill (Jasper County) look lost without their means of locomotion in this photo believed taken in the latter part of the 19th century. (Photo courtesy Mrs. Eugene Carley, Petal)

ROSE HILL SCHOOL IN 1901 — This picture was made in 1901 of the students at Rose Hill School. See legend accompanying picture for identifications. The school was under the direction of Mr. A. E. (Lonnie) Freeman (4) who received his Master of English Literature degree from Harperville College Mississippi in 1893 at age 36. His assistant was Miss Mattie Hunt (16). The students: (1) Louis Freeman; (2) Will Booth; (3) Will Massey; (5) Sam Finnegan; (6) Tom Graham; (7) Bettie Freeman; (8) Ramon Freeman; (9) Maud Chatham; (10) Ina Merrell; (11) Myrtle Foreman; (12) Martha Aycock; (13) Maud Davis; (14) Ollie Merrill; (15) Emma Foreman; (17) Annie Avery; (18) Angie Graham; (19) Betty Lewis; (20) Azaline Lewis; (21) Ethel Avery; (22) Jeff Davis; (23) Jim Smith; (24) Eunice Foreman; (25) Witt Murry; (26) John Lewis; (27) Rodney Freeman; (28) Hattie Cooley; (29) Etta Merrell; (30) Irma Morgan; (31) Carrie Holyfield; (32) Bernice Chatham; (33) Julia Davis; (34) Claude Davis; (35) Annie Morgan; (36) Jenny Massey; (37) Linnie Foreman; (38) Lula Mae Moulds; (39) Dan Foreman; (40) Charles Fowler; (41) Charley Aycock; (42) George Fowler; (43) Will Peek; (44) Green Merrell; (45) John Chatham; (46) Laura Finnegan; (47) Kate Finnegan; (48) Sarah Finnegan; (49) Nettie Mae Graham; (50) Emma Avery; (51) Mittie Murray. Approximately half of these students still live in the Southeast Mississippi area. Picture submitted by Rodney and Ramon Freeman of Hattiesburg. Identifications made by Tom Graham of Enterprise.

Rose Hill School

**Teacher: Onie Mae MANN**
**Bottom Row:** (standing) Josephine GRAHAM, Minnie Lee LOVITT, ??, Luna Mae O-ROURKE, Lou Alice CARAWAY, Ella Mae MOULDS, Lucille HICKS married Loyd PHILLIPS, Mary REID, Margaret (Tutie) BUNCH, Lizzie TAYLOR, Julie SHARP married Sharp MORGAN, Luna Mae HUTTO married Olan REYNOLDS, Arlise LEWIS married Dan YOUNG
**Middle Row:** Maudie Lee COOLEY, Foster LEWIS, William PORTER, Kelly LEWIS, ? STARLAND married Herbert LEWIS, Sadie BUNCH, Maggie FINNAGIN, Louise GRAHAM, Mattie Grace BOUTWELL, Victor PARKER
**Top Row:** Norval COMBEST, Irvin HICKS, Silas HARPER, Earl LEWIS, Ryner HUTTO, MERRITT CHATHAM, Garland LEWIS, Buddy DANIELS, M.J. TAYLOR, Lamar ARTHUR, Lewis COMBEST

# TO DEDICATE ROSE HILL $18,000 SCHOOL ON NEXT FRIDAY; SPECIAL P[ROGRAM]

The brand new $18,000 Rose Hill school building (above) will be dedicated in an all-day program Friday, at which time J. S. Vandiver, state superintendent of education, will deliver the principal address. This was announced by Prof. T. B. Winstead, principal of the school. Thousands of patrons, school children and visitors from all sections of the state are expected to attend the dedication. At noon a basket lunch will be served free by residents of the community. The dedication will be open to the public.

Superintendent Vandiver's dedicatory address will be given at 11 a.m., immediately preceded by a band concert. Members of the state department of education will speak in the morning.

At 1:30 p.m. another band concert will be presented, following which addresses will be made by various candidates for public office. These speakers will include candidates for circuit judge, chancery judge and congress.

Professor Winstead has been principal of the Rose Hill school for the past five years. Members of the school board include W. A. Lewis, president; L. N. Boutwell, secretary; E. B. Murray, S. E. Lewis and T. F. Graham.

Plans for the modern new school building were drawn by Krouse and Brasfield, Meridian architects, and the construction work was done by Curry and Corley, contractors, of Raleigh and Jackson. The school, erected as a PWA project, will employ nine teachers in addition to Principal Winstead.

Located in the northwest corner of Jasper county, Rose Hill is approximately 28 miles from Meridian, by way of Enterprise, and the area served by the school has a population of approximately 2,500 persons. The school enrollment at present is 225.

### Fine Farming Area

The Rose Hill area is said by experts to be one of the best farming sections in Jasper county, and it is from this area that Meridian live stock buyers obtain the fattest cattle, they said.

Rose Hill was the birthplace of the first child born in Jasper county, and a school has been operated there since about 1846. This new structure is the fourth building to be used. Prior to the Civil War, two academies, male and female institutions, were located in that community.

The Meridian Chamber of Commerce and Meridian and Rose Hill business men and community leaders have for the past several months been attempting to improve the route from Rose Hill to Enterprise and thence to Meridian, which is approximately 14 miles shorter than routes heretofore traveled to reach Meridian.

A WPA project to gravel this route has been obtained and piling work has been completed. Although the road is easily traversable in dry weather, it is as yet incomplete and somewhat inconvenient after heavy rains.

"The strok[e] this graveled symbolically, ments for al[l] improved bu[t] tween Meridi[an] servers decla[re]

**Old farm house off Hwy 18**

# Montrose

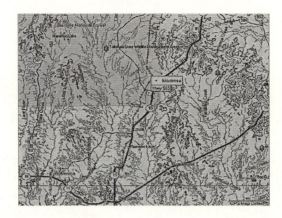

Located four miles north of Bay Springs on Hwy 15, Montrose was reportedly settled by a colony of Scots and named for James Montrose, a Scottish patriot. According to the records compiled by the noted Jasper county educator and historian, Mr. J.M. Kennedy, the village was a whistle stop on the M.J. and Kansas City Railroad between Meridian and Paulding. Local establishments included a bank, post office, numerous stores, churches, mills, gins, and Montrose Academy, established in 1841 by Reverend J.N.Waddell . The Jasper County Review newspaper was originally published in Montrose, 1890, by W.W. Moon. By 1892 the paper listed it's home as Paulding, owned and published by P.T. Lawless. Reverend Waddell's establishment of Montrose Academy in 1841 led to the villiage becoming know as the Oxford of Jasper County. However, when Dr. Waddell was elected Professor of Ancient and Modern Languages at the University of Mississippi, the Montrose Academy was closed. Jasper County was largely devoid of schools until the early 1860's when a high school was opened.

*Montrose Class of 1922~23*

*Montrose Men's Basketball Team - 1946~47*

*Downtown Montrose – Stores and Mill*

*The Montrose Presbyterian Church, organized in 1841, is the oldest church in Jasper County.*

# Dushau

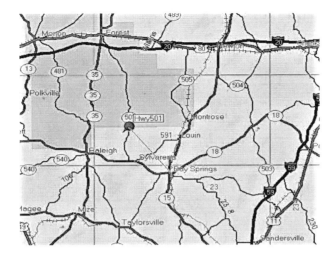

Dushau was a lumber camp community established by the Gilchrist-Fordney company. Posted below are two mentions of Dushau that were located by Mr. Robert McFarland in the Mississippi State Archives. One of these is a Jasper County News article that details the death of his Grandfather, W. J. McFarland. It was located in sections 29 and 30 T3N R10E, or about 3 miles west of Louin.

## Jasper County Loses One of Best Citizens

**W. J. McFarland Succumbs at Home in Dushau Monday Night.**

The announcement of the serious, sudden illness of W. J. McFarland at his home in Dushau, late Saturday afternoon, followed about sixty hours later by the report that he had surrendered to the Grim Reaper brought profound grief, and sorrow over the entire county. Never has a man in the county wielded a greater influence for the clean, the true, the pure than did he. In public, in private, in the home, in his church he was the same W. J. McFarland.

While sitting in the office of Gilchrist Fordney Co., Dushau, late Saturday afternoon, he spoke of an unusual, strange feeling in his head, which was soon violent. He was taken in charge by several by-standers who carried him to the porch where symptoms grew worse. He was carried to his home some two hundred yards away and spoke but once after reaching home, and every muscle save his heart and respiratory organs became motionless, never relaxing at any time, death resulting about twelve o'clock Monday night, surrounded by his wife, all his children, and many relatives

of office, that of surveyor, circuit clerk, representative and five times to the office of sheriff. Since returning to private life he held a responsible position with Gilchrist-Fordney Co., and was in that harness when overtaken by the final malady. It was with this company, possibly, that his Christian life shone most brightly and bore most fruit. He was leader of the Dushau squadron, which has held many very impressive services, and to him is followers dropped many flowers in his pathway while he saw and heard as well as had placed over his last resting place, seen only by those still on the journey. He was also a member of the masonic and woodmen fraternities. The deeds done in the body have wrought an inheritance that cannot be computed.

"Death hath made no breach
In love and sympathy, in
hope and trust,
No outward sign or sound our
ears can reach;
But there's an inward spiritual
speech
That greets us still,— though
mortal tongue be dust,
It bids us do the work they laid
down,
Take up the song where they
broke off the strain."

The Thompson, undertaker, of Laurel, in charge, the body, followed by scores of relatives and friends, was brought to the Presbyterian Church here, where he held his membership, and the services were in charge

44. D'Olive, "Reminiscences," 173–74; Hickman, "Lumber Industry," 220–21; Hodge, "Lumber Industry," 372; Hickman, *Mississippi Harvest*, 240–42, 245–47; Hickman, "Black Labor," 86. A resident of Dushau, a Gilchrist-Fordney logging camp about sixty miles north of Laurel, remembered the "quarter" where the black people lived: "I do not know much about the this section of town as I was never allowed to go there" (Elise Graham, "Dushau Days," typewritten manuscript in Lauren Rogers Museum of Art, Laurel, Miss., 3).

45. Hickman, *Mississippi Harvest*, 245–46; D'Olive, "Reminiscences," 173.

### Dushan

Located eleven miles northwest of Bay Springs, Dushan was formed in 1919 as a mill location of the Eastman-Gardner Lumber Company and was named for a representative of the company. At one time, there were several stores and a group of company houses that gave the town a population of 125. The mill closed about 1927, and by 1929, Dushan was extinct.

*This is a clip copied from a popular local Jasper County book entitled Hometown Mississippi. The community described is called Dushan instead of Dushau and ownership is credited to Eastman-Gardner instead of Gilchrist-Fordney.*

Dushau, named after Frank S. Dushau, occupied a 360-acre site. The houses, built on pier and beam foundations, were permanent bungalows of five or six rooms. Each house had running water and electricity, which set it apart from neighboring communities where hand pumps were the norm and electricity remained an exception. Elise Graham wrote of the Dushau in her recollection of life in the camp:

> The company provided its inhabitants with a house in Dushau. Most of them were small bungalows consisting of five or six rooms... All the houses in Dushau had running water which was a step up from those in the surrounding towns still operating with pumps and wells. Our houses had electricity long before the rural electric programs... Our small Mississippi town, although deserted now by the loggers and their families, will always remain

loggers and their families, will always remain alive with me. It is in this place I spent many happy times and received many of life's lessons that are with me even today."

Dushau's public buildings included a large commissary, clubhouse, doctor's office, school, and a YMCA which did additional duty as a church and community center as well as provided space for a barbershop and a traveling dentist. The commissary buildings of Camp Dushau and Camp Allenton, as is the Gilchrist Mall, were shopping centers located under a single roof. The town's post office was also located in the commissary building. The construction and operation of these camps presages the construction and operation of Gilchrist, Oregon. Quarters for the logging superintendent and school teacher were located in the clubhouse. There was a house which was occupied by the doctor whom the Gilchrist-Fordney Company provided for its employees and their families. Visitors and single loggers lodged in a two-story boardinghouse.[102]

Elise Graham, in her memoir entitled *Dushau Days*, describes life in a lumber camp operated by Gilchrist-Fordney during the 1920s. The

---

October 27, 1921.
PETITION FOR INCORPORATION
To His Excellency Lee M. Russell, Governor of Mississippi.
We the undersigned inhabitants of the territory hereinafter described desire to be incorporated as a village. Their aim in incorporating themselves as a village is for the better preservation of law and order, for the better enforcement of health regulations and the betterment of sanitary conditions, and for the promotion of the efficiency of their schools. They desire that the corporate name of the municipality shall be the Village of Dushau. They petition that the following territory may be embraced in said municipality, to wit:
The W½ of the SW¼ of Section 29, and SE¼ of SW¼ and SE¼ of Section 30, and N½ of NE¼ of Section 31, all in Township 3 North, Range 10 East, in Jasper County, Mississippi.
Petitioners show that the number of inhabitants of said proposed village is 300; and that the amount of the assessed value of real property therein is $20,000.
Petitioners further show that they desire that the following named persons shall be appointed municipal officers, to wit:
Mayor: Dr. Lovett Golden; three aldermen, E. V. Wright, J. B. Mustin, and Isom Ezell; marshall, W. J. McFarland; tax collector, W. J. McFarland; clerk, Isom Ezell; street commissioner, W. J. McFarland; that they desire that the Clerk's office shall be held by one of the aldermen; and that the office of marshall, tax collector and street commissioner shall be held by one person.
Petitioners show that there are not exceeding 100 qualified electors in the proposed municipality and that this petition is signed by more than two-thirds of said qualified electors.
Respectfully submitted, L. D. Bassett, W. O. Eddins, W. D. Shows, R. R. Bassett, J. B. Bassett, A. F. Spurvin, J. C. Bassett, W. B. Beauregard, W. C. Dawkins, B. M. Kyer, R. R. Jones, I. C. Dollar, B. W. Johnson, Ollie Barnett, J. P. Applewhite, W. E. Robert, Jno. Mustin, B. V. Wright, Wm. Chronister, Isom Ezell, H. B. Cox, W. J. McFarland, W. A. Ray, Inman Waldrup, W. F. Harrison, J. L. Nester, George May Davis, O. L. Bell, C. D. Webb, Irby Jones, O. J. Barnett, E. T Norton, Dr. Lovitte Golden, J. W. Sims, J. S. Chestnut, C. Smith, H. B. Rawson, Alex Manuel, H. Bates, R. L. Lee, A. Moffett, T. P. Brogan, A. Gavin, E. L. Batte, Lee Jordan, R. Boykin, Noble Lacy, J. R. Horne, Will Hassen, Marshall Ward, Gus Gavin, Mack Wallace, Bob Brooks, Joe Curtner, J. R. Lee, George Childree, Sam Knight, J. B. Boykin, G. E. Russum, Magnis Jones, Burt Moore, R. E. Bell, A. H. Prescott, S. D. Brogan, A. H. Waldrup, W. E. Horne, J. W. Roberts, C. I. Roberts, F. M. Rawson, Morse Prince.

# Vossburg

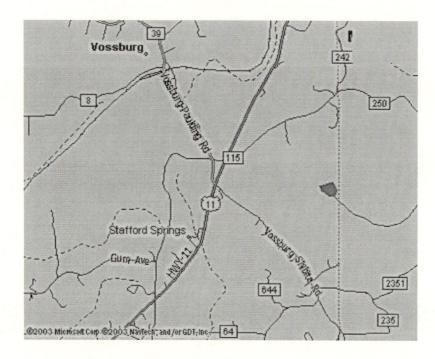

Almost everyone has a soft spot in their heart for the place that they call home. For myself, home included a special little dot on the map in east-central Jasper County named Vossburg. Although this landmark has all but vanished from the modern landscape, it was once a bustling little town and the place that my grandparents and my mother called home.

I grew up in a city, mostly devoid of woods, fields, babbling brooks, wildlife, and many of the other amenities that an adventurous young boy holds dear. As luck would have it, during my adolescent summer months, I was permitted to spend a few weeks with my grandparents. These precious weeks facilitated the creation of many good memories that follow me until this day.

Like so many other small towns built around a farm-based economy, most of the original Vossburg residents have died of old age and their children, now elderly themselves, long ago departed to earn a living amid better employment opportunities. Having little commercial value, other than for the lumber, most of the buildings have fallen to decay or have been demolished, their foundations now hidden beneath a thick carpet of forest mulch and kudzu.

Before I progress much farther, it's appropriate to present the limited amount of historical fact that I have been able to unearth regarding this village. Vossburg is located in the southeast sector of Jasper County. This territory was granted to the State of Mississippi and to the United States at the Treaty of Dancing Rabbit Creek, concluded on September 27, 1830. The counties included in the Choctaw Purchase were Noxubee, Neshoba, Leake, Newton, Smith, Jasper, Clarke, Lauderdale, and Scott. Vossburg appears to have been formally named around 1882, probably when the railroad was constructed, after William Voss, an early settler. S.R. Voss, likely a relation to William, built and operated a hotel located near a mineral spring with much the same qualities as Stafford Springs The New Orleans & North Eastern Railroad as well as the rail depot was located directly in front of this structure.

*Rail Depot circa 1930 - Persons in this photo are not identified - Automobile on left front appears to be 1925 model Durant*

*The original Vossburg Rail Depot - Replaced in the early 1950's - Replacement demolished during the late 1960's*

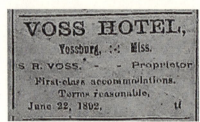

*The Voss Hotel - Built in Vossburg - c. 1890*

*The building to the right is the J.E. Bounds General Mercantile - demolished during the early 1970's. As a youngster, I shopped in this store. J.E. was quiet elderly by that time and his wife pretty much attended to customers as he watched. This store was a shotgun design with long glass display cases extending the legnth of the building on both sides. Tall shelves stocked with canned and dry goods were built on the walls behind these cases. I remember bolts of cloth, sewing thread, farm supplies, clothing, and a back room that housed simple hardware items and nails. J.E. and his first wife lived on the second floor of this building. In later years, he built a fine house behind the store and lived there with his second wife until his death.*

When you combine a rail stop, a hotel, fertile farmland, abundant water, and an enterprising group of people, you clearly have the ingredients for a town. I have no way to confirm the order in which Vossburg was built, but, from my youth, I remember some of what remained. Old Highway 11, the main thoroughfare through town, is now called the Vossburg-Paulding road. From Heidelberg and Stafford Springs, it passed by the Vossburg Cemetery and descended into the railroad hollow. The road crossed the tracks near the train depot and the J.E. Bounds store. Immediately beyond the track crossing, an intersection was situated on the north side. A road to the left threaded between the Voss Hotel and the Bounds store. It continued eastward and emerged near the current public school in Heidelberg, MS. Old 11 continued toward the north, scaling an intensely steep incline, and leveled off at the center of town. In later years, a bridge was built, on the east side of the original rail crossing, spanning the railroad hollow. The main road was rerouted from the proximity of the cemetery and crossed the bridge into the downtown area. This new road frontage brought with it additional business and residential properties.

*View of Downtown Vossburg - Old Hwy 11 - Circa 1930*

Note Turner's Store on Left side of photo. All of these buildings have been demolished. This photo was displayed in the Vossburg Post Office and was owned by Miss Grace Wells, wife of Leroy Wells. Leroy operated the Turner Store (building on the left) for many years. The huge timbers used to frame this building were sawed in Enterprise, MS and brought to Vossburg on the railroad. When the building was demolished, these timbers had to be sawed in half because they were too long to legally haul on a public road. Below are some details taken from the above street scene.

*Storefront of Chester Arledge Store - Note manual gasoline and motor oil pumps - Next Building on Right is Believed to be Dr. Stafford's Office*

*Two unidentified men talking - Unidentified man in foreground on horseback - Martin's Store and Garage is behind the white billboard. Gas pumps are beneath the covered island on the left.*

*Group of customers outside the entrance to Turner's Store. In the distance, Hwy -11 is visible as it curves toward the railroad bridge. Turner's warehouse is also visible on the left, beyond the store.*

*Turner's Store - Circa 1980 - Just prior to it's demolition*

*1893 Newspaper ad that appeared in the Jasper County Review*

Turner's was sold to Oscar Lee in the early part of the century. He later sold it to Leroy Wells who operated it until his health failed in the late 70's. It sat vacant until it's demolition a few years later. As a child, I well remember trips inside to purchase a cold Coke from the old chest type cooler. It was always dark inside because the only light was provided by a couple of open bulbs hanging from the ceiling on long wires. Several marvelous glass display cases were located in the main downstairs room. I never had the opportunity to visit the upstairs. I was told that several wooden caskets remained up there when the building was being cleared for demolition.

*A 1912 receipt from Turner's*

*Martin's General Store*

*Martin's Warehouse*

*The old Vossburg Bridge and the Southbound Southern Railways Passenger Train*
*Hanging the Mail – A pencil drawing by Al Hausman*

For those of you who don't know, the U.S. Mail used to be carried by passenger trains. The mail pole shown on the left side of this drawing was used to suspend the outgoing canvas bag of 1st class mail and held in place by a pair of hairpin springs. The train had a dedicated mail car equipped with a snatch hook that was extended from the side of the train. As the train passed, the bag was snatched from the pole and pulled into the mail car. Incoming mail was also packed in an identical bag and manually tossed out the side window. The contract postal employee who hung the mail would retrieve the incoming sack and deliver it to the local post office. This process was repeated twice per day, seven days per week, rain, shine. sleet, or snow.

*Old Rowell Homeplace - circa 1900*

*Left to right: Catherine Smothers Rowell, Arsula Starling Rowell, Godine Rivers Rowell, Mary Jane Rowell ( wife of John T. Rowell), Dora Lee Rowell (daughter of Mary Jane and John T. Rowell), Albert Matthew Rowell, Horace Rivers Rowell, an unknown friend and dog*

# The Vossburg School

Very little is known about the origins or the history of the Vossburg school. All that remains are a few scattered class photos and portions of the building foundation. Based upon oral accounts, the Rowel home was located near the school and a few early students who lived too far away boarded there. Based upon the class photos, it appears the school catered to multiple grades with a classic one room schoolhouse approach. In later years, as the public school systems and transportation improved, Vossburg children began to attend school in Pachuta. The school was closed in 1938 and the building was demolished at an unknown date.

*Approximate location of the school. GPS coordinates: N31 55.414 W88 56.299*

*Class of 1912*

*Left to Right: Back Row: Mr. and Mrs. Pennington (Teachers) 2nd Row: Dave McCormick, unknown, unknown, Jewel Sanders, Berniece Allen, unknown, unknown, Knolton Martin, Reuben Allen (brother of Berneice Alan). Front Row: unknown (half of face showing), Woodrow Martin, John Singleton, Eloise McDaniel, unknown McCormick, Annie Kate Elkins, Minerva (or Ada) Gordon, Marvin Gordon, Mamie Weems Stafford (daughter of Dr. T.E. Stafford), unknown (may be Lela Todd Lee), and Doris Lee*

*Class of 1921*

Listed from Top - #2 line is first row of students below teachers
Vaseburg School 1921

Top: Mrs Hinton - Mrs Harris - Miss Loughridge

2nd Row: Mary Lee, Rebecca McCormick, Evil Allen, Louise Eldridge, Millie Martin - Johnetta Arrington

3rd Row: Oliver Singleton, Julia Martin, Willie Mae Chatham, Bertha Martin, Alma Thornton, Mildred Stafford

4th Row: Dimon Wilson, B.J. Martin, Russell Bounds, Owen Moore, Mike Lightsey, Hector Webb, Tom Stafford, Sam Cooley, J Bordon Clyde Webb, Arnie Chatham, Owen Moore, Marvin Gardner, John Stacy Martin, Herman Cooley

5th Row: June McCormick, John Ed Cooley, Benny Ray Allen, Wilma Arrington, Rosa Lee, Lucille Leggett, Katherine Reed, Grace Osley - Doris Lee, Ivona Martin, Alice Donald, Ruby Rhoden, Minerva Borden, Mary Donald, Marino Stafford, Edna T. Lee, Frances McCormick, Mary Sue Thornton

6th Row: Lee Donald, Martin Chatham, Frances Anderson, Melvin Donald, Sam Webb, Howard Allen, Rhoden Allen, Frank Lightsey, David McCormick, Louie Rhoden, W.T. Bounds, Knowlton Martin, James Donald, Mike Lightsey, B Bo Arrington, Althea Stafford, Hassell Bounds, Forest McCormick

*The Last Class before the school was closed - 1936~37*

Left to Right: Top Row: Margret Reynolds, Sue Brownlee, Nigle Gooch, Alma West, Verda Mae Stephens, James Robert Reynolds, Burel McCormick, Carl McCormick. 2nd Row: Mary Sue McCormick, Thelma Lee McCormick, Mary Helen Ritchie, Ida Ruth Stephens, Billie Jean Martin, Betty Jean McCormick, Betty Lou Martin, Buddy Rowell, R.B. Reeves. 3rd Row: Nora Bell West, Sue Howell, Howard Donald, Billy Top Carpentin, Frank Stevens, John Brownlee, H.T. Leggett, Frances Martin, Paul McCormick

Although Vossburg is located near the eastern border of Jasper County, after the consolidated school system was introduced in the county and the local neighborhood schools were closed, Vossburg children attended the school at Pachuta, MS, located on the western border of Clarke County. I'm not sure how the school tax system worked at that time. The schools may have been funded exclusively by state taxes and the individual county taxes did not come into play.

*The Allen Brothers Playing Hooky – Digging for fish bait – Circa 1925*

# Vossburg Churches

Living in Vossburg offered three convenient choices for a house of worship. You either attended the Vossburg Methodist Church, Shady Grove Baptist Church, or Saint Peter Baptist Church. I'm reminded of a favorite joke that is attributed to the famous American writer and orator, Samuel Clemons (AKA: Mark Twain). He once said, "Man is the only animal with the true religion …. several of them!" Nonetheless, if you were not a Methodist or a Baptist who lived in Vossburg, you may have been left out in the cold on any given Sunday.

**The Methodist Church**

*The Vossburg Methodist Church - 100th Year Celebration Program*

*Interior of the church*

**WELCOME:**

It seems especially fitting for us to be celebrating the one-hundredth birthday of Vossburg United Methodist Church on The Day of Pentecost, the birthday of the Christian Church. God's love in Christ and the power of the Holy Spirit strengthened the early Christians and enabled them to spread the good news of the gospel and to keep its message of love and forgiveness alive. That same love and power has kept this church alive and touched all who have come to her sanctuary.

A church which never locks its doors is a special place. It is a haven for those troubled in body, mind, or spirit. It is a place of comfort, of peace and spiritual restoring. It is a quiet island in the midst of a helter-skelter, too-fast world. This church is such a place.

For many of you, being here today will bring back fond memories and recollections of earlier times. Wherever you may have traveled, no matter how long you have been away, you carry this church within you. The years may take their toll, wind and rain may damage, but in the heart's memory she stands beautiful and white and welcoming.

A living church is more than a building. She is all the people who worship and have worshipped together there. She is all who worked to begin her, increase her, and sustain her. She is laughter and tears. She is those who have served her and those whom she serves. She is those who have spent a lifetime here and those who's stay was brief. She is children and old folks, mothers and fathers, grandmothers and grandfathers, aunts and uncles. She is the place of living water for those who have come to her and those yet to come.

One hundred years have come and gone. For those many and full years we give thanks. But what of the years ahead, the next hundred years for which we can hope? It is our privilege and loving task to preserve this beautiful little church so that those who follow us might be touched by her as we have been touched, that Christ's healing message of sight for the blind, freedom for those who are prisoners and comfort for all who mourn, might long ring from her sanctuary.

Yours in Christ,

Rev. Jim Ballard

---

THE ORDER OF WORSHIP

VOSSBURG UNITED METHODIST CHURCH

THE DAY OF PENTECOST

May 30, 1982

Rev. Jim Ballard ................................................ Pastor
Rev. R. M. Matheny ................... District Superintendent
Rev. C. P. Minnick ........................................... Bishop
Rev. James D. Slay, Sr. ........................... Guest Speaker

Special Music .................... Holders United Methodist Choir
THE PRELUDE
THE INVOCATION
A Hymn "The Church in the Wildwood" ................. 121
The Affirmation of Faith
The Responsive Reading ........................................ 325
The Gloria Patri
THE PASTORAL PRAYER
THE LORD'S PRAYER
A Hymn "Amazing Grace" ....................................... 43
WELCOME & ANNOUNCEMENTS
THE OFFERING
A Hymn "Rock of Ages" .......................................... 76
THE SERMON ........................... Dr. James D. Slay, Sr.
A Hymn "Blest be the Tie" ...................................... 87
THE BENEDICTION
THE POSTLUDE

"Enter to Worship, Depart to Serve"

CENTENNIAL SPEAKER:

Dr. James Dudley Slay, Sr. is known and loved throughout the entire state, wherever Methodists are gathered together. He has been referred to as one of the giants of this conference. Dr. Slay has served in the various capacities of District Superintendent, Pastor, and Counseling Elder for over forty years. We are grateful and appreciative that he and Mrs. Slay can be with us today.

\*\*\*\*\*\*\*\*\*\*\*\*\*\*\*\*

A BRIEF HISTORY:

Our thanks to Mrs. Sarah Drake for the use of the following material from her history of Vossburg United Methodist Church, "In Search of Water." The history was compiled with the help of Mrs. Etta Boultou Martin and Dr. James D. Slay, Sr.

### The Preface

Water is urgently needed to sustain life. Yet how much we take it for granted. We turn on the tap without realizing where the water comes from other than from the pipes - forgetting or not knowing the source.

In my homeland there were many springs. Water was most plentiful. We knew where the springs were and how we could get to them. The one nearest our home furnished our needs. The path to the spring was so well worn I could almost find it in the dark. The many daily trips to get water for household use were a part of my duties as a member of a family of eight. And the wash-day pilgrimages were repeated often. While the wash-pot boiled near the spring I would lie on the grass beneath the sycamore tree and look up at the blue sky and wonder about life and what would happen to me.

On Sundays we would go to the little church in the village and listen to one tell of a different kind of water. The year was about 1930. Many in our country were hungry and life was difficult. We got food from the land and the earth gave forth its water. And at the church we found hope.

Twenty-two years following the death of John Wesley the first Annual Conference of the Methodist Episcopal Church was held in Spring Hill, Miss. The time was November 1, 1813. The heart warming experienced by John Wesley was repeated again and again. The circuit riders went forth to tell their good news. The circuits were large in those days and the preachers were kept busy trying to minister to the sparsely settled region. The saddlebags were both libraries and ward-robes. It was not easy.

They traveled by horse-back and studied the Scriptures by lamp-light. They built upon the ruins brought on by the Civil War. In spite of cold, heat, floods, cyclones, disease and fire, the circuit riders carried their message forward.

In 1882, sixty-nine years following the first annual conference, seven new Methodist Societies were organized. One of them was at Vossburg. These early Christians along with others helped to establish churches, schools, a hospital and an orphanage in the state. Some of the schools were the Seashore District High School in Hattiesburg, the Brookhaven, Brandon and Montrose District High Schools. The ministers served as teachers and administrators.

A parsonage was built in Vossburg in 1883. The property for the church was purchased June 9, 1884 from S. R. Voss. The neat wood-frame sanctuary has provided a place of worship for both Methodist and Baptist. When the church bell rang on Sunday mornings the people gathered for lessons provided by the Methodists. Evenings, in the early days, were devoted to programs by the Baptist Young Peoples Union. Preaching came by the way of circuit riders, visiting or traveling preachers from both camps.

The Vossburg United Methodist Church was organized in the Meridian District under the auspices of the Methodist Episcopal Church, South, in 1882. In 1939 it became the Methodist Church at the Unification Conference in Kansas City, Missouri. The Evangelical United Brethren Church united with the Methodist Church in 1968 to be called the United Methodist Church. In the early days this little church was a part of the Enterprise, Forest and Newton districts. In 1908 it became a part of the Hattiesburg district. It is now, again, in the Meridian district. In 100 years this church has been ministered to by 43 pastors, 26 presiding elders and 30 bishops.

## PASTORS OF THE VOSSBURG CHURCH

| | |
|---|---|
| J. B. Baldwin | Thomas Hewitt King |
| Lyman Carley | McKendree Marvin Black |
| Daniel C. Langford | D. Elton Brown |
| William C. Hines | Denison C. Napier |
| Benton Solomon Rayner | Bruce Nicholas |
| Ralph Bradley | G. C. Aston |
| Jules Victor Penn | Cliff B. Smith |
| Robert Barnes Downer | Benjamin M. Lawrence |
| William Monroe Sullivan | J. Bruce Vardaman |
| James Madison Corley | James Thomas Weems |
| Paul Douglas Hardin | C. V. Bugg |
| Robert S. Gale | Ned T. Keller |
| Charles E. Evans | Keith R. Hagenson |
| William DeFreeze Dominick | Gaines McCago Thomas |
| William James Dawson | John Floyd Carter |
| James William Ramsey | James R. Meyers |
| Henry J. Maddox | Charles Olan Miller |
| John Henry Jolly | Ronald Stanley |
| William Gibson Forsythe | John Cornell |
| Stewart Calhoun Moody | James Dudley Slay, Sr. |
| Walter Preston George | Jim Ballard |
| Patrick Henry Howse | |

## THY PRESENCE NEAR

We stand today where our fathers stood
And hear a distant sound;
We hear them preaching, praying, singing -
We stand on holy ground!

We crawl first, and afterwards we walk -
Then we a running go;
But along the Christian pathway we
Are still a crawling so!

Help us to probe deeply in our souls
And try to speak for Thee;
We are so dull, so blind to the truth
We fail to hear and see.

We're not big enough to do Thy work
Within our strength alone;
Our prayer then is for Thy presence near
That we might carry on.

Dr. James Dudley Slay, Sr.

*The only grave in the church yard. There is no adjoining church cemetery - Rev. Theo S. Norman*

*The last faithful members of Vossburg Methodist Church - Standing on the church steps - circa 1980*

Sherry Allen, Ann Thomas, Francis Brewer, Dan Brewer, Una Logan, Harold Logan, Verda Mae Brewer, Dewey Brewer, Donis Brewer, Ann Stafford Petermann, Randy Brewer, Herman Dykes, Wessie Dykes, James Thomas, Bobby Stephens, Sandra Thomas, Larry Hillard, Grace Wells (wife of Leroy Wells), Lena Lightsey, Bonnie Mae Martin (wife of Robert Martin)

*A members recollection and painting of the original Shady Grove church building*

# HISTORY

## SHADY GROVE FIRST BAPTIST
## A CHURCH WITH A MISSION

Shady Grove First Baptist Church was established as a Cambelite church by William G. Bounds and others in the year of 1845. Mr. William G. Bounds was buried in Shady Grove Cemetery in 1847.

In the years following the 1850's through the year of 1867 difficult and trying times came upon the church. John Chapman Bounds, son of William G. Bounds, was licensed to preach in 1866 by the Shady Grove Baptist Church, but died before he could fill the pulpit. The 200 some church members both white and black began to part as the white families could not look after all the blacks scattered around the county. Other preachers were having to give up their pulpits and take jobs close to home to support their families. Brother Ferrell still came on the 3rd Saturday and Sunday to preach for us, while he continued to preach over at Ebernezer and Beaverdam Churches.

In 1887 Shady Grove Baptist was again flourishing, a Bro. Hall came as pastor and many new members by family names of Martin, Bynum, Morris, Voss, Heidelberg, Ellis, Cooleys, and Thatchs joined the church. In 1890 others like the Walkers, McDonalds, Herringtons, Odoms, Arringtons, came to join Shady Grove. During these times the church took a strong stand against immorality and sin; even to kicking members out of the church and withdrawing fellowship from them until they straightened out their lives. The church also served as the schoolhouse and community gathering place for socials. Mr. A. A. Allen taught school here in the year of 1890 and following years. At the Associational meeting that year, Brother Martin, who wrote for the Standard, Mr. Obe Robinson, Brother Turner, Brother Thigpen, Willie Thigpen, Brother Clark Shows, Brother Tolbert, a teacher of the Indians, and Brother Hall covered the Colportage work.

In the following years many pastors came to serve at Shady Grove Baptist; men like W. A. Roper in 1898, A. J. Thames in 1901, L. E. Hall in 1904, C. G. Elliott in 1905, H. M. Collins in 1910, J. F. Hailey in 1913, Bro. Hayes in 1916, Rev. Hendrix in 1918, J. B. Garrish, Bro. Chris Chisholm, Bro. J. W. Lee, R. A. Venerable in 1919, Bro. Hendrix again in the year of 1922.

# HISTORY

It is uncertain which association Shady Grove served with up to this time, but during these years Shady Grove sent messengers to Lebanon and Jones Associational meetings, supported foreign mission board, and aided the Pleasant Grove Church in ongoing support. Other minutes from 1922 to 1945 were apparently destroyed in a fire.

In 1945 Bro. Hendrix, pastor, along with Mr. Bert Ellis on the 3rd Sunday in August started Sunday school at 3:00 P.M. following the morning services. A number of families began to take part, the Speights, Thomas', Kennedys, Travis' Merrells, Allens, Penningtons, Cooks, Martins, Stanleys, Lyons, and Bounds. Others joined the church and Sunday School as time passed on, the Hensons, Donalds, Eddins, Johnstons, Lees, James, McDaniels, Phillips, Rileys, Thatchs, Sanders, Thorntons, Sanfords, Arledges, Ritches, Hollands, Chancellors, Bennetts, Herringtons, Blackledges, Elkins, Reads, Smiths, McKees, Moseleys, Touchstones, Walters, Chathams, and others in later years.

In 1946 a new building was built and is still in use today. The first service in the new building was on November 17, Dr. Van Harden preached the first message in the new church while Bro. Hendrix was still pastor.

Dr. D. A. McCall served during the first part of the year in 1947, while Rev. Grayson came in October of that year. The new Shady Grove Baptist Church was dedicated October 3rd of 1948 with Dr. W. E. Greene preaching the dedication service and the Clark College Quartet singing after the noon meal. In 1952 Rev. Burch was pastor, in 1954 Rev. J. W. McGrew was pastor, the parsonage was built and they became the first residents. In 1961 Rev. John Daniels was called as pastor and in 1963 E. C. Moss became pastor. Others came into the church, the Sellers, Whites, Schletts, Davis'. The church was remodeled in 1964, a baptistry, new Sunday School rooms, were added and a kitchen. Bro. Moss did most of the work himself. The year of 1967 brought improvements as Mrs. Doris Wilson gave a new organ and hymnals and the church was air-conditioned. In 1968 the name of the church was changed to Shady Grove First Baptist Church. The Merrell family gave a marble plaque engraved with the new name and placed it over the doors in front of the church. Mrs. Velma Speights gave a baptistry painting in honor of Mrs. Minnie Thomas and Mrs. J. E. Bounds gave the vestibule and steeple in honor of Mr. J. E. Bounds. In 1969 Rev. Moss' son, Mike Moss and Frank Travis Anderson were licensed to the gospel ministry. In 1977 Rev. Harold Wilson was called as pastor, in 1981 Rev. J.W. Williams and in 1985 Rev. Sharber Smith was called as pastor. The sanctuary was remodeled with new carpet, cushions for the pews and painting of the sanctuary.

# HISTORY

Many of the elders have passed on and others have moved away. There are many new faces like the Boultons, Roberts, Welborns, Rowells, Solomons, Williams, Gillis', Harrisons, yet many of the family names remain from the early church.

In the year of 1994 more new faces arrive as Rev. Ervin "Leon" Parnell and family move into the pastorium. The church continues to grow spiritually and numerically as the Henningtons, Broadheads, Ulmers, join the church family. New office furniture, a typewriter, and copier were purchased. The painting of the fellowship hall, kitchen, Sunday School rooms, and pastor's office all have a fresh appearance. The church has also incorporated and at present are waiting for new carpet to be placed in the fellowship hall and Sunday School rooms.

On July 16th 1995, Shady Grove First Baptist Church celebrated our 150th anniversary in our "Lord's" service. This coincides with the 150th anniversary of the Southern Baptist Convention this year. Like the S.B.C., Shady Grove First Baptist knows our "Lord" has "empowered us for the unfinished task." A great day of celebration with Dr. Edward L. McMillan, Exe. Secretary of Mississippi Historical Commission of the Mississippi Baptist Convention and Jasper Association presented plaques and certificates to the church for service and dedication to and in our "Lord's" work. We at Shady Grove are thankful to those who served our Lord well in the past and trust that not only we, but others who come will continue in their labor of love. Trusting that as our Lord tarries we would not lose sight of the call to the unfinished task for our "Lord!" Matt. 28:18-20.

Thanks to all who helped, to those sources of information; Jasper Co. News Aug. 29th, 1957 Edition, Mrs. J. E. Bounds, Mrs. Bell McGrew, Mrs. E. C. Moss, Mrs. Velma Speights, Mrs. J. T. Merrell. To all the church clerks who over the years that kept up with historical events, and to the historical committee that labored long hours with Bro. Leon to make this available for us of the Shady Grove First Baptist Church, as well as friends of our church.

Yours in His Service

*Rev. Ervin L. Parnell*

Rev. Ervin L. Parnell
Pastor

# CHURCH FAMILY

*I was glad when they said unto me, Let us go into the house of the Lord.*
    Psalms 122:1

# Later Years

Up until about 1930, a gravel Highway 11 ran through Vossburg. However, the road was rerouted and paved. Vossburg became a side route, off the beaten path and the economic impact was negative.

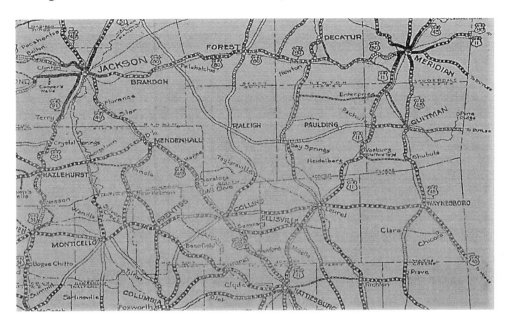

*1928 Mississippi Road Map showing Highway 11 as unpaved and routed through Vossburg*

*Site of the Mid Donald home. During the early 1940's this site was used to set up a traveling motion picture theatre. On Saturdays, an unknown gentleman hauled a large tent and a projector to the site. After erecting the tent, the truck, which housed the projector, would be backed up to one end of the tent. Old westerns and horror movies would be projected onto a pull-down screen at the opposite end of the tent. Admission was $.10 for children and $.25 for adults. Blacks and whites sat within the same tent, segregated by a center isle between the folding chairs.*

*The old Blackledge home*

*The Blackledge Store*

*Old Highway 11 through the center of town*

*The old Oscar Lee Home, once surrounded by one of the most beautiful ornate iron fences that I have ever seen.*

*The old Thornton Home and the Lee pecan groves*

*Remains of the old Vossburg Post Office*

*Previous site of the Turner Store. The present day Vossburg Post Office is on left.*

*The new Vossburg Bridge. This is the third bridge to be built in the same location. The first burned during the 60's. The foundations of the second washed out. Two warehouses and several store once occupied the vacant land on the left. Martin's garage and several stores occupied the land on the right. It's hard to imagine that this was once the center of a town.*

*Road that descends into the railroad hollow (the original Highway 11 prior to the first bridge) Martin's and J.E. Bound's Stores were once located on the right, as was the Voss Hotel.*

*Foundation remains of the Vossburg Rail Depot – A sad testament to days gone by*

*The Vossburg Spring which supplied water to the Voss Hotel. Hotel was located to the left.*

*The Vossburg Cemetery*

*The Old Eddins Home*

*The Old Eddins Store*

# Heidelberg

The ancestral roots of Heidelberg can be traced back to the Palatinate region of Germany. Following the French invasion of the 1680's, and the religious persecution that followed, many Protestant Germans fled the Rhine River region. Large numbers of these refugees immigrated to England and, later, sailed to the new world colonies located in North Carolina. The majority earned a living by farming, slowly migrating westward, clearing new lands as the unfertilized soils lost their ability to sustain a decent yield.

The first recorded Heidelberg was a colonist named Christian Heidelberg, appearing in records during the early 1700's. Christian fathered two sons, one of which was named John Christian Heidelberg. John's son, Thomas Christian, was born in North Carolina during the late 1760's. In 1800, he moved his wife and children to Georgia. Around 1817, the family moved westward into the piney woods of the Mississippi Territory. He established himself in this new land and was living near Bogue Homa Creek as late as 1830.

Thomas' son, Thomas Christian Heidelberg, Jr., established his home on Beaver creek, between the present location of Heidelberg and Vossburg. He married a young woman by the name of Jane Risher, from the Vossburg area. One of their daughter's married Captain Edward Stafford, for whom Stafford Springs is named. Another son of Thomas, Samuel Christian Heidelberg, established a large farm in the Paulding area. Samuel would father and raise fifteen children, five of whom served in Army of the Confederate States. Despite engaging in numerous battles and being twice wounded, one of these sons, Washington Irving Heidelberg, returned to found the town of Heidelberg.

Around 1870, W.I. Heidelberg settled on a plot of Jasper County land that he had purchased prior to the war. With a demonstration of strong character, he persevered the difficult times afforded by the difficult years of reconstruction period. He managed to construct a fine home, marry, and began a family. His business ventures would grow to include a considerable farming enterprise, a general mercantile store, a cotton gin, and a gristmill.

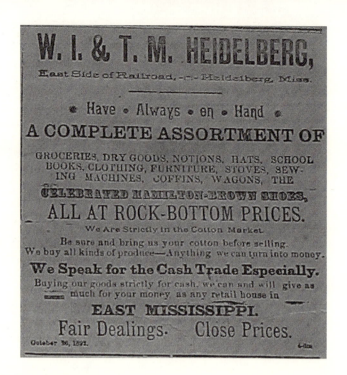

In 1882, on his own land, he laid out the present location of Heidelberg town. Included in this plan was a right of way that he presented to the New Orleans and Northwestern Railroad. This gesture ensured that a proposed Paulding to Mobile railway line would route through his community. A grid work of Streets was surveyed and numbered one through twelve. In all, the town encompassed one square mile, extending from Beaver Creek to old Highway Eleven

The railroad accepted his offer and with this key asset came enterprise and commerce. Farmers in the surrounding areas were soon routing their goods through Heidelberg. Numerous travelers were also passing through the fledgling town. Realizing yet another opportunity, Washington built a camp house to accommodate those who were in need of shelter. Other business would soon spring up along Ochs Street, the main street through town. T.M. Heidelberg, a brother of W.I., would establish another general mercantile. Abney & Travis would establish a business that included an undertaking service. Gaston and Sprinkle General Mercantile was another prominent establishment.

*Ochs Street – circa 1900*

*Heidelberg Rail Depot*

It is recorded that Heidelberg had six doctors and one dentist. A local inventor, C.R. Reid, operated a small manufacturing operation for seed planters. The first barbershop in town was owned and operated by Irving Reid, a black barber. In 1900, S.C. Wilkins opened a two-story hotel across the street from W.I. Heidelberg's General Store. W.A. Morrison operated a horse and buggy rental service to salesmen and other travelers who needed transportation to the outlying communities. Four cotton gins, several restaurants, a beef market, a millinery shop, and an ice plant were also opened.

*One of the four cotton gins*

A post office was also built on Ochs Street. The first postmaster was Daniel.W.Gatlin. In 1900, S.C. Wilkens, owner of the hotel, was appointed postmaster. He relocated the post office to his business until the facility was destroyed by fire. Before residing in the present day location, the post office occupied space in the Bethea Grocery, W.A. Morison's store, and the Common Wealth Bank building.

Heidelberg's first bank was opened in 1904 with S.W. Abney serving as president and Sam Morgan as the cashier. A large sawmill was opened in 1910 and the relentless harvest of the abundant virgin timber began.

The first school one-room was built during the early 1900's. A second school, located on North Magnolia Avenue, was destroyed by fire.

*The Wilkens Hotel – Post Office*

As the public road system came into being, the original Highway eleven was routed through Heidelberg, Stafford Springs, and Vossburg. This was an unpaved gravel road and remained such until the early 1950's. (Highway Eleven was later rerouted, bypassing both Heidelberg and Vossburg) Travel during the early part of the century was mostly conducted by railroad due to the poor road conditions. This was especially true during the wet seasons.

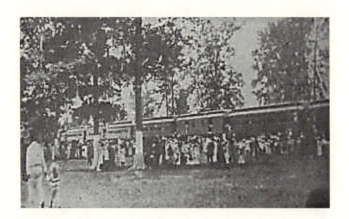

*Photo of an excursion train at the Heidelberg Picnic Grounds*

Three churches were built within the town, a Baptist, a Methodist, and a Presbyterian. A large picnic area was also constructed on the east end of town and was used by the Brotherhood of Trainmen as the destination of an annual excursion. Special trains were run from Meridian and New Orleans to the site.

The Thornton's opened a Ford automobile dealership during 1921. The cars were shipped by rail from Detroit and displayed along Ochs Street. Prices ranged from about $450 to $700, depending on the model and features purchased.

*The 1921 Ford Line*

*The Abney Ford Dealership*

*The Abney Service Station*

*Abney Homeplace*

In 1943, oil was discovered beneath Heidelberg and brought a burst of new life into the area. At that time, there was only one telephone in the entire town, located in one of the grocery stores. Many of these shallow wells have continuously produced crude for nearly sixty years. In a posthumous display of business savvy, it was determined that W.I. Heidelberg had retained the mineral rights to the land that he deeded to the railroad, a decision that proved profitable for his heirs.

*Some Current Heidelberg Oil Production*

*Ochs Street – 2003*

*The Mary Weems Parker Memorial Library - Wife of Dr. W.H. Parker*

*The Confederate Memorial Monument was originally imported from France and erected in 1911*

# The Heidelberg Oil Boom

## The Heidelberg Oil Boom

As early as 1929, surveyors employed by the Gulf Oil Company recognized the geological signature of oil in the proximity of Heidelberg, Mississippi. In 1933, the Eastman-Gardiner Company established a drilling site on the Morrison lease, but, for unknown reasons, elected not to follow through. Using seismographic and core drilling techniques, Gulf Oil continued their exploration during the following years and outlined what was believed to be a huge underground oil structure. In October of 1943, Gulf established a drilling site on the Helen Morison lease. W.G. Ray, a contract driller, was hired to sink the well and oil was finally discovered on December 23$^{rd}$.

The exciting prospects of wealth saw the value of land soar within the town. Resident lots began to sell at $100 per acre. Within a mile of the well, oil royalties sold for $200 per acre.

On January 27$^{th}$, 1944, the Helen Morison well was completed and the production was recorded as 160 barrels of 23-degree gravity oil per day. Gulf Oil constructed four 500-barrel storage tanks near the well and laid pipe to a rail loading station south of Heidelberg on the Southern Railroad.

A second well was drilled on the Helen Morison lease and proved to be more prolific than the first. When drilling was completed, 209 feet of oil-saturated sand was reported. In March of 1944, *The Dixie Geological Survey Report*, an oil industry trade journal, proclaimed, "Heidelberg may prove to be Mississippi's largest reserve!"

The third Heidelberg well was drilled on the Mack Lindsey lease and, unexpectedly, rather than oil, it produced 20 million cubic feet of natural gas per day. Another well was drilled on the property that brought in plentiful quantities of crude. Soon thereafter, independent drillers joined the action and *Dixie* reported: "Heidelberg, Jasper County, Mississippi, is fast beginning to look like an oil field. Production derricks have been erected on the two producing wells and the derrick is still up on Sun No. 1, Mack Lindsey, which gives a total of about 12 derricks that can be counted from the high hill at Gulf's No. 1, T.D. Lewis. The oil at Heidelberg was selling for 82 cents per barrel. (May 18, 1944)

*Sherman Adkins - Interstate Oil 1946*

One of the better wells was drilled on the H.W. Husbands* property by an independent, Graham and Lewis. The well drillers employed a perforation technique and the well ultimately flowed at a rate of 1,896 barrels per day. Mrs. Effie Husband, who was reported to be a very poor woman, was soon to become a very rich woman.

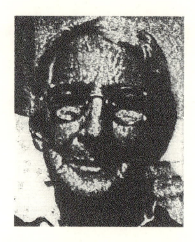

*Mrs. H.W. (Effie) Husbands*

The oil field development continued at a blinding pace and there were 104 producing wells in Heidelberg by the end of 1945. The extensive effort and investment exerted by Gulf Oil had been rewarded.

In January 1944, the pony edition of *Time* Magazine carried a story about the Heidelberg boom. In February 1945, *Collier's* Magazine carried the following article:

### Ole Miss' Strikes It Rich

By Harry Henderson and Sam Shaw

Eleven fields are now in operation and wildcats are being drilled in twenty-five counties. The greatest drilling activity is near the little town of Heidelberg … But the whole state is swarming with geologist, roustabouts, scouts, roughnecks, tool pushers, riggers, drillers, lease hounds, wildcatters, speculators, lawyers, tipsters and gypsters, ant that crowd of fast operators who appear wherever money is made and lost hand over fist …

Lease hounds track geophysical crews to try to dope out the area they are converging on, so they can jump into its center and grab some of the leases. The geophysical crews get up in the middle of the night and drive 60 miles in a circle to escape them …

The competition is frantic and fantastic not only for leases and royalties, but for everything from a hotel bed to a square meal.

All of the major oil companies and several scores of independents are drilling and exploring Mississippi's substrata. They have unleashed a flood of money, millions in leases and drilling with royalties still to come in what has been one of the poorest sections in America.

Southeastern Mississippi, which has become the focal point of the boom, has never known such wealth. Here there were never plantations, but only small farms, worked by farmers who were too poor to buy slaves.

Until thirty years ago, much of it was pine forest. Now most of this has been cut off, leaving scrubby, stumpy land almost too poor for cultivation, to be ravaged by erosion …

From the oilman's view, probably the most significant fact about this Mississippi discovery is that the search for oil has now moved eastward.

The big change is in people's pocketbooks – money. For the first time in their lives they all have it.

One of the men who will probably end up a millionaire as a result of the discovery of oil is chubby B.C. Burns who runs just about everything there is in Heidelberg to run, namely, a cotton gin, a general store, a cement agency and a trucking firm. Burns came to Heidelberg sixteen years ago fresh out of the University of Alabama's school of commerce … he managed to build up a profitable business and put the profits back into land. He now owns 700 acres and has two good wells, and has an interest in four others.

*B. C. Burns*

The king size good luck story of Heidelberg is Harry Eddy, a big, slow-footed whittler with a downhill gait, whose cup overfloweth with ironic amusement at his new wealth. He owns 1,805 acres in Wayne, Jones, Jasper and Clarke Counties, with seven wells and more to come.

*Harry Eddy (on right)*

Two young Mississippians named Evon Ford and John Clark from Smith County got in on twelve wells by loading a car with $10,000 cash and pulling farmers in off the street. Then while one offered a farmer cash for his royalty, the other phoned a companion in the courthouse who gave the man's title the once-over. If it looked clear, they bought it.

Mrs. [Effie] Husbands accepted $100 from a strange man for a third of her royalty. A few days later, her son Norman, to whom she had given some land, accepted $280 for a third of his royalties. Not until a sister got $5,000 for a similar share did they realize the value of the rights. (*Collier's* Magazine, February 10, 1945)

Many of Heidelberg's residents achieved great wealth during the oil boom. A substantial oil field support industry developed in the area as well. Eventually, the majority of the oil reserve was exhausted. The final numbers were impressive. Some 250 oil wells on the Heidelberg field would yield over 175 million barrels of oil. This ranks the Heidelberg field as Mississippi's third largest find. Even today, a few of the wells continue to produce.

Reference:

Hughes, Dudley J., *Oil in the Deep South*: a history of the oil business in Mississippi, Alabama, and Florida: 1859 – 1945 / Dudley J. Hughes ISBN 0-87805-615-7 Published for the Mississippi Geological Society and available from the University Press of Mississippi

In the referenced printed articles, Mrs. H.W. Husbands is referred to as Mrs. W. H. Husband. Per a family member, William Henry Husbands was her son. She married only once to Henry W. Husbands.

# Heidelberg Schools

*This is the 1939 Graduating Class at Heidelberg High School. These were the names written on the back of the picture:*

*Front row: Eugie Stamper, Eloise Thomas (Valedictorian)*

*2nd row: James Morrison, Lila Rae Touchstone, Francis McDonald, Laverne Pittman, Thomas Bonner,*

*3rd row: Catherine Bergin, Maxine Eddy, Oneida Morris*

*Back Rows (names not necessarily in order): Walter McDaniel, Steve Lee, Tommie Loper (Salutatorian), Jessie Mae Lowery, Whitney Sims, Joseph Carr, Lavoy Craft, Miss Nell Bayliss, Horace Bergin*

*L to R: Glenda Spurlin, Barbra Pauley, Judy Adkins, John Newton Satcher – Early 1950's*

*Homer Holmes (School Principal '50's) and wife Thelma Holmes*

*Mr. Fortenberry – Band Director Early '50's*

*Miss Smith & Jerry Adkins hiding behind the bush*

# Mineral Springs

Jasper County does not suffer for water resources and I suspect this feature was especially appealing to the early settlers. Especially in the eastern sections of the county, there are many springs, creeks, and rivers that dot the landscape. Beyond the basic needs of water and before medical science evolved into modern standards, water that tasted of minerals gathered a following for it's curative benefits. Several sources for this mineral water were found in eastern Jasper and in nearby locations. Some of these springs managed to achieve nationwide fame.

## Stafford Springs

Before the days of the interstate highway system, cross-country travel in this nation was conducted mostly on the network of federal two-lane highways. A classic example, US-11, meandered through Mississippi from Meridian down to New Orleans. About forty-miles south of Meridian, along a series of rolling hills and two miles southeast of Vossburg, US-11 passes through a largely forgotten spot of historical importance named Stafford Springs.

Stafford Springs came to be named after a confederate veteran who settled near the town of Vossburg following the War of Northern Aggression. Soon after his arrival, Captain Edward W. Stafford made an interesting observation. The few remaining Choctaw Indians, who had managed to evade deportation by the Federal Government to the Indian Territory in Oklahoma, often brought their sick or ailing to drink from a mineral water spring located in his pasture. The Choctaw called the spring "Bogohama", or "Water of Life" and, as Stafford observed, many of those who drank appeared to profit some relief.

*Edward W. Stafford*

*The Original Edward Stafford Home*

*Edward Stafford Home in later years of decay*

One thing led to another and it wasn't long before the white man had adopted the Indian's belief in the spring. It is reported that the water was sent out for testing and a Congress of Medicine, held in Chicago, IL, proclaimed it to offer great benefit to those suffering from Bright's disease and other kidney and bladder ailments. As testimony to the curative qualities spread, a group of capitalists formed the Stafford Mineral Springs Company, Limited, and incorporated in Louisiana on May 19, 1892. The oficers are listed as follows: President: C. Livingston, Vice President: Dr. Rudolph Schiffman, both of St. Paul Minnesota, and G.L. Colburn, Secretary and Treasure, of Stafford Springs.On March 7, 1893, the group formed the Stafford Mineral Springs and Hotel Company, Limited and soon built a bottling works that could produce two railroad carloads per day. The Stafford Inn, described as "a large and comfortable hotel, with wide porches, airy rooms, comfortable office, bath rooms and all modern conveniences," opened in 1899. The owners promised that "rates are reasonable".

Thereafter, people began to travel from all over the country to bathe and drink from the waters of life. Most of them arrived by rail in the town of Vossburg, met by a taxi carriage and ox drawn wagon loads of mineral waters.

*1902 letterhead used by Stafford Mineral Springs*

*1902 Invoice*

*One of the original five-gallon carboys used to ship the mineral water. This one survived for many years beneath my grandmother's house and, nowadays, has become a flower vase.*

*One of the smaller one-quart consumer jugs. I have managed to find two of these with the paper labels still intact, despite the fact that they are over one hundred-years old. One was located in Connecticut and the other in New York - a long way from Jasper County.*

Stafford Mineral Springs Water was sold in "Carboy, Bottle, or Jug," and always contained the registered trade mark, a "'RED HEART' and the word BO-GO-HA-MA, printed upon it in White Letters upon a black background". The half-gallon bottle was apparently colorless with a single-part finish, for use with corks, and paper label. On the label was printed STAFFORD/MINERAL

SPRINGS/WATER above the red heart with THE/BO-HO-GA-MA/(WATER OF LIFE) OF THE INDIAN in an upward sweeping arc. On both sides of the heart were claims for the water's curative properties followed by finer print that is illegible in the drawing in the booklet. The final lines stated Stafford Mineral Springs & Hotel Co. (in script)/of NEW ORLEANS, LA. [1]

*The Public Fountain housed in the Gazebo that was situated in front of the Hotel near US Hwy -11*

*The Old Hotel from a 1906 Promotional Booklet*

*Facade of the Hotel from a early promotional flier*

*Visitors posing on the Water Wagon*

*Stafford Springs Hotel Property Main Entrance - Highway 11 - circa 1910*

*Close up of Welcome Station on Highway 11*

*Detail of foot bridge. Directly behind bridge, two women standing and talking. To the left beside a tree,*

*a lone man standing.*

*Detail of Gazebo. Lone woman standing to the left. Two women standing at doorway. Lone woman standing behind gazebo. Upper right, lone man walking toward gazebo. In the background, the old hotel porch banister can be made out as well as hints of the hotel structure.*

*The original dirt and gravel US-11 looking north - C 1928*

*Young girls posing at the Stafford way stop on US-11 - C 1928*

*Young lady posing on the Stafford waystop bench on US-11. Hotel can be seen in the background*

*Quiet walkway leading to the hotel - C 1928*

Dr. Schiffman and his partners owned stock in the Stafford property until 1918, when it was transferred to A.L. Staples of Mobile, Alabama. In 1925 Staples and company sold the property to a group of Meridian Mississippi businessmen, reported to have included a Mr. Repshur and a Mr. John Perry. For a short period of time, this same group, or Perry alone, also held the local landmark known as Lake Waukaway. In 1930, Dr. E.M. Gavin purchased the property and moved his family to the site. The following are some photos from the Galvin ownership.

*Dr. Evan Moody Gavin with children Anita and Charles on the hotel grounds C. 1937*

*Anita and Charles Gavin C. 1937*

With the advances seen in medicine during the 20th century came a loss in faith by the general public for the curative powers of mineral waters. Clients stopped coming and the resort fell victim to economic hardship and decay. The Great Depression certainly played a role in the reduced patronage. Sadly, the old hotel was torn down around 1956. I personally remember riding down to the site with my grandfather to purchase some of the used lumber. He used it in the construction of a house which, as of 2003, remains standing in Vossburg.

Parallel to the demise of the health resort, new life was introduced into the property. In 1952, the site was subdivided. The Gavins withheld their home site while selling the hotel properties to a Florida investor by the name of Landstreet. Landstreet, and possibly others unknown, also owned the Pinehurst Hotel in Laurel, MS, the Hotel King Cotton in Memphis, TN, and the Nobel Hotel in Blytheville, AK.

Thanks to the popularity and affordability of the automobile, America was becoming a mobile society. Motels were springing up along the highway systems and Stafford Springs seemed like a strategic location. On the opposite side of US-11, a modern motor lodge and a café was constructed.

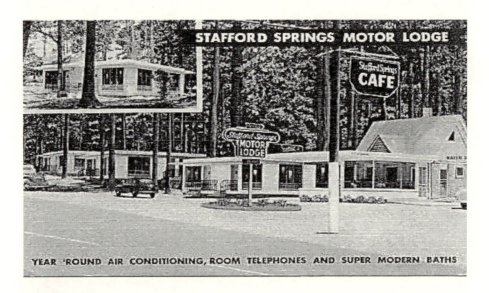

This facility was operated from around 1952 until Interstate I-59 replaced US-11 during 1967. Soon thereafter, the loss of passing traffic brought with it deep economic hardship.

# The Stafford Springs Dude Ranch

In 1961, John L. and Dorothy Blanks assumed management of the Stafford Springs property. Mr. & Mrs. Blanks, seasoned Gulf Coast motel veterans, who had previously managed the Trade Winds Motor Court in Biloxi, orchestrated a major overhaul of the facility. In addition to the upgraded motor lodge, a Dude Ranch theme was added. Horses, trail rides, authentic Indians in costume [*a Choctaw indian who went by the name of Cooley Jim. He also worked at the summer camps for children held at Lake Waukaway*], chuck wagon meals, a stagecoach, and a horse drawn hearse (rumored to be the one used to transport Jesse James to his final resting place), were listed among the attractions. The Dude Ranch operated for a number of years, but there simply wasn't enough business to prevent the inevitable demise of the facility.

*John Blanks*

*Dining Room in the Old Hotel*

*The Highway 11 Stafford Springs Cafe*

*Interior of the cafe*

*One of the newer motel duplex buildings that replaced the hotel*

*Interior of motel room*

*The unusually large swimming pool*

*The old gazebo and the spring fed drinking fountain*

In about 1958, I remember my grandfather stopping at Stafford and taking me inside the old stone sided water building. Inside, a black employee, wearing rubber boots, was working to manually fill a large number of glass jugs. This was accomplished by positioning multiple jugs on a workbench and filling them with a water hose. Wooden crates, specifically designed to cradle the glass bottles, were used to ship the water. At that time, the train no longer stopped at Vossburg and they were forced to ship the water by truck. The volume sold was apparently very low and a majority of the business stemmed from local customers. I'm not sure of the exact date that bottling of the water ceased, but I'm sure that it had stopped by the time that the property was converted to the dude ranch theme.

For a while, the motel rooms were rented out as apartments and the restaurant was opened and closed by a few different owners. For a number of years, William "Little Bill" Martin, of Vossburg, operated a gas station in the remains of the old stone sided water building, first built in 1886.

All known commercial activity ceased at Stafford Springs during the 1980's, somewhat short of a centennial celebration. Nowadays, the large roadside sign and a few of the abandoned motel buildings are all that remain. On the opposite side of the sparsely used US-11, a private residence stands near the original site of the resort motel. Despite all of this disruption, Bogohama continues to flow, just as it did when the Choctaw first discovered it.

*The remains of the Motor Lodge Restaurant building with the Dude Ranch sign in the background*

*The remains of one motel room duplex*

*A home that now occupies the site of the old hotel. Concrete in foreground is the old curb that surrounds the reclaimed motor lodge swimming pool.*

# Stafford Springs Post Cards and Memorabilia

Spanning a couple of decades, I conducted a active search for anything related to Stafford Springs. The following items are a few items from the results of that effort. Some of it was bought, some borrowed, and some generously given.

Stafford Inn, as seen from the Highway, Stafford Springs, Miss.

The Grove, Stafford Springs, Vossburg, Miss.

Stafford Inn, Vossburg, Miss.

The abundant growth of native forest trees surrounding the Inn, results in an atmosphere that is hard to duplicate, Stafford Springs, Miss.

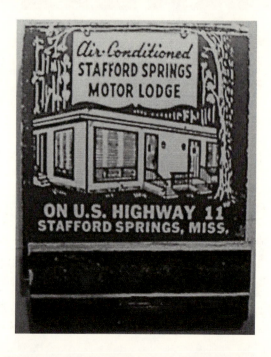

Stafford Springs is not only a delightful overnight stop but you will enjoy spending a week or a month. Ultra modern, reasonable rates, year round air conditioning, room telephones and excellent food.

Old Colonial, Established 1892.

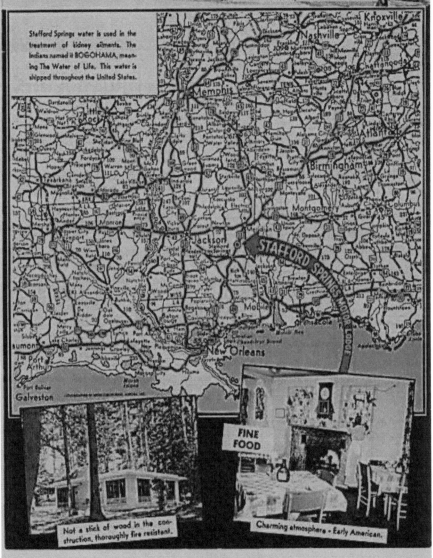

Stafford Springs water is used in the treatment of kidney ailments. The Indians named it BOGOHAMA, meaning The Water of Life. This water is shipped throughout the United States.

Not a stick of wood in the construction, thoroughly fire resistant.

FINE FOOD

Charming atmosphere - Early American.

Horseback riding. Charming bridal trails.

Walkaway Springs and Bathing Beach, 36,000 gallons of water per hour. Two miles on good road.

# Other Mineral Springs

By all known accounts, there were three commercial mineral water springs established near Vossburg during the late 1800's. Newspaper articles and US Geological records reflect that two of these springs, Stafford Springs and Lithia Springs, were engaged in significant commercial enterprise wherein they bottled and shipped mineral water on a global scale. The activity of the third spring, the Vossburg Mineral Springs Company, is not clear. The records of the United States Geological Survey do point to two major players: Stafford Springs and Lithia Springs. Other than a statement contained in the newspaper clip posted below, I have not been able to find any record of the Vossburg Mineral Spring water being bottled or shipped. Only one hotel is known to have operated in Vossburg, The Voss Hotel, so it is likely that the Vossburg Mineral Spring Company was somehow affiliated.

*Clip from Jasper County News - circa 1900*

A few years ago, while I was searching for information relative to Stafford Springs, I ran across an E-Bay item associated to Jasper County. The offering was for a printer's bottle label proof for the Vossburg Mineral Springs Company, recovered from the files of a defunct New York printer. At that time, I had never heard of a Vossburg Mineral Springs Company and assumed that this must have been an alternative brand once marketed by Stafford or Lithia Springs. I bid on the item and won the auction. A few years later, I have come to realize that I most likely own the sole remaining label of a Vossburg Mineral Springs water bottle.

Based upon personal accounts, the Lithia spring and the spring house (possibly other structures) were located on the north side of the railroad tracks, west of Vossburg, by a relatively short distance (a mile or less). I have been in contact with one individual who, as a child, observed the remains of the spring house and some foundation stones.

# Mariah Springs

Although located north of Eucutta, MS, Mariah Springs was well known to many residents of eastern Jasper County. If visiting in that area, it was a great place to water the horses and to collect some drinking water. This spring is amazing in that it flows like a creek instead of a common spring. I was told that this property was named for a female slave who was given the land in appreciation for her loyal service.

*Mariah Springs – Located north of Eucutta*

# Jasper Swimming and Fishing Holes

Blessed with good water resources, Eastern Jasper County residents had several excellent choices for aquatic recreation. In several locations the free flowing springs were dammed to create lakes to power sawmills, grist mills, and cotton gins. These lakes were also used as swimming and fishing holes and the recreation qualities outlasted the initial purpose in every case.

## Utopia Lake and Fish Camp

*This is a picture of Utopia Lodge located on Old Highway 11 just south Of West's Grocery near Vossburg, Mississippi. During the early 50's, the Utopia Lodge and Fish Camp was owned by J.W. Barnett, Sr. At the time this photograph was taken, the facility was managed by Bob Siebels and his wife Tommie Loper Siebels. It was a great place for locals to unwind, and weary tourists on Highway 11 could stop for a good meal of fresh caught fried fish and have a good night's sleep. Once Interstate Highway I-59 was opened, travelers stopped taking Highway 11 and the Lodge went out of business*

*The Home of J.W. Barnett, Sr. and his wife Myrtle Howell Barnett. This home and his grocery store were located just up the hill from the Utopia lodge going south on Highway 11.*

*Bob Siebels, Tommie Loper Siebels, Barbra Siebels, and a Big Bass - 1954*

*Dave Boney with Mac McCormick sporting a typical day's catch*

*A.E. Prine, of Heidelberg, MS*

**Lake Bounds**

Lake Bounds is located in Clarke County approximately 5 miles east of Highway 11 off the Vossburg / Shubuta road. This lake is located on private property and was closed to the public a few years prior to the death of the previous owner, Trudy Bounds Gatlin.

It is my understanding that the millpond and the gristmill was built by Trudy's father. The date of the construction is unknown, but speculated at around 1890. The pond is fed by a huge spring that produces many thousands of gallons per hour. As a result, the temperature of the water remained around 60 degrees, even during the blazing Mississippi summers. In the younger days of the facility, the water was crystal clear and around 15 to 20 feet deep at center. The soil in the area has a high sand content thus making the lake's bottom and shoreline naturally clean and swimmer friendly.

I'm not sure when Mr. Bounds first grasp the idea of declaring his pond to be a recreational site, but I would speculate that many young boys helped him with the concept. From inception through the 1980's, Lake Bounds became a staple of local family recreation. On any given weekend, the road to the lake would be lined with parked cars. Picnic lunches, watermelons cooling in the water, music, and the happy squeal of young children filled the hollow.

The swimming area was divided into three sections by floats attached to ropes. A shallow children's area was situated near the millrace. A second rope was designed to keep swimmers from venturing into the upper, undeveloped, section of the lake. The main section comprised the balance and included a thick oak diving board and a pontoon raft.

The raft was approximately 10 feet square with flotation provided by four fifty-five gallon steel drums. A long bamboo pole was normally provided to propel the raft about the lake. More often, all of the passengers would sit on one side of the raft and kick their legs to propel the craft. A common raft dweller's sport was a King of the Hill contest whereas the winner was the only party who didn't get tossed into the lake.

A lifeguard was always on duty and you could rest assured that he was a highly qualified swimmer. I once heard that a part of the qualification was to swim the length of the lake, underwater, which was no small task.

Miss Trudy's standards were always high and she had no problem showing you the way out if you didn't conduct yourself in a suitable manner.

I've never spoken to anyone who doesn't remember a trip to Lake Bound's without producing a broad smile. Like so many other elements of life, the facility was a component of a simpler time that has now passed.

*From left to right: Catherine Lowery, Tommie Siebels, Bobbie Siebels, Vannah Merrell. - Circa 1946*

*Note the sandy hill on the opposite side of the lake. A steel cable was strung above the lake. You could climb this incline and slide down the cable suspended by a pulley. The object was to let go above the deep water and make a big splash.*

*Bobby Siebels playing in the lake, circa 1946.*

In the background: A dressing room or bathroom located on the dam. A sign is posted on the corner of the building that reads: PAY AS YOU ENTER – TEN CENTS. The spillway is visible directly behind Bobby.

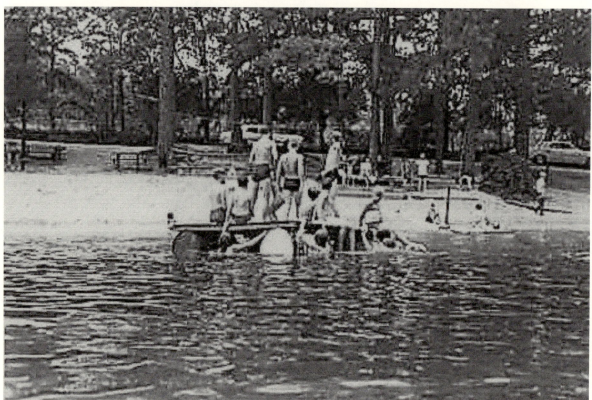

*The old concession building*

During October of 2003, I revisited Lake Bounds and captured some photos of the millpond, the grist mill, and the old store. The condition of the buildings is rapidly degrading and I'm glad that I was able to collect the following photos.

The millpond is now very shallow and filled with moss. Old diving board is still there on the right. Concrete millrace is visible on the lower left. Sand beach is almost gone. Picnic pavilion, site of many happy family reunions, remains on right.

*The dressing rooms*

*The Grist Mill*

*Peeking between the cracks - Mill Interior*

The old scales used to calculate the tare weight fee for grinding corn or wheat. The miller was normally paid with a percentage of the grind. Note the old stoneware pitcher on the lower right.

During the Summer of 2007 I had the opportunity to visit Lake Bounds again. What I found was sad. The foundation of the mill has collapsed and is in a condition of demise. This site is private property so there is likely no salvation. However, I'm glad for the great memories and the luck to have collected some good photos while the mill was intact.

*A newspaper photo from better days*

# Lake Waukaway

*The Cooley-McDaniel Cotton Gin & Gristmill - Lake Waukaway*

*The man at the left, with the hat, is Andrew Jackson McDaniel. Others in the photo are unknown. A.J. McDaniel came to Jasper County MS from Newton County MS, between 1865 and 1870, where his parents, Asa McDaniel and Irena Walker McDaniel, owned a farm of about 200 acres. His father, Asa, died Jan. 5, 1865 in Newton Co. The farm was sold for delinquent taxes in 1874. At that time his mother, Irena, moved to Jasper Co. Typical of those times, the property taxes could not be paid because the reconstruction era governor, Dealbert Ames, raised taxes tenfold between 1870 and 1874. Aside from the Choctaw Indians, the Cooley & McDaniel families were the first known owners of the Waukaway property.*

## A History of Lake Waukaway

You won't find it on a map or listed in any travel guides, but Lake Waukaway, Mississippi, located off Clarke County Road 391, a few miles east of Vossburg, is an amazing gem tucked away in the annals of east-central Mississippi history. The Choctaw people who once inhabited the area called the location, Waukaway, due to the converging of three huge springs. The name translates into "cool and flowing waters". Following the Choctaw Purchase concluded on September 27, 1830, one of the first European settlers to own the property was a fellow by the name of John Cooley. Some years prior to 1865, Cooley, and others unknown, constructed a combination cotton gin and a gristmill at the site of the abundant springs. Somewhat later, Andrew Jackson McDaniel, who was married to Nancy Ann Cooley, John Cooley's daughter, acquired the mills from his father-in-law. The property later passed into the hands of a gentleman by the name of Perry.

Around 1929, the Laurel Mississippi Rotary Club purchased the property from Perry and developed it into a recreational site. They also hired Mr. Howard Allen to manage the facility. Six years later, Mr. Allen purchased the facility along with 120 acres of land. Howard Allen operated Lake Waukaway as a family business until 1978. His home was located at the site, upstairs from the offices and concession buildings, and the business was a full time venture for himself, his wife, and their three children. For some forty years, the people of the surrounding communities came to love their excursions to Lake Waukaway as well as their interactions with the Allen family. In the summer days before air conditioning, Waukaway remained open until 10:00 PM, thus allowing many patrons a place to cool down following a long and hot workday.

In addition to swimming, Howard Allen strove to add other Waukaway attractions. Through the years, there were alligators of all sizes on display, white tail deer in a pen, 7-pound striped bass, and a tame school of blue gill bream that would eat out of your hand. During the 1940's, he sponsored group camps for churches, Boy Scouts, and underprivileged children. Through the 1950's, a private two-week camp, with an Indian theme, was held. A Choctaw Indian named Cooley Jim was on resident making crafts as well as bows and arrows. The climax came in the form of kids donning Indian costumes and holding a "War Party". During the 1960's, participation in these camps came to an end as the various organizations established their own private facilities. In it's place, a small RV park was added to the eastern area of the lake.

In 1978, Howard Allen passed away. Sadly, the Lake Waukaway that so many of us loved ended as well. The property was sold to Mr. Gene Garrick, who established the site as a christian retreat. Presently, the private facility remains in operation.

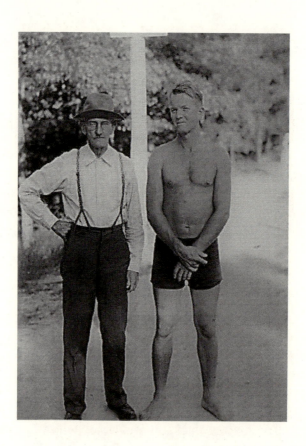

*Howard Allen (right) with Oscar Lee*

# Some Lake Waukaway Photos - Past & Present

*Early photos prior to any major commercial improvements*

*Photo from later shows some landscaping refinements*

*Cecil & Denny Allen – 1927*

After major refinements to the lake were completed, some advertising of the facility began.

*A clip from a Stafford Springs advertisement*

*An extremely brave swimmer jumping off the famous diving tower*

*Personal photos submitted by Dr. Mark Allen*

*Jerry and Judy Adkins*

*A typical weekend crowd during the 1960's*

During 2003, I revisited the Waukaway site and recorded the following photos. The facility is no longer open to the public and I deeply appreciate the staff of the facility for allowing me access onto the grounds.

*The original entrance road and parking area*

*The old entrance gate*

*The old entrance staircase. The building on the right is new and was once the site of the Allen home. The office and concessions were located on the ground floor.*

*A shot of the old kid's pool, much like it used to be. The slide may actually be the original.*

*A general shot of the lake. Gone are the diving platforms. The inflatable things are obviously new. The docks are configured about the same.*

*It's clear that the depth of the lake is far less than it once was. I'm not sure if this was a natural change or intentional.*

*A shot of the secondary lake below the dam. As I remember, this was home to some pet fish.*

*While wandering in the woods, I stumbled across this relic. It's the old platform from the diving tower.*

Lake Waukaway

# Phalti Lake

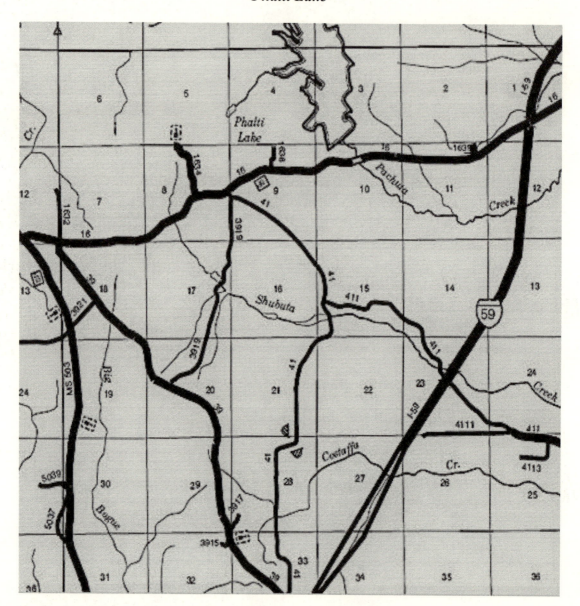

Phalti Lake, located on private property in eastern Jasper County, once served as a popular recreational destination. Both local and extended patrons visited the site as a vacation destination. The railroad transported patrons into the village of Pachuta, who were then transported to Phalti via horse and buggy. It is unclear if lodging was subsequently provided at Phalti or at Pachuta.

Although I have been unable to learn the complete history of the lake, I have obtained several old and current photos of the property. Based upon these photos and a collection verbal accounts, the following is an attempt to piece together the puzzle. If you have any knowledge of the lake's history or can offer any corrections, please contact me.

Based upon early USGS survey maps, Phalti Lake(s) may have once been known as Lewis Lake. These older maps indicate a Lewis Lake Dam at the current Phalti site. In any case, it's apparent that the lakes were constructed for the purpose of supplying water to a sawmill. The old foundation piers of this mill remain in the lower lake. Other testimonials support the existence of a water powered wheel that powered a sawmill.

*Old Photo of the Dam*

These old photos seem to indicate the presence of a hand dug canal or flume system. In other parts of Jasper county, similar systems were used for logging and sawmill operations.

*Notes on the edge of this photo flag the presence of a barn and an overseer's house in the background of the photo.*

In later years, the property was converted into a private residence as well as a recreational faculty for the public. The principal residence, located near the upper lake, remains in good repair and is currently used by the present owners.

*The upper lake is fed by several flowing springs. In turn, the lower lake is fed by the upper lake. Swimming was only allowed in the upper lake.*

If you look closely in this photo, you will recognize a arch bridge that leads to a camping area. Central to this camping area, you will note a white canvas tent.

A sizable concrete swimming pool was built and supplied water by the upper lake.

*Spillway from the swimming pool. Notes on the edge of this photo record a calculation of approximately 18,500 gallons per minute being discharged from the upper lake.*

*Below the dam of the upper lake, a picnic area included an impressive fountain. The head pressure of the upper lake provided for a naturally gushing spray of water that shot several feet into the air. Fish were kept in this fountain, as they are still are.*

In addition to swimming and fishing, I am told that Phalti was used as a camping destination for local boy scout groups. The property also included a sizable dance hall. This dance hall was being used up until the early 60's and may have been the original lodging destination of the early vacation visitors.

*Remains of the Dance Hall*

All forms of public activity have come to an end at Phalti. The site remains as peaceful and inviting as ever. Many fond memories were created on these grounds and I trust that the site will remain treasured by all who had the opportunity to enjoy it.

# Pachuta

Prior to and following the acquisition of this section of the Mississippi Territory, European settlers migrated into the virgin forests of Jasper and Clarke counties. Most of them soon established small hard-scramble farming operations. For unknown reasons and at an unknown date, a village was formed in the current location of Pachuta. This area was situated along the route of a stagecoach road that ran from Mobile, AL to the booming city of Paulding, MS, and may have been the site of a way station.

Although a post office was established at Pachuta in May of 1856, the village was not formally named until 1882 when a map was drawn up for the newly chartered New Orleans and Northwestern Railroad. Captain William. H. Hardy, who assisted in the development of the map, submitted the name. It is unknown if the word represented a nearby creek or was the name of a local resident family. The Pachuta surname is fairly common, originating in the Slavic regions of Eastern Europe, and this may lend credence to the latter speculation.

*Hicks Home in Pachuta*

The first school, a "pay" school, was formed in 1846 and taught by Malcolm Logan. Classes were suspended during the War Between the States, but reinstated in 1866. Classes were held in a two room dogtrot building and continued there until the public school system came into play in 1921.

With the introduction of the railroad, the long established northern industrial base looked to the vast untapped timber resources of the south. A turpentine still and stave mill was built within the town and served as a catalyst for growth. Several general mercantile businesses and other buildings were established along a centralized strip parallel to the railroad right of way. Land for a rail depot was contributed by Major M.F. Berry, a Confederate veteran, who also assisted in the first land survey of the town. Streets were established, including a Main Street that ran North and South on the East side of the railroad. In 1890, an act of the Mississippi legislature incorporated the town.

Growth in the town was slow and steady with additions of several small businesses, a bank, and medical services. The timber industry maintained a presence as the leading industry with several large sawmills being established. One major example was the Mayerhoff Mill, which was a large enough operation to include a commissary.

Around 1900, when US Highway 11 was routed through Pachuta, the route followed the main street. The additional width and easements required that all of the businesses be relocated to the east side of the highway, a layout that remains unchanged.

Consolidation of Mississippi schools began in 1921 and Pachuta was selected as the proper site for a regional High School. Elementary students from the communities of Orange, Paulding, Pine Hill, Souinlouvie, Silver Hill, Vossburg, and Harmony continued to attend local schools while High School students would attend Pachuta. In compliance, a large school was build at the location of East Chestnut and Poydras Streets. During the following years, an auditorium, grammar school, and a gymnasium building were added. As the aforementioned local schools were closed, the elementary students joined the upper clansmen.

*Pachuta Consolidated High School*

The growth of Pachuta crested in the 1940's and 50's only to fade when Interstate I-59 replaced US Highway 11 in 1967. The once thriving village has become a largely forgotten landmark along a sparsely used byway. Most of the businesses have closed and many of the buildings are now gone. The Pachuta School was closed during 1962. With the exception of the gymnasium, all of the school buildings have been demolished.

**Main Street (Highway 11)**

*Site of the Pachuta School*

*The original gymnasium - the sole remaining school building*

*Sign Over the Entrance Door to the Gymnasium – Bleachers - Lunch Room*

# Claiborne

*Once located west of Heidelberg, MS - Jasper County – Photo taken in 1922~1925*

# Oak Bowery

This is a picture of the Oak Bowery School class of 1911. The class was taught by D. V. Bankston, who is now 87 years old and living in Bay Springs. Class members shown are, bottom row, (left to right), D. V. Bankston, Maggie Collins, (deceased), Erma McDonald, N. M. "Dink" Collins, Sam McDonald, (deceased), Willie McDonald, J. C. McLaurin, (deceased). Top row, (left to right), Essie Collins, (deceased), Gabe Collins, (deceased), Bessie McDonald and C. Risher.

# The Jasper County Review

The *Jasper County Review* newspaper was established in Paulding MS in 1890. J.A. Mayer served as the founding editor. During 1892, the name was briefly changed to the *Weekly Review,* then back to the *Jasper County Review* with T.P. Lawless serving as the proprietor and editor. During 1917, under the direction of W.J. Shoemaker, the *Jasper County Review* was merged with the *Bay Spring News* to become the modern day *Jasper County News*.

During the tenure of Mr. T.P. Lawless, copies of the *Jasper County Review* were retained during a time period of 1892 through 1895. These issues were carefully preserved and photographed. It is totally impossible to include this volume of material in this book so I will only present some information regarding Mr. Lawless and a sampling for the newspapers.

*T.P. Lawless*

THOMAS PETER LAWLESS was born 31 Dec 1864 in "Irish Town", a community of Irish settlers, located three miles west of St. Michael's Church in Paulding, Jasper Co., MS. He died 5 May 1920, and he was buried at St. Michael Cemetery. Correspondence between his parents during the Civil War reveals that his father had his last furlough home in Mar, 1864. His father died 3 Oct 1864 in a CSA hospital in Richmond, VA of pneumonia. When Tom Peter Lawless was 5 years old, his widowed mother married Timothy Dailey. The Daily family moved to Bassfield area in Covington Co., MS. A new county was created, Jefferson Davis Co, and Bassfield was put in the new County. Tom Peter Lawless remained in Paulding with his childless aunt & uncle, who reared him through his teen years, Martha Jane Brogan (his mother's sister) & Michael Hanley (her husband) treated Tom Peter Lawless as if he were their own son, giving him love, attention and education. He taught school in "Irish Town". 2 Feb 1887 he & Mary Lillian Street (a daughter of Solomon & Charlotte Lyon Street) were married. They were the parents of 7 children, 3 of whom died in infancy. The others were Hilda, Mary Marths, Neri (Sr. Annunciata) and Thomas Peter, Jr. During the 1890s Thomas Peter Lawless, Sr was editor of THE JASPER COUNTY REVIEW. Mary Lillian Street Lawless died in 1902 at Baxterville, Marion County, MS. When a new county was created, Lamar Co., MS, Baxterville was in the new county. It was at Baxterville where T. P. Lawless, who was in the lumbering business, met Dixie Catherine Webb who had gone there to teach school. She was a daughter of A. G. Webb & Nancy Hathorn Regan. On 5 May 1903 they were married by Fr. O'Riley at the Webb home in Columbia, MS. They were the parents of John H. Lawless, Michael Hanley Lawless, Sarah Kathlene Lawless, Dixie Christine Lawless, Patrick Boyd Lawless, and William Webb Lawless. Some of Thomas Peter Lawless' ancestors are listed below.

1. Parents
   John Thomas Lawless + Elizabeth Ann Brogan

2. Grand parents
   William Lawless + Rose Ann McCourt (both from Co. Meath, Ireland; no info from Ireland)

3. Great-Grand Parents
   James Brogan (born in Ireland) + Katherine

*Patrick B. Lawless*
*Dec 1988*

*Biography of T.P. Lawless*

*Front page from 1892 issue of Jasper County Review*

*Front page from 1893 issue of Jasper County Review*

# JASPER COUNTY REVIEW.

LAWLESS & STREET, PUBLISHERS.

VOLUME 4.     PAULDING, MISSISSIPPI, WEDNESDAY, JANUARY 17, 1894.     NUMBER 16.

*Front page from 1894 issue of Jasper County Review*

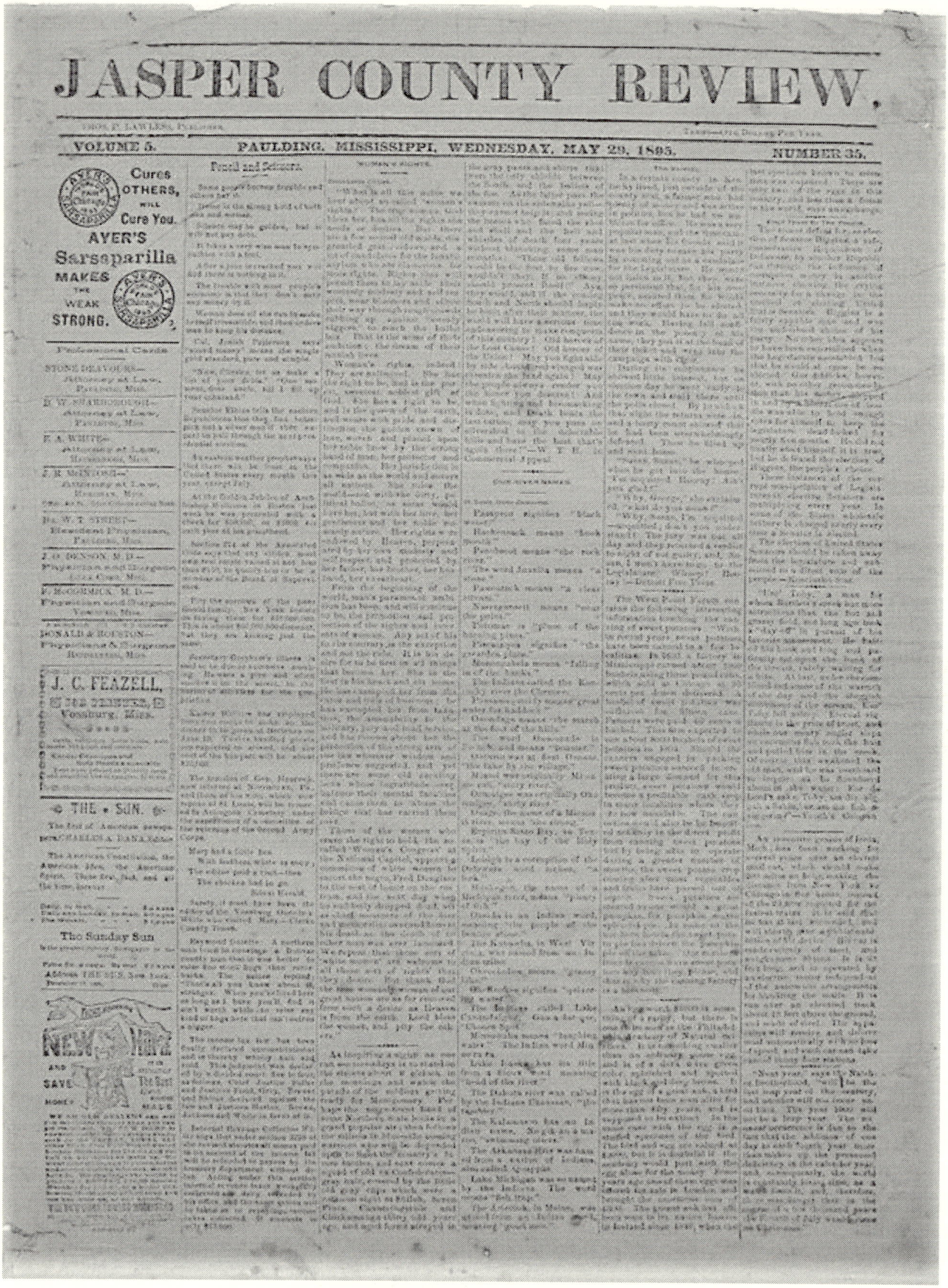
# JASPER COUNTY REVIEW.

VOLUME 5. PAULDING, MISSISSIPPI, WEDNESDAY, MAY 29, 1895. NUMBER 35.

Cures OTHERS, WILL Cure You.

AYER'S Sarsaparilla MAKES THE WEAK STRONG.

Professional Cards

J. C. FEAZELL,

THE SUN.

The Sunday Sun

*Front page from 1895 issue of Jasper County Review*

The following are a collection of clips from this newspaper collection. Most are associated with the eastern section of the county.

## Professional Cards.

**Dr. C. W. BUFKIN,**

PHYSICIAN AND SURGEON,

VOSSBURG, MISS.

Offers his services to the people of Vossburg and surrounding country.

Chief Health Officer of Jasper county, and consulting Physician to Stafford's Springs.

---

**F. McCORMICK, M. D.,**

## Physician and Surgeon,

VOSSBURG, MISS.,

Offers his professional services to the citizens of Vossburg, Paulding and surrounding country.

---

# HYDE'S

## CHEAP CASH STORE,

Vossburg, Mississippi.

We invite the attention of all self-interested people; we ask you to call upon us before you purchase your goods; we are sure to save you money.

WE BUY FOR CASH AND SAVE THE DISCOUNT; WE SELL FOR CASH AND AT A SMALL PROFIT.

**J. C. FEAZELL,**

**JOB PRINTER,**

Vossburg, Miss.

Cards, envelopes, letter heads, note heads, bill heads and circulars.

Cards, Envelopes and Note Heads a specialty.

Your name printed on 25 lovely cards and beautiful line of samples, 10 cents.

---

**BLUE RIDGE HIGH SCHOOL.**

This institution, for both sexes, is located in the southwestern part of Jasper county, ten miles west of Heidelberg. Its object is to prepare colored teachers to teach in the public schools and for college. In its course of study, all the common school branches adopted by the county will be included. Board can be had in private families from $5 to $6 per month. Tuition from $1.00 to $1.50 per month. It began its first session Monday, December 4, 1893, and will continue for ten months. For further information, call on or address

S. T. GAVIN, B. S.,
Furman, Miss.

December 6, 1893. 10-3m

---

**HYDE'S**

CHEAP CASH STORE,

Vossburg, Mississippi.

We invite the attention of all self-interested people; we ask you to call upon us before you purchase your goods; we are sure to save you money.

WE BUY FOR CASH AND SAVE THE DISCOUNT; WE SELL FOR CASH AND AT A SMALL PROFIT.

**SEE FOR YOURSELF.**

Give us one trial and we will have the pleasure of the second. WE MEAN WHAT WE ADVERTISE.

A specialty made of FLOUR, COFFEE, SUGAR, And only the best grades kept. Best flour—our full patent—"Empress," $3.90 a Barrel. Highest cash price paid for all country produce. Cotton a cash article at market price.

W. M. HYDE.

**Reduced Rates From Vossburg.**

Commencing July 20, 1894, and continuing until October 28, 1894, will sell round-trip tickets to Meridian for $1.45 and to New Orleans for $6.40. Limit for return five days from date of sale.

W. M. HYDE, Agent.

---

W. M. Hyde, Vossburg, will buy your cotton, pay you full market price and pay you the cash, and then sell you goods cheaper than anybody. You do not meet with this proposition, as is the practice of many buyers: "I will give you $60, but you must close out. You can't do better, there is no use trying the market." We want our friends to realize all possible and urge them to try all who pretend to buy.

# The Civil War

Volumes have been written on the subject and I am unqualified to add very much. However, while doing family research I did learn that this war deeply effected everyone who lived in Jasper County and all parts of the nation. I learned of two Great-Great Grandfathers who served in the Confederate Army, one who volunteered and one who was conscripted. Both of them survived the ordeal. One was wounded twice, shot through the hand at Chickamauga and in the head at Franklin. One account of the war that I found to be fascinating came from a Jasper County native by the name of J.R. McCormick.

## Thomas R. McCormick

### Submitted by L. McCormick

Thomas McCormick was born on March 3, 1841 in Vossburg, Mississippi. In August of 1861 he enlisted in Co. H, 27th Regt., Miss. Inf., know as the "Jasper Blues". The following is his account of his capture, escape and return to Mississippi after being taken prisoner at Lookout Mountain. Thomas McCormick died in Meridian, Mississippi on August 22, 1919.

My Escape from Prison:

I enlisted in August, 1861 from Jasper County, Mississippi and rendezvoused at Marion Station, Miss., the 12th day of September, 1861, taking the train at DeSoto., Miss. Remaining in camp at Marion Station about three months; then went to Pensacola, Fla., and from Pensacola to Warrington, Fla., and there remained until the following summer, when we left there and went to Mobile; remained in Mobile until September, and then went to Chattanooga, and were formed in brigade under General Walthall. In a few days we took up our march with General Bragg through Tennessee and Kentucky, where we fought in the battle of Perryville; From there we fell back to Knoxville, Tenn., and from there to Shelbyville, Tenn., then advanced to Murfreesboro, where we met Rosecrans in battle about the 26th day of December,1862, lasting eight days. After the battle we fell back to Shelbyville, Tenn., where we wentinto winter quarters, and remained until next Summer.

From Tennessee we fell back to North Alabama, after which we advanced to the Battlefield at Chickamauga, where we fought Rosecrans on the 18th, 19th, and 20th, of September, 1863. After that battle we advanced to Chattanooga, Tenn., taking up line of battle on Missionary Ridge; from there we moved to Lookout Mountain, and later fought the battle of Lookout Mountain, which took place on the 24th of November, 1863; there I was captured by the enemy and carried to Rock Island, Ill., prison at which prison I was kept until Oct. 1, 1864.

When we reached the prison it was very cold day, and we had to wait around the gates for hours before we were carried inside; the object of waiting being to search every one for contraband of war. I was placed in Barrack 8, and fared very well for a few months. Then our rations were cut down to about one-third of a soldier's rations; it was so scant that we could hardly live on it, and we were told that they were retaliating for the way the Andersonville, Ga., prisoners were treated. Men were so starved that they would even go into the gutters and gather the fragments of meat that were thrown out from the barrels, and even climb the trees and gather the dead twigs and sticks from the trees. They would also gather the bones from the cook rooms, and boil them in the cans and get the oil from them, which they would sell for 5 cents per pint. This grease I would buy, put into my flour and make johny cakes to sell to the soldiers who happened to have the money. One of my company had some money which he loaned me, and with this I bought flour and tobacco, which I sold from a little stand. When I made enough money to spare I would buy something to eat, always dividing with my mates, Jim Lott, Tom Morris and Frank Lightsey.

## Plan to Escape.

This prison was surrounded by a plank wall or fence twenty feet high, with a parapet on top, where sentinels were posted about every thirty of forty paces. Three other prisoners Fred Morgan, Joe Morgan and Wesley Mayfield, and I, planned to make our escape; our plan being to dig under the wall or fence; the place we selected was in one corner of the prison. We selected this place because there had been a new fence built, cutting off twelve barracks, and this fence had no parapet, and of course no sentinel, so we in going under at this place we had only one sentinel to watch. On the night of Oct. 1, 1864, we went to a point near this place, and Joe Morgan volunteered to go forward and dig under the fence, which he did with a carving knife procured from the kitchen. He made the excavation and went out. We remained back, and while we were waiting, the lamplighter made his rounds, and we hid under a barrack until he passed safely out of sight, when we again got together and attempted to go forward. In the mean time Fred Morgan, who was a little in advance of us, said that Joe Morgan had been caught on the outside, and that he heard the sentinel say, "The next one who comes we will bore him through", and we believed this to be true, retired to our barracks and went to bed. This, however, was a false alarm, and Joe, after waiting for us for a while, returned to the barracks, woke us up and told us everything was quiet and ready for our escape. This was probably after 12 o'clock at night, so we said goodbye to the other boys we were leaving behind us, and started out again on our dangerous undertaking, for dangerous it was, as the sentinel was walking back and forth continually, and we were in full view until he turned his back to walk from us; when he did this we crept across the deadline, which was forty feet from the prison wall, and crawling flat on the ground until he turned again walking back toward us, when we lay perfectly still until he went forward again. We continued this until we reached the fence, where the excavation was made under the fence, where we fortunately went out. Our plan was that we should all get together at the corner of the prison on the outside, as, necessarily, we had to separate in making our escape, but I failed to get with the other boys, through some misunderstanding.

After searching for them some time and failing to find them, I made for the bayou which surrounds the prison. Reaching the bayou, I took off my clothes, tied them to my back, and right into the water I went, determined to wade as far as I could, and if needs be to swim. I found that the water was not deep enough in any place for me to swim so I waded right through all right and reached the opposite bank, where I found I was in the suburbs of the city of Rock Island, Ill. After dressing I did not pause here, but struck out directly south, down the river, avoiding all roads during the day. Late in the evening, while passing through a apple orchard, I gathered some apples, and went to a ravine where I sat down to eat them, and while there a man, whom I suppose was the owner of the place, passed so near I could have almost touched him, but he did not see me. After he had passed on I continued my journey. Then I came to Rock River, which I swam. After getting through the small village, I took to the woods again, going down to the bank of the Mississippi River. I concealed myself in a cluster of bushes, my object being to wait until it was dark, so that I could get a boat in which to go down the river. While waiting there I saw a skiff coming up the river, with two men in it; I saw them land and fasten the boat just above me. There was also a boat tied at the landing where I was ambushed. I waited there until dark, when I went forward to secure the boat. Just as I was getting near the boar I heard some one coming from the house. I lay flat on the ground perfectly still, and he did not discover me. He went down and fixed something about the skiff, and then returned to the house. When all was quiet again I examined the skiff and found it locked with a chain to a rock. There were, however, two oars lying loose in the bottom of the boat, so I went further up the stream, where the two men had left the boat, and I found it merely tied with a rope. This boat was without oars, so I went back to the other boat, procured the oars from it, and got into the boat and went down the river. After going some distance, and when I was far enough away to avoid pursuit, I pulled my skiff up to the bank for the rest of the night.

The rain was falling and I could not lie down, so I set under a little bush until daybreak next morning, when I resumed my journey down the river in the rain. I continued down the river all day, stopping that night at a farmhouse on the bank of the river, went to the barn and found it filled with new mown hay. Into this hay I went, thinking I would have a good night's sleep, but no sleep came to my eyes through all that night, as I was cold, wet and hungry, having had nothing to eat since I left the prison, except the apples about which I have spoken. At the first intimation of day I got out and went back to my skiff, and continued my course down the river. I stayed in the skiff until about 11 o'clock, and being thoroughly worn out, and thinking I was near Alexandria, Mo., I landed and took it on foot, and there was a plain road running along the bank of the river. After traveling this road for about two hours, I came to a village which was Fort Madison, Ia. Here I inquired the distance to Alexandria, Mo., and was told that it was about 150 miles. The second day about noon, cold and hungry, I resolved to go to a farm house on the bank of the river and get something to eat. On my way up I saw four cavalrymen ride off, and saw that they wore the blue uniform. However, after seeing them leave, I went up to the gate and hailed, an old man came to the door and invited me in. In a short time dinner was announced, and I was invited to partake, which I did thankfully. During my conversation the old gentleman asked me where I was from, and I told him from a little town up the river, the name of which I do not remember. He asked me if they were husking corn. I told him they were. Then he asked me many questions about John Jones, and other people he called by name, whom he knew, and of course thought I also must know. I ate heartily, and as fast as possible under the circumstances and even then, when I had finished, I felt as though I had not half enough.

But to go back to Fort Madison, which town I reached with $3.10 in silver. The first thing I bought was ten cents worth of tobacco. I then went to the ticket office and bought a ticket to Alexandria, Mo., which cost me $3. The boat arrived at 5 o'clock in the afternoon. I went aboard, and took a deck passage. After getting on the boat supper was announced, but I had no money with which to buy supper, so I sold a gold ring which a young lady put on my finger the night I left Desoto in 1861. This ring I sold for 30 cents, and with 25 cents of this money I bought something to eat. I found on the boat several sacks of onions, of which I ate to my hearts content. About 12 o'clock the boat landed me at a point from which I could take a train to Keokuk, Ia. While waiting here for a train a Yankee approached me for a trade to substitute for him, offering me $500.00. At first I concluded to take him up on this trade, my purpose being in making the trade to go to the front and make my escape across the line; but upon investigation I found that he wanted me to return to Davenport, where I would be mustered into service. But Davenport being right across the river from Rock Island Prison, and not caring to take my chances near that prison again, I did not consummate the trade. I took the train for Keokuk, Ia., and landed in that town about sunrise the next morning with 5 cents in my pocket, left from the sale of the ring. With this 5 cents I bought a pie, on which I made my breakfast.

Here I waited to catch a boat, which landed me in a short time at Alexandria, Mo. I then took up my march west of the river to a place called Winchester, Mo., where I had a cousin living two miles west of the town. I reached my cousin's home about eight o'clock at night, told him who I was, and that I had escaped from prison. He took me to his house, where they prepared supper for me, and gave me a feather bed to sleep on. The next morning I felt as though I had been beaten all over, and could hardly stand on my feet, which were blistered from my marching the day before. I remained with my cousin from Thursday until the next Wednesday when my cousin's wife took me in a buggy eighteen miles and dropped me about four miles from Canton, Mo. My cousin gave me $20 in greenbacks and had my clothes laundered. Just before reaching Canton I met some pickets, whom I asked what was the trouble, and they remarked that they were expecting Gen. Canby and his forces, and I said to them, "Give him a hearty reception", and I passed on. Arriving at Canton, Mo., I found the little village filled with Yankee militia.

When night came on I went to a vacant store house, and slept soundly until about 5 o'clock next morning, when I heard a boat whistle. As soon as the boat landed I went aboard and paid my passage to St. Louis. After getting to St. Louis I found a boat bound for New Orleans, about to leave, on which I took passage. I went to the cooks room and made arrangements to assist the cook. On the next day this boat arrived at Cairo, Ill., and turned it's cargo over to another boat, and stopped there. I transferred to a Memphis boat and arrived in Memphis on Saturday morning following. After getting to Memphis I found the City filled with Yankee soldiers, and the streets blocked with bales of cotton. After being there for some hours I made a trade with an Arkansas farmer to go out with him that evening, but he failed to meet me. That night I went to the hotel and put up.

The next morning was Sunday; I took in the City with a Yankee detective. In the evening I went out to the pickets that surrounded the City, to make my escape but finding it difficult returned to the city, stopping at another hotel that night. The next morning I went to the wharf and found a boat getting ready to leave, South, and as they pulled the gang-plank in I got aboard and evaded the guards. After getting aboard I found that this was a government boat carrying supplies to the army at the north of White River. On the way down the boat was fired into by our men from the banks of the river. This boat anchored in the middle of the river at night, and during the day I saw no opportunity to make my escape from the boat to the Mississippi shore, so when the boat arrived at the mouth of the White River, where there was a large army, I knew I must have a pass to get on the boat again, so I went to the commander of the post and told him I was on a wild goose chase, and had been down there hunting work, but finding no work I want a pass to go back home. He asked me where I lived, and I told him I lived in Winchester, Mo. He asked me many more question and gave me a pass to return, and I went aboard the boat. The boat landed me Saturday morning in Memphis again. I went ashore and stayed around the city until evening. I saw there was a boat loaded to go North, and just before night I went aboard, when it took its leave, and landed at Island 37. I got off and was taken in by one of the residents of the island and allowed to stay all night. He suspected me as being an escaped prisoner and questioned me very closely. The next morning I made arrangements to work with him, and had by this time made up my mind that he did not intend to harm me, so after breakfast he saddled his horse and was about ready to leave, when I went to him and told him that I was an escaped prisoner and wanted him to assist me in getting away from the island. He would not help me get off but gave me directions how to get off of the island. I told him that was all I wanted, so he asked me to mount the horse behind him, which I did, and rode with him to the head of the island, where I got in the company with two of Capt. Forrest's scouts. I mounted behind one of them and rode across the chute to the swamp on the other side, where they told me they could go no further with me, but gave me directions how to proceed toward Corinth, Miss. Then I set out on foot, and traveled toward Shelby station.

The scouts had given me names of the parties with whom I could stop that night. After leaving them and when I had traveled until the middle of the evening, or later, I met a man who was riding a mule and talking on the roadside to probably fifteen or twenty Negros. I fancied he was a Yankee and intended to pass him by but when I approached him he halted me and asked who I was. I demanded of him who he was, and that this juncture he leveled his pistol at me, and said at the same time that he was a confederate. I told him I was also a confederate. He questioned me very closely, and finally decided that I was what I claimed to be, invited me home with him. As we went towards his home we met a neighbor of his, in company with a confederate scout, to whom Dr. Peyton introduced me. The soldier proposed going down to Memphis the following Wednesday evening to capture a horse for me to ride from there on to Corinth, Miss., but not being mounted nor having any arms, of course, he said it would be no use for me to go; so Dr. Peyton and I went on to his home where I remained three weeks. While there I was employed as overseer, and went out to his farm and helped pick a little cotton. During my stay his wife carried a bale of cotton to Memphis in a wagon. The cotton weighed 500 pounds, and sold for $550. Among the things which happened while there, a party of Jay Hawkers killed a farmer, and the citizens and the scouts ran them down and killed them, and Dr. Peyton secured one of the horses for me, gave me both greenback and confederate money, and started me on the road to Corinth. I went by way of Jackson, Tenn. While on my way from Jackson to Corinth I met a brigade of our cavalrymen making a raid into Tennessee but I went on my way to Corinth, Miss. where I sold my horse for $400, and rejoined the army again. This was the later part of November. The Company I was put into was Captain Gallagher's company, Col. Weir's regiment. I applied for a furlough after getting in camp, but failed to get it, and in about twelve days

Col. Weir was ordered with his regiment to Buckatunna, Miss. to meet Griensau's raid, and when we arrived at Shubuta, Col. Weir gave me a pass to go home. I dropped off at Shubuta and found neighbor Leroy Morrison there with a lead horse, which he gave me permission to ride home. I mounted, in company with him, and rode out to my father's home, reaching there Dec. 10, 1864. Mr. Morrison asked me not to make myself known, wanting to see if my parents would recognize me. When reaching my father's we went in and sat down by the fire, and my father and Mr. Morrison talked for some time when my father inquired, "Who is this you have with you?" when I remarked, "Father you do not seem to know me." "I do not", says he, "unless it is Thomas." I had changed so much that he did not recognize me.

T. R. McCormick

Co H 27 Miss Reg Walthall's Brig

# World War II

Beyond the service and sacrifice of many Jasper youth during this war, others were effected in a equally unsettling way when the government established a flight school and a practice bombing range at Key Field in Meridian, Mississippi. While the school was conducted in Meridian, a live bombing range was established south of the field in Jasper County. All of the residents who lived in the condemned area had to abandon their homes and farms. For the duration of the war, training and live ammunition runs were conducted on this range. Following the war, live ammunition continues to be discovered on the land. No one complained because they all comprehended how important the efforts were.

The aircraft utilized at Key Field were numerous. We do know that fighter training for the P-51 Mustang was conducted there.

# Forgotten Cemeteries

One thing that I have learned about the practices of the past, the celebration of a grave site was not revered by all. Graves were often placed near a home site or near a church. Markers were often home made from wood or crude stone carvings. Sometimes the markers were just a native rock. As a result, these grave sites are scattered and often impossible to pinpoint. If you have family records that reference a cemetery, you are lucky. But, don't expect to find a etched stone if yo go there. There were some exceptions and they are hard to find. A couple of examples are as follows.

### Hodges Cemetery

Located on private land, north-east of Old Salem Cemetery. Reference map and GPS coordinates.

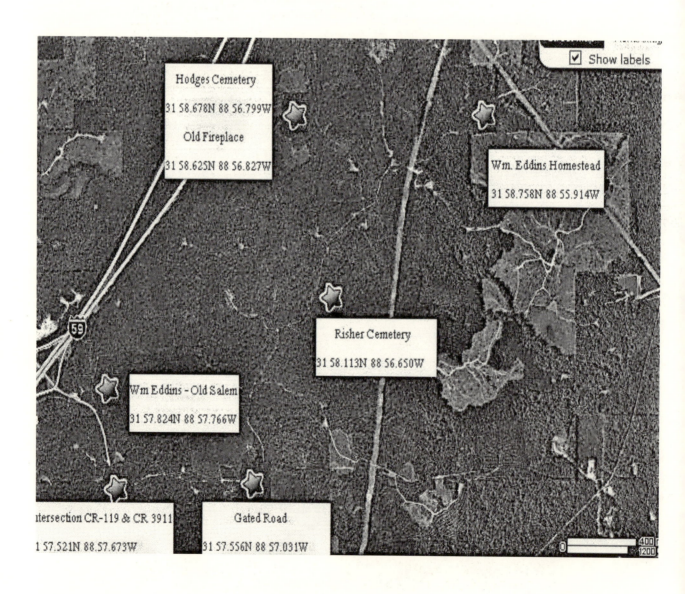

# The Risher Cemetery

Located on private land, north-east of Old Salem Cemetery. Reference map and GPS coordinates.

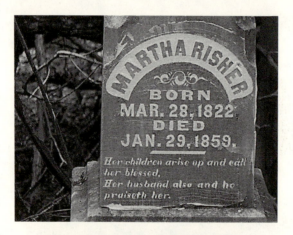

MARTHA RISHER
BORN
MAR. 28, 1822
DIED
JAN. 29, 1859.

Her children arise up and call
her blessed,
Her husband also and he
praiseth her.

J. A. RISHER
BORN
JAN. 31, 1856.
DIED
SEPT. 29, 1868.

God gave, He took, He will
restore.
He doeth all things well.

# Obscure Jasper County Locations and Post Office

This being the last chapter in this book equates to the foot note category for all things forgotten that should have be included. My limited research simply did not uncover enough to warrant a dedicated chapter for many Jasper communities that are likely dear to many. Nonetheless, I feel that I have done my best.

*Stafford Springs Tea Room*

*Bus from the Stafford Springs School*

*The Mineral Springs School*

*The Pine Grove School*

# Jasper Post Office Locations

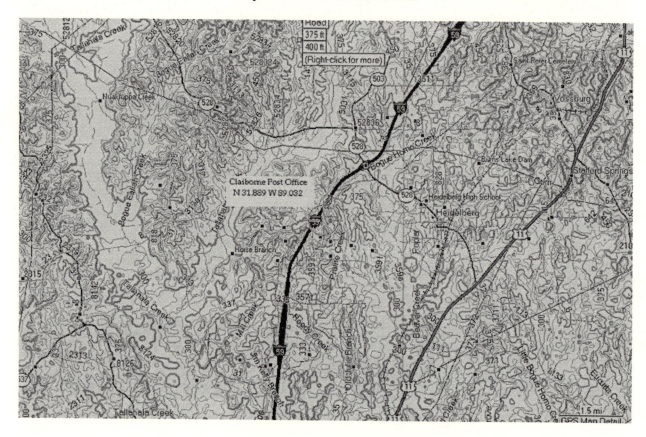

*Claiborne Mississippi*

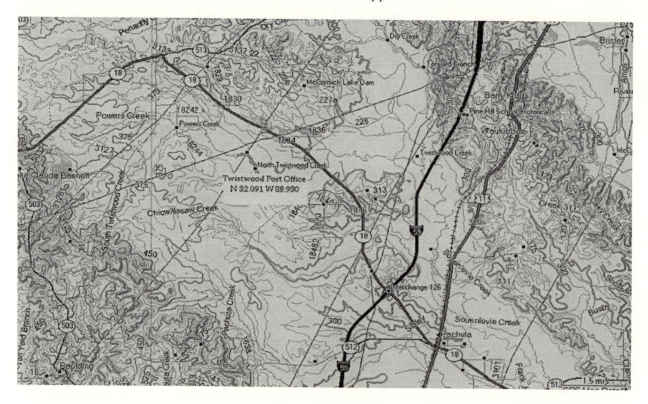

*Twistwood Mississippi*

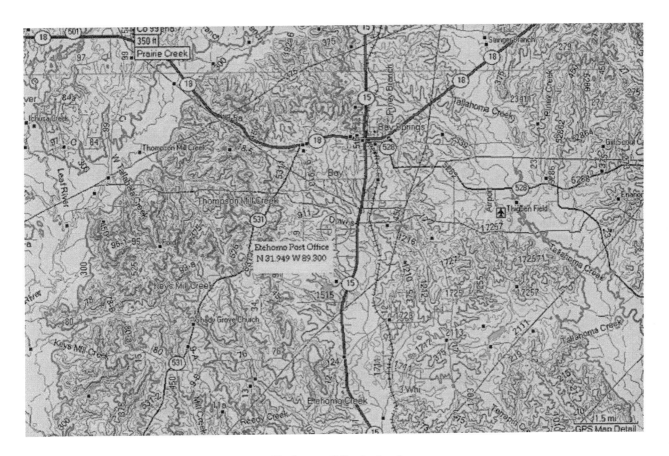

*Etehomo Mississippi*

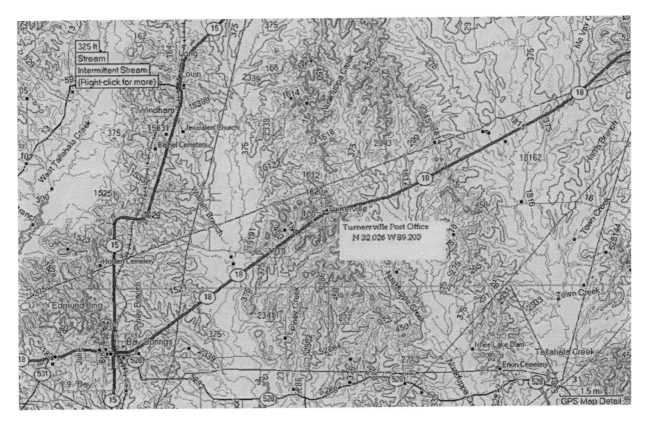

*Turnersville Mississippi*

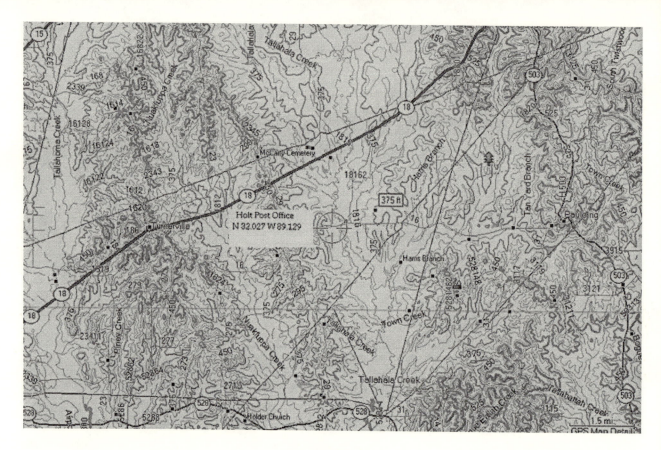

*Holt Mississippi*

*Moss Mississippi*

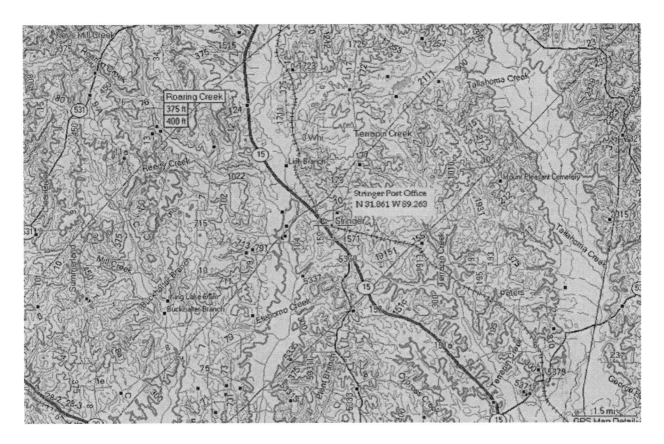

*Stringer Mississippi*

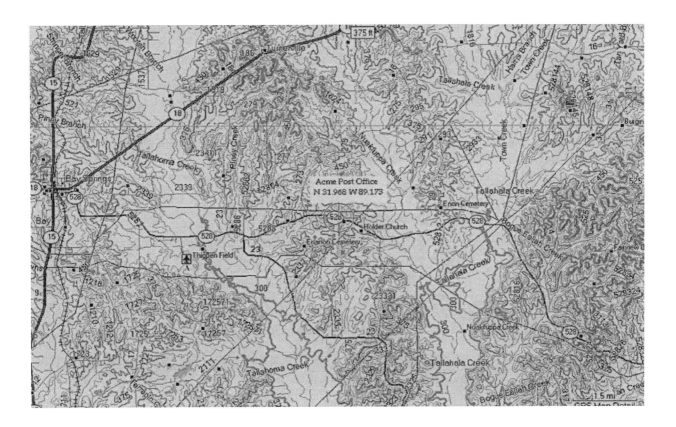

*Acme Mississippi*

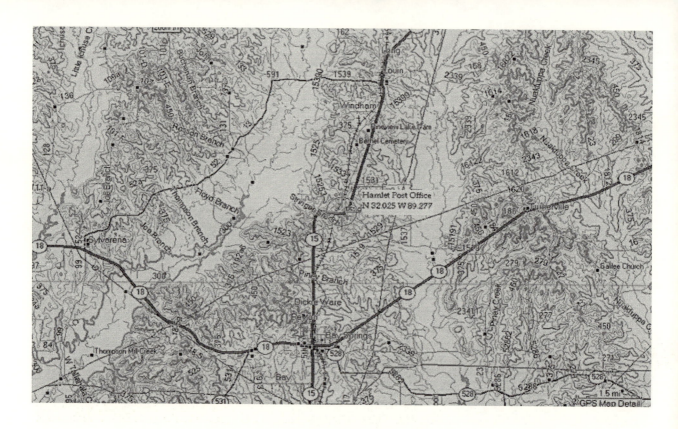

*Hamlet Mississippi*

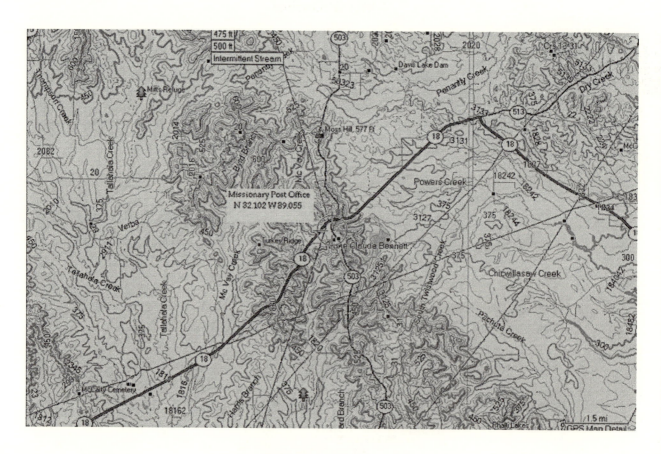

*Missionary Mississippi*

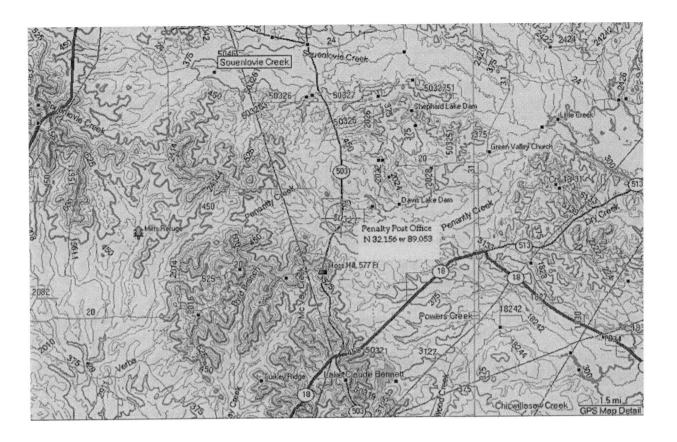

*Penalty Mississippi*

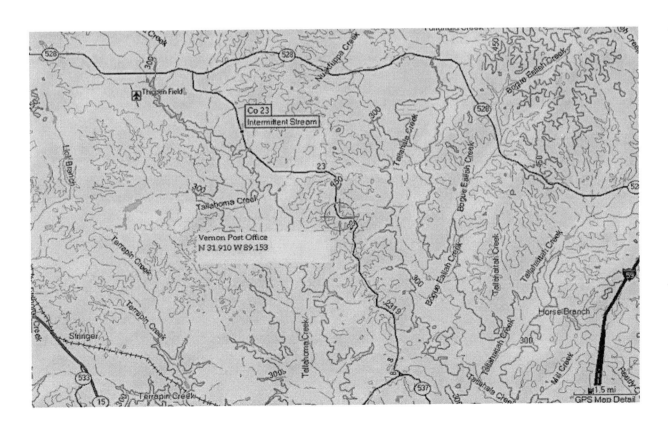

*Vernon Mississippi*

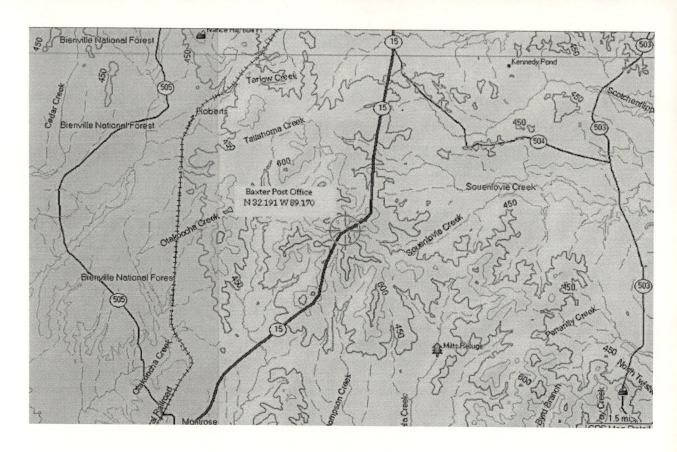

*Baxter Mississippi*

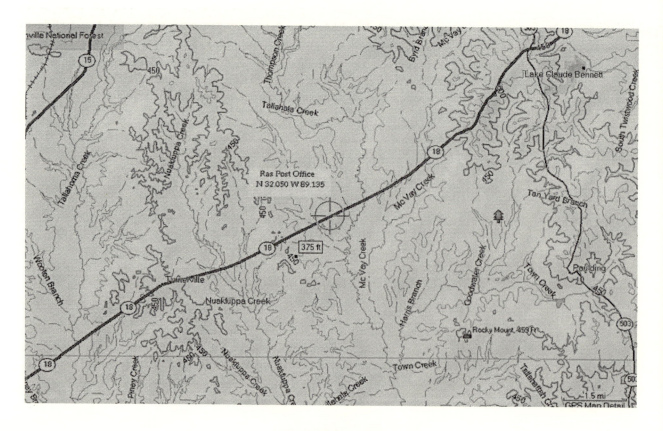

*Ras Mississippi*

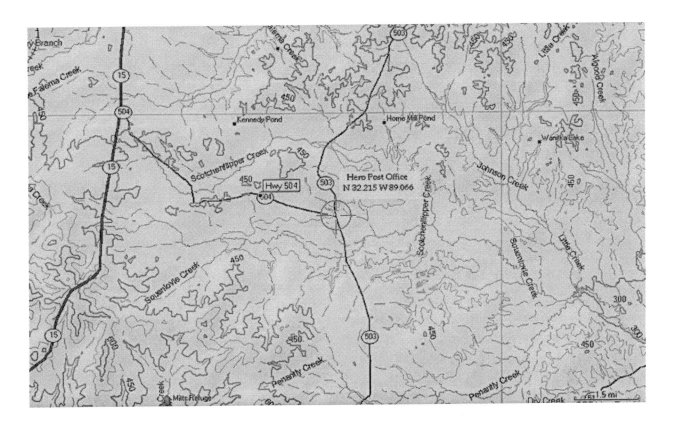

*Hero Mississippi*

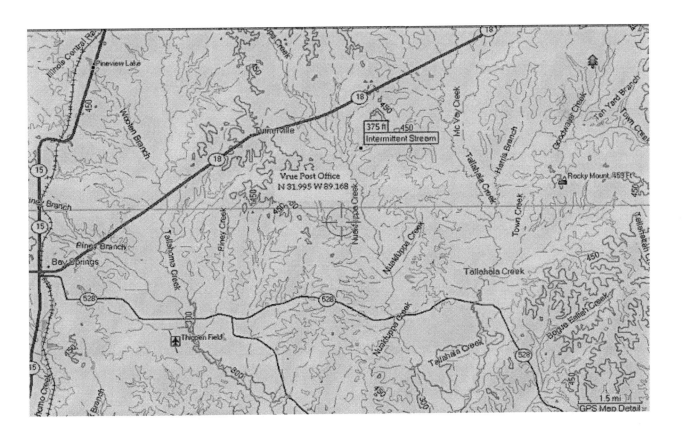

*Vrue Mississippi*

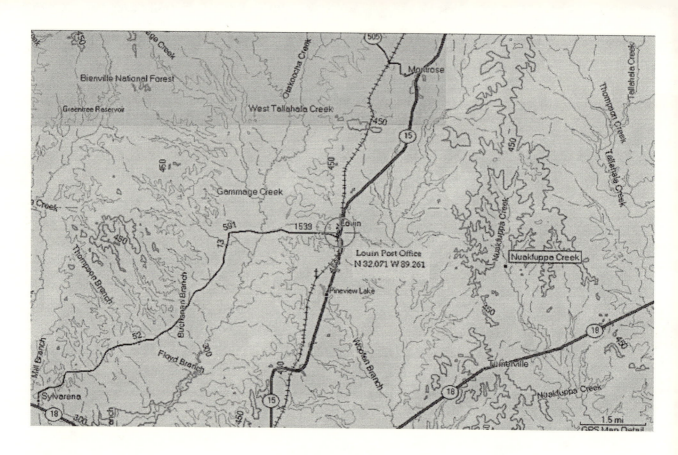

*Louin Mississippi*

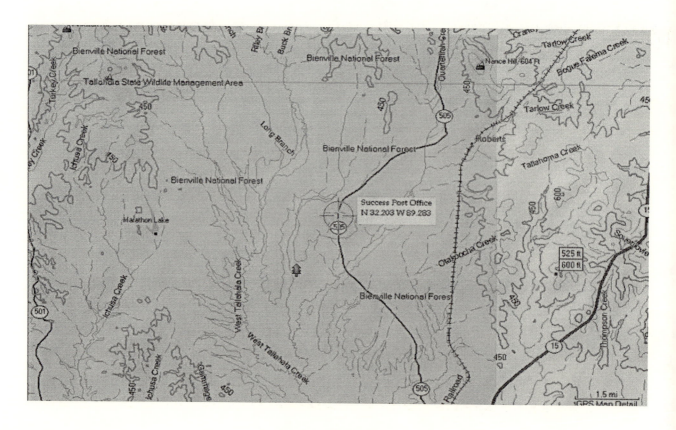

*Success Mississippi*

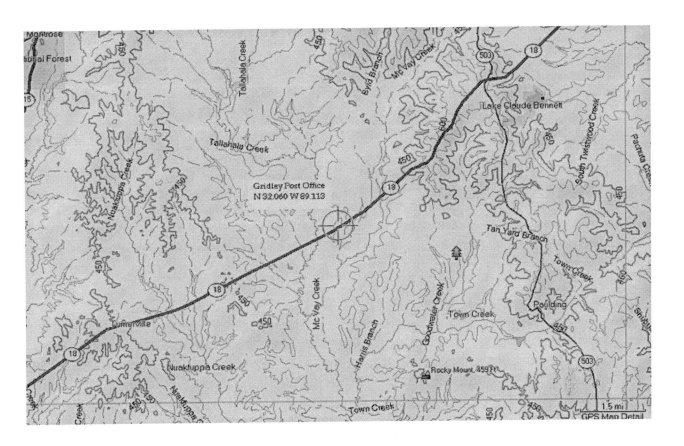

*Gridley Mississippi*

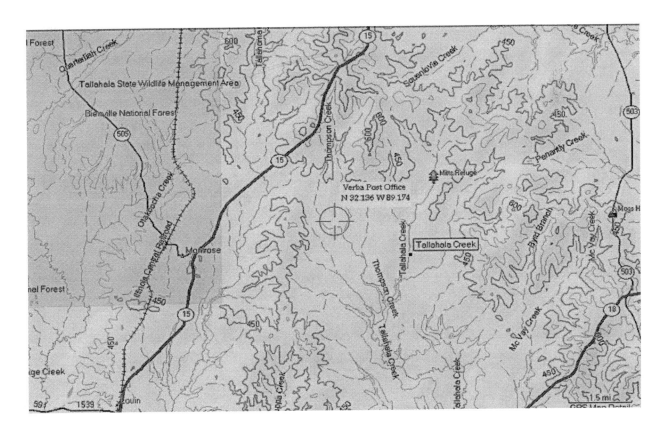

*Verba Mississippi*

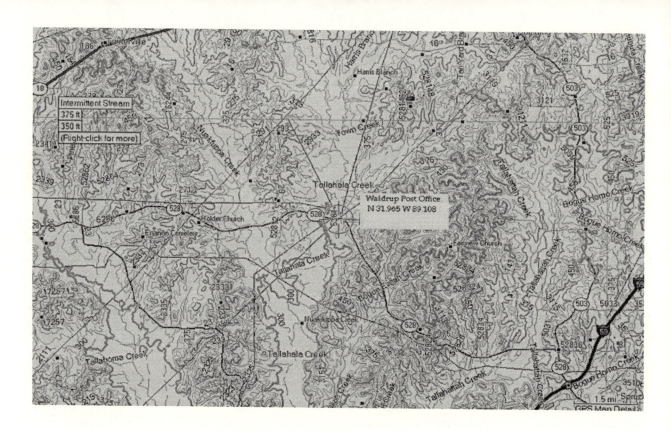

*Waldrup Mississippi*

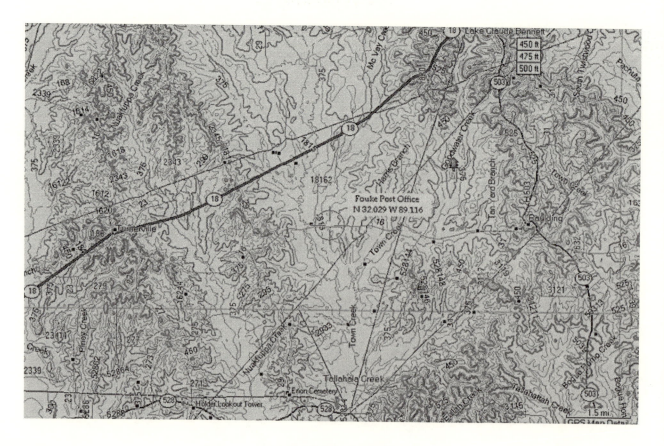

*Fouke Mississippi*

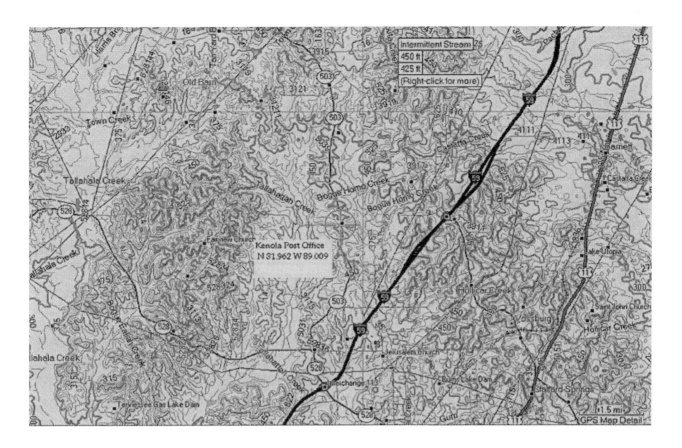

*Kenola Mississippi*

That's all folks!

Made in the USA
Columbia, SC
29 May 2018